THE STEPS

12 Secrets To Raising Happy and Successful Kids

Andrew Watson, MD
Charles Watson, MD, PH.D.

The Steps: 12 Secrets To Raising Happy and Successful Kids

Translation from Portuguese to English by Luís Guilherme C. P. M. Ferreira

Legal Disclaimer

This book is for educational purposes only. The views expressed are those of the authors alone. The reader is responsible for his or her own actions. Neither the authors nor the publisher assumes any responsibility or liability whatsoever for the use of or inability to use any or all information contained in this book, and accepts no responsibility for any loss or damages of any kind that may be incurred by the reader as a result of actions arising from the use of information found in this book.

DOWNLOAD THE AUDIOBOOK
AND HAVE A GREAT EXPERIENCE

https://adbl.co/34ctxgn

CONTENTS

DEDICATION

This book is dedicated to our parents, Maria Claricia and Luís Fernando. For always believing in us.

CHAPTER 01 — THE BABIES' WIZARD

"The delicate balance of mentoring someone is not creating them in your own image, but giving them the opportunity to create themselves."

—*Steven Spielberg*

"Do you want me to put that in the magazine?" asked Helena, the chief publisher, while shaking the sheets of paper with the text that Estela had just written over her head.

"What's wrong with it?" Estela replied, frowning. "You asked me to write about education in Brazil! That's exactly what you have there."

"I can't publish this, my dear! You already know that since the publisher was bought by the Letters Corporation, we can no longer publish depressing articles. Their policy is to transmit a message of well-being, emotion, and happiness. You keep harping on the same string: teachers are unmotivated; the students are illiterate; blah, blah, blah . . . It makes me feel like I'm going to cry. I want different articles: uplifting and bold."

Estela put her hands on her waist and exclaimed, "Oh! I didn't know I was supposed to lie!"

"That's not the case at all! I want you to bring me solutions. I want to make my readers feel inspired, not sad. I want a new angle on the topic, and I know you can do it. You are a great journalist, and I love your work. Not only me, but also your readers, your fans."

"My fans?" Estela raised the corners of her lips in a subtle smile.

Helena settled her big body on the chair and answered, "You are quite controversial and charismatic. I see how many commentaries every single one of your articles generates. And your blog? It's a success! Maybe Letters' approach is too idealistic, I agree. I was once your age too, and I know how it is. However, today we need to subject our work to the bosses; otherwise, we will all get fired."

Estela thought about freedom of the press and a time when she felt she could write any text, believing her writing depended only on her imagination and information sources. She did not expect journalism to suffer such an abrupt transformation after the advent of the Internet.

"You asked me to write about education in Brazil, and you expected me to be optimistic! I have to be realistic."

"Think outside of the box; approach the topic from a new perspective. Go after the bright spots, the gems, the projects that are working out! In such a big universe as the Brazilian one, there must be some pedagogical practices working properly in our education system. Search for it! I can't publish this. I'm sorry."

Estela left the room displeased. She reread the text and could not agree with Helena. The article she wrote was an accurate picture of what she saw in practice: a general indifference regarding the learning-teaching process, that left students inadequately prepared and that was sending an improperly qualified workforce to the labor market. So, she decided to post the article on her blog, since it had no connection with the magazine. She was imagining how the readers would react to the rant, when the phone rang. It was Victor, her boyfriend.

"Whenever you are ready, gorgeous, you can come down! I'm down here waiting for you."

"I'm coming down right now."

Victor had parked his car right in front of the publisher. He had just bathed, thus looking even more beautiful and smelling all good. He gave her a big hug and a kiss, saying, "Let's have dinner somewhere different!"

After walking down several avenues, they stopped at a restaurant they had never been to before. Since both were hungry, they went to the nearly empty buffet. They took their plates and cutlery, while a curvy woman was giving instructions to a little boy with straight hair just in front of her.

"You are going to tell me what you want, all right? You just need to read these rectangles here."

The little boy nodded and started reading. "Sugar beet with aplicot..."

They walked a little bit.

"Moloccan couscous. What is Moloccan couscous?" the little boy asked, mistakenly switching every *r* with an *l*.

Estela raised her eyebrows and whispered in her boyfriend's ear, "Is it possible that a boy, this young, can read the names of the dishes?"

"Moroccan comes from Morocco, it is a country in Africa," the mother explained.

"Impelial shlimp!" the little boy shouted.

Estela and Victor looked at each other. They had never seen such a young boy reading, especially words as complex as those.

Estela could no longer hold her curiosity. She approached the woman: "I'm sorry, how old is he?"

"He has just turned five," answered the boy's mother.

"I want shlimp," said the boy, interrupting them.

"All right, son." The mother placed a small portion in the little boy's plate.

"Wow! I'm surprised. How can he read so perfectly already?"

"Yahoo! Flied banana. I love flied banana."

"What a prodigy!" Victor exclaimed, sharing the same enthusiasm as his girlfriend.

The boy's mother smiled, embarrassed, and gestured with her hands for them to go ahead of her and her son. The couple politely rejected the invitation, shaking their heads while holding the empty plates in their hands.

"Did you force him to read, by any chance?" asked Estela.

There was no answer. Thus, Victor continued the idea, inquiring, "Isn't it prejudicial, at such a young age?"

Suddenly, both the mother and the son stared at the couple. The woman had a reprehensive look, and the boy was confused.

Estela was about to justify herself when she examined the boy's round face. Behind the dark glasses, two characteristic eyes silenced her. The boy had Down syndrome.

There was a pause that lasted a few seconds. The mother, noticing the sudden embarrassment felt by Estela, explained, "He has psychomotricity, speech therapy, and reading activities at a clinic in Ibirapuera. You probably know it . . . it's called Awake Clinic."

"No . . . I don't know it, unfortunately. But I'm already amazed!"

"Joaquim is very diligent."

"I'm better at reading than Lucas," the little boy said.

The boy's mother blushed.

"Congratulations, Joaquim," said Estela, encouraging him. "You are very good at reading."

"I'm hungry. I want the flied banana."

They all laughed. Victor and Estela left the mother and the little boy alone.

While sitting at the table, Estela took her cellphone from her purse and typed three words on Google: Awake, Ibirapuera, Down.

She found the clinic website and saved the link on her favorites. She replaced the cellphone into the purse and then placed the napkin on her lap.

Victor drank water from his cup and commented, "The boy impressed you, didn't he?"

"And he didn't impress you? He saved my day. I haven't told you, but today Helena refused to publish my text about education."

"Really?"

"Yeah! She said that I was not presenting any solutions, just pointing at negative aspects and common places. She said I should have gone after the brilliant points, the gems of the educational context. Ah! But see how lucky I am . . . Joaquim is exactly what I needed. How can a little boy with Down syndrome read so well? He can read better than most children who are seven years old. He is just five. What is he experiencing that is different from other children?"

"I don't know. What is it?"

Estela cut a cherry tomato in two.

"That's what I'm going to find out."

The next day, once Estela arrived home, she opened her laptop and checked her e-mails. Most of the messages were censuring her article about education. Words such as *deception, trivial,* and *boring* stood out. She had to admit that Helena was right about refusing to publish the text.

She remembered the boy who was at the restaurant and opened the Awake Clinic website. It was a beautiful place, specialized in children with disabilities. Its founder was Dr. Michael Jansen.

"Who is this guy?" thought Estela.

She searched the Internet for "Dr. Michael Jansen."

Thousands of results appeared. She clicked on the first link, "The Wizard of the Babies," and entered a respected newspaper website. There, she saw a photo of a gray-haired man surrounded by children wearing nothing but diapers, with trisomy 21. Below, in bold: "I never accepted the judgment and referred to Dr. Jansen. It was a long and arduous battle, but it was worth it. Today, Yasmin is nineteen years old and is successfully studying law, in her second year."

She read the whole article, and her curiosity inflated.

She went to another website: "Englishman Dr. Michael Jansen, naturalized as Brazilian, is nominated for the Nobel Prize in Physiology or Medicine. The neuroscientist was formally nominated Wednesday (13) for the Nobel Prize by the Swedish professor Mathias Berg, due to his theory of reshaping myelin, neuroplasticity, and neurogenesis. In the letter published by the newspaper *Västerbottens-Kuriren*, Berg argues that Jansen was one of the people who contributed the most to the new neurology, making it a little bit more accessible . . ."

However, it was the next article that excited her the most, not due to the topic itself but because it was written by Roberto Fonseca, a friend from when she was a trainee at April Publishing.

She immediately called him. A sleepy voice answered. She looked at her watch: ten o´clock. It was not that early.

"I'm sorry, Roberto. Did I wake you up?"

"No . . . No . . . You can speak."

"I was reading an article that you wrote about short attention span about two years ago. Do you, by any chance, still remember the doctor you interviewed, a man called Michael Jansen?"

"Of course!" Roberto's voice suddenly sounded quite awake. "What happened to him?"

"Nothing that I know of. It's just that I'm writing an article about what is still functioning in the Brazilian education system and I've found he is developing an interesting work regarding children with disabilities. I just read the article that you wrote, and I would like to know how he is and if it is worth interviewing him."

"I had to divide myself in two to get that interview published. His schedule is quite busy; at least it was back then. I don't know how it is now, because he retired from São Paulo University. Maybe he has more free time now. Look, he is an outstanding guy! I had planned to stay an afternoon with him, but I ended up staying for five days. He took me to visit his clinic, allowed me to meet the children with short attention spans, taught me about the treatments they perform, and even told me about the things that were going to happen next . . . He is a genius in all aspects, and I learned a lot from him. The students, residents, everyone calls him 'the Wizard.'"

"'The Wizard'? I have just read an article about 'The Wizard of the Babies' . . ."

"That's it, that's his nickname. However, to be quite honest, he looked more like a Sherlock Holmes to me: astute, observant, always trying to get as much information as possible from his environment. I used to ask myself, 'How did he know that?' And his eyes almost always answered me, 'Elementary, my dear Watson!' He knows everything deeply; he is a walking encyclopedia. Meet him for ten minutes, and you will be impressed. Stay with him for five days, as I did, and the experience will change your life. Furthermore, he is extremely humanitarian, a benefactor . . ."

"Incredible! Well, then I need to interview him no matter what. It seems like he is exactly the person I was looking for."

"Good luck! I hope you can do it. You will see I'm not exaggerating."

A few weeks later, Estela finally managed to get the interview with Dr. Michael Jansen. They arranged to meet at Awake Clinic, with a tight schedule, at nine o´clock on a Wednesday. Estela impatiently waited for it, full of expectations.

On the scheduled day, she woke up indisposed, not feeling like eating breakfast as she usually would. She believed it was due to tension.

She arrived at the meeting place a little bit early and stayed at the institution's big hall for a while, with her journalist sensors turned on, observing everything around her. She noticed that Awake was quite a busy clinic, with many parents who were bringing their children for daily activities. Looking at the children's faces, she saw that most of them had some kind of disability. Nevertheless, there were also some who were apparently without limitations.

Close to the scheduled time, Estela pressed the elevator button for the sixth floor. She felt confident and looked at the mirror: her dark and straight hair untangled; her suit aligned; her makeup light, highlighting just her cheeks. She had the image of a decided journalist.

When the doors opened, she saw herself in a vast and bright space where the glass walls showed the gray sky of São Paulo. In the room, there were flowerbeds with white and purple orchids, and a scent of rosemary energized the atmosphere. She approached the secretary and checked her presence before snuggling into a soft armchair next to the two women who were reading magazines of the competing publisher.

She was still observing the place when three men in black suits left the office in front of her. Then, Dr. Jansen showed up. He was much taller than Estela had imagined and had an upright posture that transmitted surprising vigor for a person who was seventy-two years old. However, what impressed her the most were his eyes: they had an electric blue tone that no photo could capture. In that first glance, she knew she was facing someone utterly different from everyone else.

Dr. Jansen stared at her and gave her his hand to greet her while saying, "Good morning, Estela." His voice sounded serious, powerful, with a slight British accent that was almost imperceptible. "I'm sorry I couldn't receive you earlier. I knew that you called several times asking for the interview."

"It is true." Estela smiled at him, showing her deep dimples in both cheeks. "I was looking forward to meeting you. I've read a lot of articles about you. It is an honor to be here."

The room where they entered was also quite large and offered a fantastic view, where one could see the trees and the lake from Ibirapuera Park[i]. At the same time, it was cozy and intimate. They sat on a big white L-shaped sofa.

"Would you like something to drink? Tea, juice, water?"

"No, thank you."

"What about something to eat?"

"No, thank you. Can we start the interview?"

"Sure! Make yourself comfortable . . ."

She took the cellphone from her purse, placing it at the center table, and pressed the red microphone button on the screen.

"Ready," she said while quickly fixing her hair. "Michael . . . Can I call you Michael?"

He nodded. He was focused, with his chest facing forward.

Estela kept talking, trying to be as natural as possible. "One day, I met one of the clinic patients, by chance, in a restaurant. I was impressed by how quickly he could read the name of complex dishes, despite being too young to do it. I was even more surprised when I found that he had Down syndrome. I was astonished, thinking, what are you doing differently here at Awake Clinic regarding educational practices, to promote the education of children with disabilities? And, going a little bit beyond: is it possible to extrapolate that methodology to our children who are considered 'normal'?"

Dr. Jansen took a little longer to answer, looking like he was considering his reply. Staring at him silently, Estela remembered the deceased actor Paul Newman. They looked alike: the straight nose, strong jaw, and gray hair. He was still a good-looking man, masculine, appearing to be twenty years younger than his chronological age.

"Look, Estela. The method we use is an individualized teaching-learning process in which we conceive each child as being unique. Thus, each one is different, has an individual profile, their own identity. We don't work only with children with trisomy 21 but also with children who have autism, neonatal anoxia, Asperger's, consequences of encephalic vascular accidents, dyslexia . . . The treatment, in that sense, is specific according to each disease, to each health problem. Now, answering your question, we can't extrapolate the psychological education treatment of children with disabilities to the academic development of all children. It is not a 'ready-to-use' treatment."

Estela looked at her new shoes. She was not expecting to hear this. She thought Dr. Jansen would have answers to all her questions.

"However, we also have protocols for children who were born, like you said . . ." he made a significant gesture with his big fingers, mimicking quotes ". . . normal."

Estela widened her eyes and exclaimed, "Really? You have protocols for children with no disabilities?"

"Why the surprise? Most of the parents who monitor their special children have children without disabilities. And they also need to be stimulated, don't you think?"

Estela nodded. Dr. Jansen got even closer to her.

"Can I tell you a secret? . . . I know you."

"You know me?" she asked, frightened.

"Yes. You were not the only one who did your research, Estela. I also learned a little bit more about you, since you were going to interview me. I've read your articles and seen your blog, including the post regarding the broken education system in Brazil. You blamed the government, the lack of infrastructure, the low quality of the teachers, the lack of general knowledge by most people . . . You did not mention the people that I intimately believe to be the truly responsible ones . . ."

Estela felt her cheeks burning and asked, "Who?"

"The parents. I know that at first, it seems odd, but when the parents want their children to have a high-quality education, nothing you mentioned matters. Are those aspects barriers? Of course! However, none of them are responsible for the situation you portrayed. If parents want to, they will provide a first-class education to their children . . . If they don't act and hope to receive the right knowledge on a silver plate, then, yes, you are right about everything and our education system is irretrievable."

Dr. Jansen stood up from the sofa and paced back and forth.

"Let me explain it better, to avoid appearing to be unseemly. In more than forty years of work with children with disabilities, I've found parents who are so stubborn that they managed to convince me their children could move forward. They celebrate each small success like a big victory, and small step after small step, the children progressed, the achievements added up, and after years of treatments, those who we labeled *irretrievable* were on their way to becoming people with autonomy. Discredited children got back on their feet because their parents were wholehearted—parents who managed to prove that my first impression was wrong."

"Blaming parents for the success or failure of their children isn't a little bit too harsh?"

"Many parents don't know what to do for their child to respect them, be conscientious, or listen, because they, themselves, never had someone they could simulate. In the end, it is the lack of knowledge and the lack of experience that generates the educational problem as a consequence. The cycle will break when parents know their children are their responsibility, yes! And it is education with quality, that tries to understand the person entirely and globally, that paves the only way there is to produce a difference in that child's future."

"Oh! That is why you think parents are the most important factor for a high-quality education..."

"Without a doubt!"

"And the sooner these parents realize that, the better."

"Of course!" Dr. Jansen smiled, as he saw he was being understood.

"And what is the protocol Awake Clinic has for 'normal' children? Could you tell me a little bit more about it?"

Once again, the doctor considered the question before answering, "The protocol is called the Steps. And from all of our interventions, it is the one that has the best results. The Steps is completely based on the progress of neurology, neuroscience, and psychology during the last forty years. We have several children that follow this program, or that have already followed it, with nearly absolute success." The eyes of the doctor sparkled while mentioning the protocol. "By being stimulated since childhood, they don't become 'normal' children, but rather genial! They jump to above the average in all ways, becoming a dot outside the curve. It's impressive ... their progress. Furthermore, this is the only protocol that does not require many adjustments from child to child. It depends more on the learning speed of each one and the parent's availability."

Estela smiled, relieved. She knew right from the beginning that she was on the right path. There was just one other aspect disturbing her. "I didn't understand one thing. If you have that excellent protocol, wholly based on scientific evolution, which was already tested and approved, why don't you make it public? Wouldn't it be interesting?"

Dr. Jansen remained silent again while deliberating about the question before answering, "Estela, I would love if other people could have access to this kind of knowledge, but do you think there are a lot of people who are willing to change their lifestyle for their children? I don't think so. Most of them want nature to raise their descendants; they hope their genetics are blessed and will overcome everything else. The mentality is, 'Don't worry, and everything will be all right. I will worry when the time comes. I mean, if anything goes wrong.' Who am I to tell them, 'Follow this, and your child will be the highest exponent, he will have more opportunities than you have ever dreamed'? I can't do that . . . Most of them would suspect my ideas and would label me as a charlatan; the others, even if they believed me, would not follow my ideas."

"But you have already seen results ..."

"Here at Awake, we have a situation that falls outside the typical pattern. The parents who look for us are different. They put their children first. They are the ones working two times harder. They are the ones who follow the most difficult and most rigid protocols. The results come from their effort. Even if the child with a disability can't manage to develop adequately, their parents will develop their potential."

This time it was Estela who waited until every sentence had been understood.

"So, you ensure that the Steps work?"

"I see the results every day. In the end, it is our big project. It is what makes me wake up early and come to work. I'm privileged, Estela. In my life, I have the mission of helping children achieve their potential regarding their cognitive, psychomotor, and affective skills. I love seeing the progress of these children. And neuroscience is currently finding methods that help them develop even more. I'm sure that we are doing our part, due to the parents and children that come here looking for us, and at the same time, I'm trying to change the minds of those around us. I see our actions as several continuous waves that spread the results and cause an impact, not only locally, but also in other spaces and spheres, quite far away from here. When people see the results from our work, they start believing that it is possible to improve education for everyone."

"You said that you see results every day. How many children have already followed your protocol?"

"Thousands," Dr. Jansen spoke without thinking. "And I repeat, most of them with absolute success. Those children who are a part, or were a part, of this education project are emotionally healthy, brilliant, and multitalented."

"And what is the ideal age to start the protocol?"

"The ideal is before conception."

"I don't understand. Before conception?"

"Yes, both the mother and the father have to wish for this child. Both the mother and the father have to be in synchrony and truly love each other so that this love reflects on the child and establishes an even stronger bond between them. It is clear that the mother suffers less from stress during pregnancy when the father gives love to her and the baby. Several studies have already shown that exposing the fetus to a high level of hormones related to stress, especially cortisol, can be harmful to the baby in the long term."[ii]

"How can it be harmful?"

"In several different ways[iii]. From raising the risk of diseases to reducing the baby's growth, changing the times for the development of tissues, diminishing the size of the brain, damaging the system that is used to answer stress, changing the baby's temper, and even impacting the expression of specific genes."

Estela laughed. "The problem is that everyone is constantly stressed..."

"Yet it is not all the kinds of stress. Harmful stress happens when stress is too frequent or intense."

The doctor stood up swiftly and went to the bookshelf. While using his index finger to point, he looked through the books until he found one called *The Ice Storm: An Historic Record in Photographs of January 1998*[iv]. He took it off the bookshelf, passed his hand through it, and gave it to Estela. She started leafing through its pages randomly.

Dr. Jansen explained, "January 1998 was one of the worst winters Canada has faced. The natural disaster resulted in hundreds of towns and cities having no electricity. About five million people had no heat, and tens of people died. Imagine yourself in that cold, without a heat source or electric light."

Estela watched the photos of the devastation, uprooted trees, snow, chaos. It made her face turn pale. Dr. Jansen continued: "Depending on where the person lived, that nightmare lasted from a few hours to up to six weeks. Many bridges fell, the army had to rebuild the electric grid. It was a matter of life and death. Imagine that you were pregnant and experiencing that storm, rolled up in blankets, shivering cold, in minus ten degrees centigrade, praying for everything to get back to normal, begging for your child to stay longer in your belly, since accessing the hospital would be impossible and if the child were to be born now, he or she would die..."

Estela's pulse accelerated.

"Researchers from McGill University in Montreal decided to investigate what happened with the children of those who were pregnant while suffering the consequences of that disaster.[v] In June 1998, hundreds of women fulfilled surveys about the stress level they faced during the storm. Following, their children, who were already around five years old, were assessed. The result: the children who were exposed to high levels of intra-uterine stress had a lower development of language and lower cognition skills, or in other words, a lower IQ. In subsequent studies, it was found that these children were more obese[vi] than other children."

Estela closed the book and returned it to Dr. Jansen, who replaced it precisely where it had been.

"Besides love between the couple, affection for the baby, and low stress, the mother must practice physical exercise during pregnancy, ingest vitamin supplements, such as omega-3 and folic acid in low doses, and of course, adopt a healthy and balanced diet—many fruits and vegetables—while being careful to avoid becoming overweight or underweight. All of these aspects are important for the baby to be born ready."

"Omega-3?"[vii]

"Yes, omega-3 is essential both for the baby and the mother. DHA helps the development of the brain and the eyes, while the EPA strengthens the immune system and adjusts the inflammatory response . . . Studies show that high consumption of omega-3 by the mother reduces the risk of allergies in newborns, can improve the child's IQ by a few points[viii], can enhance the child's ability to focus[ix], and can also diminish the dangers of premature birth[x] and pre-eclampsia . . ."

"Interesting. What else do you recommend to pregnant women?"

"That's it. There is no secret. Or did you think we made mothers put earphones on their belly while playing Mozart?"

"Not at all, of course . . ."

"I know a mother who did that. Unfortunately, it produced no results. The child doesn't even like classical music!"

Estela smiled, exposing her white and aligned teeth.

Dr. Jansen added: "So you just have to follow this set of simple measures for this baby, that is inside of you, to be ready to become one of the many winners of nature."

Estela concealed a smile. She didn't understand the comment but made sure to let the doctor know, "No ... I'm not pregnant. I just came here for the interview."

Dr. Jansen took a hand to his forehead. "I'm sorry for the mistake. It's a force of habit. Mothers come here asking for recommendations ... You know how it is ..."

"It's all right. I understand... Tell me more about the Steps, Doctor."

"The protocol is constituted by twelve steps in total. We equip the babies with the necessary tools to be able to maximize their learning experience, capture everything around them with higher clarity, and better absorb the contents of books and daily events. Later we cultivate the principles that will guide their lives. That's because even with fertile soil, we have to give the necessary instructions regarding discipline, proactivity, consciousness, coexistence with other people, respect . . . Lastly, we close the cycle. In that stage, we do what we know should be done because we gave them the foundation that allows them to become complete adults, which will make a difference in the world."

Dr. Jansen had just ended his considerations about the twelve steps when the phone sounded distantly.

"Wait just a moment." The doctor quickly went to his table, picked up the phone, listened for a while, and answered: "You can tell them that I'm finishing here and that I will call them quite soon. Oh, Adelaide . . . Can you come here then, please? Thank you."

He returned to her, walking slowly. Estela anticipated him: "The two ladies are complaining about the delay?"

"You are right! I want to conclude my exposition by introducing you to an exceptional person."

The secretary opened the door. She was a brunette, about fifty years old, and quite small.

"Here you have Adelaide, my right arm here at the clinic. Adelaide, tell Estela the story about your boy, Guilherme."

Adelaide twisted her short legs, then said: "Guilherme is my pride."

"Tell her that when you started working for us, you would bring little Guilherme here and that he followed all the steps according to our guidance . . ."

"It is true."

"And that sometimes I had to be a little bit hard with you."

"Yes . . ."

"Tell her, was it worth it?"

"Of course."

"Tell her who Guilherme is today."

"He is a neurology resident in Paulista Medical School."

"Tell her everything! That he was the first one in the entrance exam. That he made his money doing a small physics course. That despite working double shifts he was first in his class and passed all the postgraduate training he had but chose to go to Paulista because of his bride . . ."

"It is true, Doctor."

"And that soon he will become a huge contributor to the Clinic, as we will hire him . . ."

"That's you who are saying it, Doctor . . ."

"Here you have one of our examples, Estela. A resilient mother who believed in the potential of her little boy, a true winner son."

"And I've raised him alone," added Adelaide.

"So, you see it is possible."

Adelaide got closer to the doctor and whispered to him, "Doctor, the two ladies outside are angry . . ."

"I'm already going," Estela said to Dr. Jansen. "I came here so you could teach me how our children can learn to read sooner. However, I'm leaving with the impression that I have to learn a lot more than that."

"That's because teaching goes beyond reading and writing," the doctor said. "Here at the clinic we extrapolate: we teach our children how to relate, have a rich intellectual and affective life, have friends and pleasure, achieve success, and also—and why not?—make money. Do you doubt that the human brain was made to go beyond the limits that we pre-establish for ourselves? We see so many examples of people that leave us speechless while they change the world where we live, making it a much better space technologically, scientifically, artistically, socially . . . I believe we are predestined to do more than we are currently doing. If there are people in the media that insist that we have the power to wipe out the world, there are also people that defend our ability to fix it, to make it increasingly better. Thus, Estela, when you get to the sixth or seventh month of pregnancy, I will be pleased to explain further what I told you today. Who knows if your child will not become a Guilherme . . ."

"Or a Patricia or a Yago . . ." Adelaide suggested.

"And so many others . . ."

Estela understood that Adelaide was observing her, gazing at her belly.

"No, I'm not pregnant. That is quite far from happening."

"Well, when you become pregnant, you already have the invitation," the doctor concluded.

Estela stopped the recording, somehow disturbed, picked up her purse, and straightened her silver suit. Once again, she shook Dr. Jansen's firm hand, determinately looking at those two magnetic blue eyes. Then she shook Adelaide's warm, moist hand.

While leaving the room, she felt a little bit envious of Roberto, her colleague, because he managed to spend five days with the doctor. She agreed with him: Michael Jansen was a fascinating person.

But pregnant?

She got on the elevator and quickly looked at her body, which was not showing anything other than a lean belly and her well-shaped legs. If she were overweight, it would be possible to understand the mistake.

"Me, expecting a child?" she thought. "Imagine how crazy that would be! Where did he get that idea from? It's not time yet. First, I would need to get married. Then, I would have to enjoy time with my husband for a little longer, and only then could I think about having a baby. That's like seven light-years away."

She did some math, and her age surprised her. "Thirty-six years old is a little bit too late for the first child." She decided on a shorter period: four years.

A yellow light immediately appeared in her thoughts. She remembered that she had forgotten to take the pill one day in the current month. Should she worry about it? No, it was just a coincidence. After all, although he looked like a Sherlock Holmes, with a gentleman's posture and a sharp intellect, he had no grounds to guess something like that.

Unless he was a wizard.

She went outside the clinic, to the sidewalk, and the valet returned with her car, an old Clio. In the traffic, the yellow light became red, and she even became sure that whether Dr. Jansen was a wizard or not, he deliberately left her conscious of her pregnancy.

Could it be possible?

"Who knows, after practicing for so long, maybe he has a sixth sense that allows him to know that I'm pregnant?"

"No, that's absurd!" she answered herself.

However, no matter how much she denied it, her own sixth sense was now screaming and alarmed. She was two days late with her menstrual cycle, but that was normal during the tumultuous days of quotidian life. During the times when she was attending the university, her period was regular, but now, with the daily stress, it was a little bit irregular, sometimes being three days late.

Anyway, she decided to clear the doubt. She stopped at a

pharmacy, nearly panicking, already imagining the developments of her own life. She went straight to the end of the establishment, near the young pharmacist at the desk, who was sitting on a small stool, staring closely at his cellphone.

"Do you have pregnancy tests?"

"Obviously," he crustily answered.

"How much does it cost?"

"It depends. Let me check the computer. We have cheaper ones, and more expensive ones."

"You can give me the most expensive one, please." She was not willing to save money at that moment. If she bought the cheaper one and it gave a negative result, the doubt would persist. She checked the expiration date on the purple package, which stated the test had an accuracy of over 98 percent. She went to the cashier and saw the orange containers with omega-3 capsules on the shelf near him. She impulsively picked one up, paid for the two items, and while leaving, gave some coins to the tramp who stank like urine and was "watching after" her car. When she sat in the car seat, she felt slightly nauseous.

"Stay calm; come on! You are not even pregnant yet."

The probability was gradually higher as she remembered each signal, each symptom.

She got home and quickly read the package instructions: it detected, with high accuracy, the hormone hCG, human chorionic gonadotropin, from the beginning of pregnancy.

She sat on the toilet, making sure the urine would not pass over the line that delimited the "maximum." She took the little rod out, placed it on the granite sink, and waited the five minutes that were recommended. Her heart was hammering against her thorax. She felt anguished, walked from one side to the other, wishing that the result was a negative but instinctively knowing she was lying to herself. She went away from the pregnancy test, to the kitchen, and in three minutes she was back to the bathroom, seeing that a second line was forming. She waited, watching the two lines becoming more intense, unequivocal.

Then, Estela put her hands over her hair, allowing a scream to escape.

She was pregnant.

CHAPTER 02 — GESTATION

"There is a moment of conception and there is a moment of birth, but between them, there is a long period of gestation."

—*Jonas Salk*

Her head was still revolving in panic. The test had to be wrong! How could that happen? Should she tell her boyfriend now? How would he react? She decided not to say anything to him before being sure about the result. The information in the package indicated the test had an accuracy of 98 percent, so there was still 2 percent left for errors.

She called her gynecologist office. She begged the secretary to get her an appointment as soon as possible. It was urgent.

"I only have time on Thursday, next week . . ."

"Can't you fit me in? Is there any chance at all?"

"Maybe. Give me your number. If any patient requests to reschedule, I will call you."

She drove to the publisher, feeling disoriented. She was not paying attention to the traffic and then to her work colleagues. It was impossible to stay focused.

Karen, a reporter, a friend from work, who was next to her table, took off her glasses and commented: "Today is not a good day, is it?"

"Not good at all ... I just found out that I'm pregnant," she said abruptly.

"That's wonderful!" Karen exclaimed, looking genuinely happy. She got up and hugged Estela.

"I'm afraid, my dear friend," Estela admitted in a whisper, "I don't know what is going to happen with my life."

"Oh, my dear!" Karen started, speaking and holding both her arms. "It is going to change a lot but certainly for the better. My children are my treasure. You will see ... Once the initial shock passes, you will handle it perfectly."

Her cellphone vibrated in her purse. It was a call from the gynecologist.

"Can you make it by 6:30 p.m.?"

"Yes! That's perfect!"

"Well, then you have an appointment."

It felt like the afternoon lasted forever, Estela's anxiety was so high. Once she completed her workday, she went straight to the consulting room. Dr. Lucimara had been her gynecologist for the last three years, so they already had a certain degree of intimacy. She told her about what she suspected and started crying.

"Stay calm, Estela," the Japanese doctor said, caressing the hands of the future mother. "You don't need to get all upset. It's not the end of the world. You have a child, a life inside of you! Do you know how many women try to get pregnant and fail?"

With quite polished handwriting on a pink prescription pad, Dr. Lucimara requested a beta-hCG blood exam, which was more trustable than the pharmacy tests, as well as other urine and blood tests.

She gave Estela the requests, complementing it with a soft look. "Easy ... There is nothing to be alarmed about."

Estela attempted to calm down while going home. She needed to get rid of the feelings of fear and anguish so the idea of having a child could start taking root.

She was preparing for a bath when Victor called. "Hi, my love," he said, sounding like he was in a good mood. "You didn't even call me to tell me about how things went at the clinic."

"At the clinic?" she nearly stuttered. "Oh, with Dr. Jansen? Everything worked out perfectly."

"You waited so long for this interview that you didn't even remember me. Can I come over? I miss you. Then you can tell me everything: how he is, if it is true what they say about him ..."

"Not today," she replied, looking at the pink prescription in front of her. "You can come tomorrow. I have lots to do, and I'm late. Have a good night!"

Estela hung up the phone, feeling bad about how abruptly she spoke with Victor, and went to sleep, emotionally exhausted.

On the following day, the reporter woke up in another mood, more positive and less fearful. Still fasting, she had her blood collected and went out for a productive day at work.

Around four in the afternoon, she accessed the laboratory website and saw that there were already some results. She immediately identified the beta-hCG, which was positive. So, it was true! She was pregnant.

She called her boyfriend and asked him if he would come by her apartment later that night.

"Of course!" he replied, sounding excited.

She was happy with the answer and tried to get done with work early so she could go buy some things for a romantic dinner.

Back at her place, she was cooking dinner and thinking about the day that she found Victor, almost a year ago. It was at a party promoted by an advertising agency, and a lot of young and beautiful people were there. Suddenly, Victor got closer and started chatting. Estela analyzed him: a little bit taller than 1.8 meters, with a broad chest, discretely muscular arms, honey-colored eyes, full hair, and a purposely careless beard. He had a beer in his hand but was sober. He asked who she was, what she did . . .

At that moment, she did not yet know that Victor was the son of the agency owner, and she was also not aware that he was the golden boy of advertisement. Until that moment, the only thing she knew was that he was sexy, had a light voice, and . . . exhaled testosterone.

He took her dancing and couldn't hold himself back, kissing her on the dance floor.

Eleven months later, the chemistry was still intense, and they spent time together almost every day, which strengthened their feelings for one another and slowly replaced a merely casual relationship. Estela loved him; she really did. The other side of the coin also seemed to be true, since she was his longest-lasting relationship . . . until now.

The intimacy created by the time spent together made them less careful regarding protection, making them take unnecessary risks, and there it was, the result: 12,400 of beta-hCG.

After cooking, Estela had a bath and sprayed the perfume that Victor liked the most on her neck, and put on a pair of tight jeans and a white shirt with lace. She carefully did her hair, used black mascara to highlight her already long eyelashes, and applied a light gloss over her full lips.

Victor knocked on the door, and she opened, with an indescribable look.

"Wow, you are so gorgeous!" he said before embracing her like a hungry animal, kissing her while holding her in his arms.

"We need to talk . . ." she said.

He instinctively retracted, scared. "What's wrong? We are good, aren't we?"

"I want to know something. Look right into my eyes and tell me, without blinking: do you love me?"

"Of course I love you!" he quickly and convincingly said. "I do love you. Why? Don't you love me?"

"I do! But something unforeseen happened . . . Something that was not planned."

Estela stopped talking, searching for courage within herself to say the words.

"I'm pregnant."

Victor instantly went from tan to pale.

"Pregnant? You are kidding, right?"

"No, I'm not kidding. I'm pregnant," Estela reaffirmed. "I found out yesterday, but I used a pharmacy test. Today I did a blood exam, which confirmed it."

A deathly silence floated in the air.

"I don't know how it happened . . ." Estela attempted to explain herself while examining the expressions on her boyfriend's face. "I never missed the pill. Maybe I forgot it once last month."

Victor was silent, although his eyes expressed a feeling she had never seen: anger. She waited until he spoke. However, the silence remained for what seemed like long seconds, and, when he finally spoke, he spoke too loudly. "You were so irresponsible! How could you be this irresponsible? I trusted you! I don't want a child now. I'm twenty-eight, for God's sake!"

"But . . ."

"Don't you see that we never spoke about having children? Because it was never in my plans." Victor looked at her as if criticizing her, as if she had planned this pregnancy. "What are you going to do now, Estela?"

She identified the subliminal rejection in his words. She raised her chin and replied, "You are not suggesting I should have an abortion, are you? If you are, know that I would never do such a barbaric thing to our child! He is here inside of me, and I already want him, I already feel love for him."

"You are placing words in my mouth . . ."

"If you don't want to shoulder this, it's okay. I will take the responsibility . . . However, our relationship is over, right now."

Victor thought for a little while and finally said slowly and in a low voice: "I don't know . . . I need some time," while walking backward. "I need some time. I came here today thinking I would have a nice night; however, you blew it. I don't feel like eating, talking . . . like anything."

He reached the doorknob, opened it, and left without looking back.

"Don't run away from me!" Estela shouted like it was an order.

"I trusted you," he quietly said while closing the door, leaving her alone.

Estela felt her throat closing and a considerable need to cry, which she decided to swallow. She placed her hands over her womb. She had her child with her. If they were the only ones, that was okay; she would take care of providing the best for her child. She would assume all the responsibilities alone. Even though Estela was trying to hold them, the tears ran down her face, uncontrolled, blurring her makeup. She was wrong. Victor was not the man of her life. Instead, he was a spoiled kid who did not know how to assume his obligations.

She went to the door and locked it.

She could barely sleep during the night. Millions of unnecessary worries came and went, forming a continuous emotional teeter-totter. She needed to go back to her life, and she needed to regain control. She needed to sleep.

In the morning, she remembered the interview with Dr. Jansen, which she did not have the time to transcribe yet. She played her cell phone and allowed the doctor's deep voice to fill the air while she prepared something to eat. Suddenly, she found herself sitting at the kitchen bench, taking notes about what he was explaining on a yellow writing pad while the pungent smell of coffee was waking her. If, before, the interview with Dr. Jansen was to please her boss, it now had a new meaning, a much more important one: the information could change the future of her child.

She needed to calm down since stress was not good for the baby. She also needed to exercise and eat properly. However, she didn't know how much exercise she should get. How much weight should she gain? Inside her, there was an immense desire to return to Awake Clinic and ask Dr. Jansen for more tips. She wanted to meet the doctor as if he was her ally. However, she had to accept waiting until the end of gestation, the interval between the sixth and the seventh month, to return to Awake, as suggested by the doctor. Meanwhile, she would clear her doubts with the gynecologist, Dr. Lucimara.

When all the blood exams were finally ready, she got a new appointment with her.

"Congratulations, my dear, you are pregnant!" Dr. Lucimara seemed excited about the result. "But wait, what is this beta-hCG value? Maybe you have twins?"

Estela gulped. "What?"

"It could be . . . According to your menstruation date, the reference value of this beta would be up to 2,600. The 12,400 value you have is a very high number . . . Just don't worry about it, okay?"

"I won't worry about it. I'm terrified about it! If taking care of a child is hard, imagine two."

"I will order an ultrasound to make sure you have one baby. Well, how did your boyfriend react?"

"What? Well, it's been a week since I last heard from him. He asked me for some time . . ."

"Men! He will come back. He is just scared."

Estela was not there to talk about Victor. Instead, she wanted to clear her doubts. She had so many things to ask her. "How much weight should I gain during pregnancy?"

"It depends on your body mass index, or BMI, and also on the fact that you can have one or two babies. If you only have one . . . You are 1.65 meters tall, and your weight is 57 kilograms, right?"

Estela nodded.

Dr. Lucimara got the glass calculator near the computer and entered the values.

"Your BMI is 20.9, which is considered normal. Thus, you will gain between 11.5 and 16 kilograms until the end of pregnancy."

Estela imagined herself weighing 73 kilograms. She was going to feel obese.

"Don't look at me like that. You will lose that weight after pregnancy."

"Or not . . ."

"Of course you will. Are you exercising?"

"That was my next question. How much can I exercise and how frequently?"

"Ideally you should exercise[xi] every day; thirty minutes is enough. Of course, you can't exercise too heavily. Aerobic activity, such as walking, of light to medium intensity, is good for you and the baby."

"Do I need to stop my spinning and bodybuilding?"

"It is better if you don't exceed a light to medium intensity. What matters the most is exercising, as it will keep you in good shape, calmer, and happier."

"And does the baby benefit from that?"

"Without a doubt! If you exercise during the first trimester, when the placenta is forming, it will be richer in blood vessels, amplifying the passage of nutrients and blood to the baby. Maybe that is why exercising reduces the risk of pre-eclampsia[xii] considerably. The body movement of the mother, besides reducing the risk of gestational diabetes, trains the baby's heart, which might make him more likely to be athletic in the future. So, everything is good for you and him. The key word is *moderation* . . . At the end of gestation, when the belly is quite big and heavy, you must perform lighter exercises and avoid excessive heat. No sauna or hot jacuzzi since the heat can be harmful to the baby's eyes and brain and can increase the risk of premature birth[xiii]. Swimming and hydro-gymnastics are ideal for that phase since they cool the body and give that wonderful lightness feeling that pregnant women deserve so much."

"Dr. Lucimara, I know it is a foolish question, but do you think I can avoid getting stretch marks? My mother had so many!"

"Come with me; lie here."

Estela arranged herself on the stretcher that was behind the medical table. Lucimara pulled Estela's shirt up, revealing her belly, golden skin, and the small, light-colored hairs. She felt her stomach, pinched her skin, and gave her a prognostic: "Your skin is quite elastic and has no stretch marks, [xiv]which is a good sign. You have to drink lots of liquids, start using a good body hydrating lotion, and exercise your skin elasticity, stretching it in both ways, creating horizontal and vertical wrinkles. Like this," the gynecologist reinforced the idea, performing the movements with her fingers on Estela's abdomen. "And you have to do it many times a day. However, the most important thing is to stay inside the weight margin that we calculated before. If you become too overweight, or too quickly, there isn't a body lotion or exercise that can help you."

They returned to their respective places, and Dr. Lucimara concluded: "Your exams are great and so are you, Estela. Let's see this ultrasound and hope that it is just one baby. Then you have to start enjoying gestation."

It was hard to enjoy the beginning of the gestation period: lonely, feeling excessively sleepy and with nausea, which was increasingly more frequent. Stela's blog had also suffered changes. Instead of the original and exciting news about general culture that she usually posted, she opted for a more intimist topic, sharing with her readers that she was pregnant and her plans for the future. From that moment on, she reported everything she read about pregnancy, relationships, love, and care. Despite how strange it may have sounded, the number of people who visited her blog increased exponentially. The new readers were mothers who identified with Estela.

Being entertained by all the reading, the blog, and her work, she had the necessary patience to wait for the news: "It is just one fetus," the radiologist doctor confirmed once the exam was done, giving Estela a paper tissue so she could clean the cold gel from her abdomen. "You have no hematoma, and there is nothing irregular. Presumably, everything is good."

"Phew!" Estela sighed, relieved. "One less problem."

The tranquility acquired from the result gave her the courage to tell her mother that she would become a grandmother for the first time.

"Gee!" said her mother, quite excited, over the phone. "What great news! I'm so happy! When are you going to marry?"

Estela was the elder daughter but the only one who was not married yet.

"Oh, mother . . . Victor broke up with me."

"I don't believe it!" her mother shouted from the other side of the line. "He seemed to be a good person, an upright boy . . . How do you feel? Do you want me to fly to São Paulo to help you?"

"No, Mother, it's water under the bridge."

"Oh, well . . . When your father finds out about this, he will have a heart attack. His dear Estela, a single mother! Either he will have a heart attack, or he will go after Victor."

"Mother, please, don't tell him anything! Let me drop the bomb when the time comes."

When she hung the phone up, she became quite concerned about her father's reaction. He was short-tempered and never liked any of her boyfriends. Imagine what he would do when he found out that Victor had left her when she was pregnant!

While she was thinking about the possibilities, the house interphone sounded. The doorman wanted to know if he should let Victor inside or not.

"Yes, you can, Mr. Manoel."

Estela quickly got to the mirror, fixed her makeup, straightened her hair, and brushed her teeth. She was feeling butterflies in her belly, a crazy desire to see him again, even if it was to tell him how everything was going.

Even though Estela left the door ajar, he rang the doorbell.

"Come in!" she told him in a friendly and receptive tone.

Victor looked languid, and that momentarily frightened her. Meanwhile, that feeling dissipated when he gave her a giant bouquet of yellow Colombian roses and started apologizing:

"I came here to apologize . . . I was quite childish! It was the shock; I don't know . . . A strange feeling took me. I was mad, but as the days passed by, I started getting calmer. I tried quite hard to forget you, but everything reminded me of you. I was thinking about you the whole time. I wanted to ignore you, I really did. But I also wanted to hear your voice, hug you, kiss you . . . I needed time to understand where I was, to rediscover myself.

His eyes filled with tears. She picked up the massive bouquet and allowed him to continue: "I read what you wrote about love, about parents and children. I was touched by sanity on the inside. I understood I was doing everything wrong. I was selfish. I'm almost thirty, I have a good job, so I can't leave my child without a father. I have a father who still gives me love. I have a mother who spoils me . . . How can I take that away from my child?"

Victor was speaking under his breath as if he was quite exhausted and needing to inhale all the air that he could.

"It is you, Estela; you are an incredible woman: intelligent, beautiful, sweet . . . You are someone I want to be close to. I'm sure that I have chosen the ideal mother for my child."

He tried to clean the tears that were running freely down his face, using the back of his hand, while the words kept flowing torrentially. "I thought about it a lot. We have been through so much together . . . The trip to Gramado, the holidays in João Pessoa, our nights talking non-stop . . . We complete each other. You make me feel complete. I can't live away from you. I don't want to stay away from you . . . no, never again."

Estela heard all of this and forgot about the sorrow, disappointment, and loneliness. She threw the bouquet to the sofa and kissed him—quick and burning kisses surrounded by salty tears that mixed and formed a single feeling: love.

They wanted each other as always and as never before.

"I love you," whispered Estela.

"Marry me," supplicated Victor.

She was speechless and thought she was making up things she had not heard.

"Marry me," insisted Victor, taking a black velvet box from his pocket. When he opened it, Estela saw a golden ring with the biggest diamond she had seen in her whole life.

She held him closer, smiling.

And she answered, "Yes."

The wedding party happened against Estela's will, as she did not want anything flashy. She dreamed of something that was intimate, which was the exact opposite of what her marriage ceremony was. While organizing the party, Sílvia, her mother-in-law, defined two goals: the first was to have the wedding as quickly as possible, so no one would know Estela was pregnant; the second was to make it an unforgettable event. Using her contacts, she managed to reduce the wait list for the most famous and essential church in São Paulo, which was supposed to be booked years into the future. Thus, in less than three weeks they got married in the Sé Cathedral, which had its Gothic structure carefully decorated and was transformed into a magnificent temple, worthy of a movie that day.

The ceremony was perfect. Estela went to the holy altar, with her father, who was sobbing with emotion, holding her veil and wreath. After the exchange of vows and wedding rings, which was marked by many tears, everyone proceeded to the reception at the Jockey Club, which was quite expensive and sophisticated.

At the end of the party, the couple was exhausted, yet happy, and left without anyone noticing for their honeymoon. They flew first class to Tahiti, immersed in the dreams of their future.

When they returned to Brazil, a surprise was waiting for them. Walter, her father-in-law, gave them the key for their new house, saying: "Victor will be closer to work, and Estela and the baby can walk through Aclimação Park, which is just two blocks away from the house, to sunbathe and breathe purer air.

The apartment could match any high standard, had five bedrooms, and had four free parking spots in the garage.

"At least our children will have space to run inside here," Victor said, opening his arms in the middle of one of the rooms.

"Already thinking about the next child?" asked Estela, lifting an eyebrow.

"We won't have just one, or will we?"

"I hope not," answered Estela, who was happy, feeling the smell of the recently installed furniture.

"I always wanted to have siblings, but Mr. Walter and Mrs. Sílvia were never thrilled about it . . . So I want to have at least three children. You can start preparing your belly."

And the belly started to show up, slowly. In every antenatal visit, Dr. Lucimara complimented her: "Perfect, perfect!"

"It is a pity we couldn't see the baby's gender through the ultrasound."

"That is normal. If you want to know if it as a boy or a girl, there is a blood exam called fetal sexing[xv] that is almost 100 percent accurate."

"Even for me, considering that I'm on my tenth gestation week?"

"Yes. From the eighth week . . . It's a very accurate exam."

Without thinking twice, she took the exam. The result was precisely as she had sensed . . .

As soon as she completed the twenty-eight weeks of gestation, she tried to contact Dr. Michael Jansen again, but his secretaries and operators were an insuperable barrier. Since she could not succeed approaching him, she went to Awake Clinic one afternoon.

"Hi!" Estela got closer to the secretary. "I would like to know if Dr. Michael Jansen is at the clinic today."

"Do you have an appointment?"

"Actually, no. The doctor asked me to return once I was on my seventh month of gestation," said Estela, caressing her very evident belly. "Here I am."

The secretary, who was young and beautiful, pressed a button on her collar and placed her shell-shaped hand on the headset and said a few codes, which Estela could not recognize. Finally, she said: "Today it will be impossible to get an appointment. Maybe we can schedule for another day?"

If she tried to get an appointment on the doctor's busy schedule, that would only happen after the baby was born, she imagined.

"I will schedule it later, thank you," replied Estela with a slightly annoyed voice.

She went to the coffee shop, which was in the atrium, asked for water, and drank a few sips. When she saw that the receptionist was distracted with a couple, she stepped up the pace toward the elevator. She pressed button number 6 and saw the doors closing, and within a few seconds she was on the sixth floor. Her senses took in the glass walls, the orchid flowerbeds, and the same rosemary scent, precisely as she remembered.

She went to the secretary and called her by her name: "Adelaide," said Estela, reaching out her hand. "You are Guilherme's mother, aren't you?"

The secretary examined her with a surprised expression.

"You don't remember me . . . Dr. Jansen introduced us, a few months ago."

"Oh, now I remember! The journalist," said Adelaide, smiling. "And you were pregnant; he never fails."

"I still don't know how he knew . . . Is he in his office, by any chance?"

Adelaide looked at the table clock and answered, "No, he is on the third floor. You better hurry or you won't find him here. The doctor is going to travel soon."

"Is he?"

"Yes, he is taking a few weeks as a sabbatical leave. You better run."

"Thank you so much," said the journalist before going to the third floor as fast as possible. The floor consisted of a narrow corridor which led to offices on both sides. At the end of the corridor, she distinguished a wall with sunflowers of several sizes, apparently painted by children. She got closer and saw that over the door leaf there was silver plate stating: "Learning is a treasure that will follow its owner everywhere" (Chinese proverb).

Through the glass door, she saw Dr. Jansen sitting on a green tatami, with his legs crossed, in front of a child who was being held by the mother.

The doctor was explaining something while handling white cards with words written in bright red. "You can show the cards faster, always pronouncing the words clearly, like this: Baby bottle," said the doctor, after choosing one card. "Soother," another one. "Doll," and another one. "Cart," he kept explaining, emphasizing: "You have to pay attention to her eyes. Any indication of tiredness, such as her looking to another side or muttering, and you should stop. It has to be a pleasant activity, an intimate moment between you two, not an obligation."

"But the words of the third group are big. I thought I had to give her more time to read."

"That's what many people think. However, words are like figures for a baby who is six months old, like Clara. If you take too long, she will get bored."

The mother and the daughter noticed that Estela stopped by the door and looked there. Dr. Jansen stood up from the floor with the agility of a martial arts teacher and looked at her too.

"Good afternoon, Estela! I thought you would never show up."

Estela was surprised that he still knew her name. It was a good sign.

"I'm sorry to interrupt."

"It's okay. Can you wait for just a few minutes, until we are done here? You can sit there, in the armchair, and I'll speak with you soon."

Estela sat, observing the affection and patience that the doctor showed toward the mother and the daughter. She felt the baby kicking in her belly. She massaged what she suspected to be a little foot and whispered, "Stay calm. Mommy is here."

After a few moments, Dr. Jansen said goodbye to the mother and the daughter and came toward Estela. She stood up at the same time he was saying, "I'm glad both of you returned!" while looking at Estela's bulge. "What will you call the little princess?"

"Sofia . . ." answered a perplexed Estela. "You can see that she is a girl just by staring at my belly?"

"No, unfortunately, I don't have X-ray vision. However, I work out my memory and my observation senses daily. I remember that you posted a photo on your blog showing Sofia's bedroom."

"It is true. A month ago, more or less. However, I don't remember saying it was a girl."

"The picture spoke for itself . . . And I must compliment you regarding your blog. It is quite good, getting better every day. You can summarize complex matters quite well. I've noticed that it requires a lot of practice."

"Thank you."

"It is a pity that you have chosen today to come to the clinic when I have already packed. We have so many things to discuss . . . Just by coming here, you show that you care about your daughter's future. It shows that you were curious about what I told you last time and that you are engaged in putting our method into practice. You are different from many mothers, who only care about esthetic aspects; you are here because you worry about her future. You care about your daughter! And that's the essence, the foundation for everything. Wishing the best for your children, that's what every or nearly every parent does. However, acting, going after information, studying, reading, and deepening their knowledge about caring for their children, that is for just a few. Congratulations, you are on the right path!"

"I can come back another day. When will you return from your journey?"

"According to what I've planned, I will stay away for two or three months. I was invited to teach at Melbourne University, in Australia. Furthermore, I want to relax with my wife while being in contact with nature, to recharge our batteries."

"If I had known that before," said Estela, a little bit desolated, "I would have returned earlier, a lot earlier."

"But you are here," said Dr. Jansen. "We can still talk a little bit..."

At that exact moment, a driver, who was wearing a uniform, got closer, interrupting them. "Dr. Jansen, we have to go. It's time."

Estela dried her face, clearly feeling disappointed, saying, "I know you are in a hurry, and I don't want to delay you. Maybe we can talk while you are on your way to the car?"

"Sure, it would be a pleasure."

They both strolled while the driver followed them. Dr. Jansen explained: "The world is changing at a breakneck pace, Estela. We have climate change, artificial intelligence is increasingly more powerful, jobs are disappearing... We need skilled children who are capable and who have multiple talents, who can become adults that do not fear the future."

"I agree!" answered Estela.

"It's not just that. We need confident children, with strong and durable interior values, who have an active attitude toward life. Children who know how to live in harmony with other people. Did you know that having friends [xvi] is the highest predictor of happiness for a person? So being successful is not enough. It is also necessary to make friends."

"Really? And we can learn how to make friends?"

"Of course. Children are malleable and quickly learn how to decipher non-verbal communication, to feel empathy for others, as well as the pain and happiness of other people; they learn to care. Look at you: you are a friendly woman who expresses empathy. You have learned, over many years, how to listen and how to express yourself, how to pay attention to what other people say."

"Thank you for the compliment!"

"We are all more capable and stronger than we think. And by using the right tools, we can make the dream of a better future for all of us a reality. We must appreciate every child in their singularity, seeing that each one of them has distinct skills and weaknesses. With the right effort, as long as it is a positive effort, we can transform a child into a skillful adult, who is confident and with many proficiencies. With education, we can change society."

"You got me excited about this!"

They arrived at the underground parking and went to the black Toyota Prius. The driver opened the door that was on the passenger side.

Dr. Jansen smiled, holding the door. "It's a pity that our time . . ." he touched on the glass of his watch with his finger ". . . is such a limited resource. I promise I will teach you all the twelve steps. And I want you to share them on your blog since we have the answers for those many parents who are afraid of what will happen to their children in the future. We have to start slowly, giving some punctual guidelines gently and kindly. Change happens gradually. However, it is meaningful, thus having a cascade effect."

"I'm looking forward to it."

Dr. Jansen kindly hugged her. "Good luck with giving birth! I wish all the best for you and Sofia."

"Have a nice journey, Doctor."

Time had flown by since that goodbye. Two months had gone by, and there was no sign of the doctor . . . nor any news . . . nothing. It seemed like he had evaporated. Estela had already completed the ninth month of gestation, and the childbirth was expected to happen in three weeks, when she felt strains on her belly. In the beginning, they were soft. However, as days went by, the pressure increased gradually.

According to her gynecologist, these were false contractions, which were typical during the end of gestation. Meanwhile, they became more vigorous and efficient. During one of those strains, she felt something warm running down her legs. She looked down and saw light liquid spreading on the floor.

"Darling!" she screamed, using the wall to stand up. "Call Dr. Lucimara. My water broke!"

CHAPTER 03 — THE FIRST STEP: CONNECTION

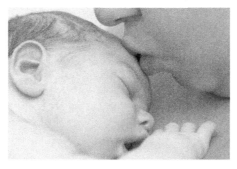

"More than anything else, it is love that separates those who become successful from those who don't. Love is the main ingredient to make adults happy. Thus, show your love to your child."

—Edward M. Hallowell and Peter S. Jensen, *Superparenting for ADD*

S cared by the contractions and the liquid that flowed on the floor, Victor immediately called Lucimara.

"Doctor, I think her water broke!"

"Stay calm, okay? But come quickly to maternity. I'm already on my way."

Victor promptly went to the bedroom and picked up the already prepared bag with all the clothes and diapers for the baby. However, he had to wait for Estela to get ready. While leaving the house, Victor spoke with the voice of someone who was thinking deeply, "When we return, our lives will never be the same . . ."

It was the purest of all truths.

Halfway to the hospital, Estela exclaimed: "Gee! I have to call my mother to let her know we are going to the hospital."

When she got the news, the mother joyfully shouted: "Yay! Daughter, stay calm. Take a deep breath . . . I'm already going to the airport to catch the next flight. Make sure you wait for me. I want to see my granddaughter being born, okay?"

Estela, however, knew how unlikely it would be for her mother to arrive in time. A new contraction sent the message that Sofia was quite close. She tightened her face in pain.

"Don't tell me she is going to be born in here?" asked Victor, in an attempt to make her laugh. "Stay calm and take a deep breath."

He was also worried. However, he was trying not to show it, so that his wife could remain calm. The traffic of São Paulo in the afternoon was intense and immobile, worse than usual, and he felt the need to drum his fingers on the wheel, so Estela didn't notice that his hands were shaking. He got calmer when he saw the maternity building.

He parked the car in the Emergency entrance and got out quickly, to get the door on his wife's side and help her get out of the car. A valet promptly took care of the vehicle. When they entered the hospital, they saw a huge line. They felt relieved when they saw the doctor, who was waving at them.

"I already opened a form for you, Estela," Dr. Lucimara explained. "Come with me."

The couple entered on the elevator smiling and holding hands, going to the obstetric center, more specifically to pre-natal, where a blond nurse was already waiting. Estela changed her overalls for a blue shirt, while the doctor was rubbing her hands, creating a yellow foam of an iodine solution that was falling on the stainless-steel sink.

"When did the water break?" Dr. Lucimara asked.

"Half an hour ago, more or less . . . at 6:00 p.m."

"Okay! I need to examine you to know if it is close to happening. I swear it will be the first and the last time, all right?"

Estela lay with her abdomen facing the ceiling, on the stretcher, watching the Japanese doctor wearing the sterile gloves. The nurse squeezed a transparent gel across the second finger of the doctor.

"Let's see," Dr. Lucimara said while closing her eyes. "Oh, my dear, we are just in the beginning," she summarized, removing her gloves, which she threw into the garbage. "But I need you to stay hospitalized."

The nurse pushed the cardiotocography machine closer to Estela, explaining everything about the procedures to her while applying brown strips on her huge belly. The device showed, in red, the number 155, however, when Estela had another contraction, it jumped to 178, signalizing the baby's heartrate. A graphic started to be drawn, on tricolor paper, pink, yellow, and white, which was strange to the couple, having no apparent meaning.

Estela exhaled heavily, with one hand on her back, breathing out all the air she had in her lungs.

"It is a pain that is worth it, Estela," the doctor commented, taking a piece of paper in her hand. "Everything is good for now. I'm going to the restaurant to have dinner because it is going to be a long night. If you need anything, just call me. I will get here in a second."

Estela's eyes wandered through the place, seeing a beautiful and well-decorated room, and the anxious face of her husband, which contrasted with the nurse's, who expressed serenity. Estela relaxed as she was in one of the best maternity wards in the country. What could go wrong?

"Do you think she will be born today?" Victor asked, stretching on the sofa.

It was already 10:30 p.m., and the impatient doctor kept entering and exiting the room. They had just applied serum in

Estela's veins to hasten the labor. So, the contractions got more frequent, more painful, and stronger. Estela had to stay up, walking from one side to another, to avoid fainting.

"Keep calm, my love!" said Victor.

"It's unbearable!" She was groaning with a panicked voice and her face red. "I want my mother! How did she withstand all this for me? I think I'm going to die! I need some medicine for the pain. I don't think this is normal."

"Dr. Lucimara told us that after the serum this would happen. Do you remember? Do you want me to call her?" Victor asked, a little frightened by the situation.

At that moment, as if through magic, Mrs. Sônia, Estela's mother, arrived, pulling her trolley bags into the room. She still was a beautiful woman, well-groomed, with short hair, brown, lively eyes, and very soft skin, which was the result of a successful mini-lift. When she was younger, she was a TV and theater actress, who had quit her career because of her daughters. The mother and the daughter hugged each other quickly before a new contraction made Estela's legs melt.

"I also went through that, my dear!" the mother said. "The pain seems unbearable, but we are very strong. You will win!"

Dr. Lucimara entered the room. When she saw the pain expressing itself in Estela's countenance, she decided to break her promise. "I'm going to examine you again, to better understand where we are at the moment."

During the procedure, she informed, "The contractions are strong, but the dilatation is not happening. We can choose one of two ways: either we wait a few more hours, or we proceed with a cesarean section."

Estela and Victor had never thought about a cesarean section, as they dreamed of normal labor. Meanwhile, in the middle of all the pain and tiredness, Estela decided, "I want the C-section!"

A few moments later, the stretcher took her to the obstetric center. Victor and his mother-in-law followed her to the door, where the doctor gave them guidelines: "One of you can be present during labor."

Victor, with the camcorder in his hands, made himself available. "I will go. I wouldn't miss this moment for anything in this world."

"Of course," said Sônia, smiling and worried. "Go! Go!"

Victor went to the changing room and wore the green uniform of the surgical center, the foot protection, the mask, and the cap. Then he entered the operating room, observing his wife, who was sitting with her back toward him, with a thin cap on her head, naked, and bending forward.

"Bend a little more," asked the anesthetist. "Yes! That's it! A little sting now."

While the doctor injected the anesthesia, an intense contraction reminded Estela of why she had chosen the cesarean section. She inhaled deeply while her legs started to lose sensitivity. She lay on the stretcher. For the first time that night, she felt relaxed. Now there was only the anxiety of holding her daughter in her arms. The waiting period was quite long; nine months was an eternity!

"That's it, smile for the camera," said Victor when he saw the expression of happiness on his wife's face.

Then he recorded agile gloves with scalpels and scissors, tweezers and compresses.

"I'm going to apply a little bit of pressure here, underneath your belly, Estela," said the doctor, leaning on her arm in the area she indicated while the hairy head of a small baby started to appear.

The hands of the doctor held the head, and with a soft maneuver that included removing a nuchal cord, she made Sofia completely appear—small, intact, wet, and active, already crying spontaneously and moving her little arms and legs quite strongly.

The doctor clamped and cut the umbilical cord and gave the little girl to the pediatrician, who wiped the small body and transported the baby to a little heated cradle.

"She is beautiful, my love!" exclaimed Victor, with tears in his eyes while shaking the camcorder.

"Congratulations, Daddy!" said the pediatrician, placing a small identifier wristband on the baby's wrist. "Sofia got a top grade: Apgar 10 out of 10. She was born at 11:41 p.m. Do you want to hold her?"

"Of course!" said Victor, with his voice choking.

The baby looked as fragile as a crystal in his hesitant arms. Suddenly, when the eyes of the father and his daughter crossed, Victor smiled in adoration. After that surprising instant, he carefully walked behind the surgery curtain, toward his wife, so she too could see the perfect little face of their daughter.

"Look at her, my dear. She is beautiful. Isn't she?"

"She is, of course. Our little princess, Sofia! Welcome to the world, my biggest love!"

A few days later, already at home, during one of many of Sofia's slumbers, Estela decided to write about the birth of her daughter on her blog. She allowed her artistic vein to flow through the message, forgetting about the pain during labor and exalting the burning love and emotion of being a mother.

Minutes after posting the news, while she was proofreading the message to find any spelling errors, she saw that the post already had one comment.

"Congratulations on the beautiful demonstration of affection for Sofia. I hope everything is going perfectly with the family. May the love you feel now fill all the corners of your home and last forever. I wish you a life full of joy, Dr. Michael Jansen."

Estela was so happy that, for a few seconds, she doubted if the replier was the doctor. She reread the message and only after making sure it was his, thanked him for his wishes, without missing the opportunity to ask if he had already returned from his journey.

Some minutes later, there was a new reply: "My wife and I decided to extend our holiday. We will arrive in São Paulo on Saturday afternoon."

Estela decided to take her chances, writing, "We will celebrate Sofia's birth, and we will have lunch with our family and intimate friends, at our apartment, on Sunday. I would love if you could both be here, if possible."

"We are thankful for your invitation, but we have a prior commitment this Sunday. If you are home on Monday morning, and if you want, I can visit you so we can start our project with your daughter."

Estela automatically smiled. He was a particular person. She answered saying she would wait for him on Monday. She could hardly wait for that moment.

As promised, Dr. Jansen went to meet Estela during the morning. At ten o´clock, he was there, at the door of her apartment —tall, upright, with a soft tan and his eyes even bluer than before. He was dressed leisurely and was holding a gift in his hands. While giving it to Estela, he said: "It's for Sofia. I hope you don't have it already."

Estela opened the wrap and saw two children's books, hardcovered, with an English text, that belonged to the Dr. Seuss [xvii] collection.

"Dr. Seuss is a good read when it is time to go to sleep," the doctor furthered. "It stimulates the babies, and they love it. Furthermore, you will improve your English."

"Oh, thank you," said Estela, placing the gift on the wood sideboard close to the sofa. "Sofia is sleeping . . . again. She will wake up soon for breastfeeding."

"You can breastfeed?" asked the doctor.

"Thank God!" sighed Estela. "Being able to breastfeed was a relief to me . . . I've read so many things about breast milk, that I would be frustrated if I was not able to . . ."

Dr. Jansen shook his head to confirm the need for breastfeeding, before commenting, "Breast milk[xviii] protects the newborn from infections, transferring the mother's antibodies to the baby. It prevents[xix] diarrhea, pneumonia, earache, and even candidiasis. Besides protecting, it increases the child's IQ[xx]. An American study[xxi], with consistent results, proved that children who were breastfed had eight[xxii] more IQ points[xxiii], on average, than those who were nourished with formula."

The doctor was passionate about the topic and continued, "It is a pity that not every woman can breastfeed! Meanwhile, every mother should try it . . . And if she can't, she should look for an expert who can identify what is happening: Is the problem in the nipple? Is it the way the breast is held? If nothing works, it is worth trying to buy or rent an electric breast pump[xxiv]. There are powerful breast pumps that can collect a lot of milk, which allows the mother to store some supply in the freezer or refrigerator."

Even though he showed how much he valued breastfeeding, Dr. Jansen did not underestimate the mothers who feed their children with formula, which he also explained: "On the other hand, not breastfeeding is not the end of the world. In that case, mothers need to search for the necessary information to promote adequate nutrition of the baby. They can try to make up for the possible dietary losses of artificial milk using other tactics. We have recipes that are gradually getting closer to breast milk on the market!"

"I still feel I'm lucky . . ." Estela confided. "Is it true that the taste of breast milk changes according to what the mother eats? I'm trying to change my diet to provide new experiences to Sofia."

"Yes, it's true[xxv] . . ."

"Oh! I still remember all the information you gave me when we first met, about the benefits of omega-3 during pregnancy. I also read about the advantages of that supplement during lactation[xxvi]. So, I keep taking those pills . . ."

Estela noticed that they were both still standing in the living room entrance and asked, "Should we sit? Come here, Michael. I asked Vera, our housekeeper, to put out a table. We have pastries, cheese bread, fruit, juices . . ."

The doctor sat near Estela.

"What do you want to eat?" asked Vera.

"The fruit salad seems great, thank you."

The housekeeper served him, and once Estela thanked her, she went straight to the kitchen.

"Finally! Today we can start the Steps; right, Doctor?" asked Estela. "Since the moment I met you, I've been thinking a lot about education. During the moments between pregnancy and giving birth, I kept thinking about the importance of preparing my daughter so she can be the protagonist of a better future. As you said, the sooner we start the process with our children, the better. There are twelve steps, aren't there?"

Dr. Jansen nodded.

"So, are you going to tell me what the first step is?" she asked, rubbing her hands.

"Knowing you, Estela, I'm sure you are already accomplishing it perfectly. The initial step is the simplest, but is also the most important one. It is the very first, and without it, no other step will produce the proper impact. The first step is the connection."

"The connection?"

"Yes, the connection. It is the foundation, the cornerstone upon which everything else will be built. We could call it *love* since it is the essential ingredient of the first step, but it goes beyond it. Loving doesn't matter if one is absent or distant. Love doesn't matter if you don't know how to express it. Thus, the mere existence of the feeling is not enough if it is not palpable, expressed through actions, such as looking into the children's eyes, knowing how to protect them when they are afraid, smiling at them when they need to be encouraged, combing their hair, touching them, hugging, kissing them for no apparent reason."

He stopped to drink juice; however, he immediately continued: "We human beings are naturally social beings. Inside of us, there is an irrepressible thirst for being loved and cared for. We need a connection with someone superior, which children usually materializes in their parents. Parents can have a lot of money, pay several babysitters, give their children everything that is materialistic. However, if children don't have a bond of affection with someone, they will always feel afflicted, needy, searching for satisfaction without ever completely achieving it. It will be hard for them to reach the emotional and cognitive success that was programmed into their DNA.

Estela observed the doctor's shining blue eyes. Since she thought that the first step would be a technique to encourage the baby to read, she was quite surprised. Anyway, she understood that Dr. Jansen's argument was incontestable.

Captivated by the explanation, she kept listening carefully to everything he was saying.

"If there is a connection, there will be no more unsafety or fear. Children will know that there will always be someone who will help them in times of need, someone to trust with their secrets, someone who will understand them, who will fight for them, who will encourage them when the time is right. Thus, children learn that they are of huge value to the world, and that is why they can become anything they desire. Furthermore, if everything works out properly, these children will transmit the love they received to their descendants, spreading it to future generations."

"Well, but that step is so straightforward. Or better, it's trivial!"

"Many parents think so. They can even think they are doing it correctly, but I see, every day, that some need to learn a little bit more about the subject."

"Do you think so? I think that most parents feel love for their children and know how to express it," contested Estela.

"Most of them feel love, that's true. Nothing is fairer, right? Your children come from you. You are dedicated to your children. You sacrifice for them. Love will exist as long as parents are not psychopaths or sociopaths. Like I told you, the feeling is not the only thing that matters. Sharing your feelings, a good daily experience, the quotidian, that's what makes a difference.

Every encounter with your child must be magical! That way, parents make it clear that they care about their children, giving them a substrate made of affection, building their relationship hour after hour, independent of the unpleasant situations of life: if you are in a bad mood or tired, if you lost on the financial field, professionally . . ."

"Fair enough, it might not happen all the time, but most parents play that role. I see love as a universal feeling, and as you said, only a sociopath could be absent."

"Universal . . ." Dr. Jansen ate a spoon of fruit salad, closing his eyes, considering the topic of the discussion before continuing. "The word *universal* was well employed. I believe you agree that animals also feel love for their offspring, right? Meanwhile, like I said, feeling and showing are two different things. I will give you an example that portrays how important it is to know how to express love correctly."

"Michael Meaney[xxvii] and his colleagues from McGill University were doing some research using rats. That was when they noticed a behavior that was so subtle that it had not been noticed before by the scientific community. Right after managing the baby rats—weighing and measuring them, as well as the normal research procedures—and replacing them in their cages, their mothers acted in two distinct ways. Some would come close to the offspring to lick him and take care of him until the little rat would get calmer; on the other hand, other rats did not do that, leaving the little rat all alone. Do you think that subtle difference produced any impact on the rat's life?"

"It did?"

"It produced a huge impact[xxviii]! When the scientists managed the rats, they were scared, and their blood was filled with stress hormones, especially adrenaline and cortisol. The act of licking the offspring reduced its heartrate and regulated anxiety, and both cortisol and adrenaline would return to their normal levels quicker. The rats who were left to their own luck and neglected became less intelligent over time, since they lost their initiative to explore new environments, and if they did so, it would only be for very short periods."

"Really? How did they measure that?"

"Both groups were left in a different environment for five minutes. The group that was constantly licked and cared for by their mothers would bravely explore the surroundings for an average of thirty-five seconds, while the other group would sit prostrate, terrified, and would analyze the new environment for less than five seconds, which means they spent seven times less time exploring . . ."

"That's an incredible difference!" exclaimed Estela, interrupting Michael's narration for an instant, before he kept explaining, moved by excitement: "Another test involved food for ten minutes. The scientist would place food in the rats' cage before scaring them by, for example, clapping, and then they would start clocking. The group that was licked by the mothers would go to the food quicker and would feed for more than two minutes in total since they would not perceive the noise as a real threat. The other group would panic after hearing the same noise, thus becoming paralyzed, and would take more than nine minutes to start eating, and even so, they would only eat for a few seconds. If we rationalize it, the rats that connected with their mothers became braver and took more risks, which are two essential qualities of successful people."

Dr. Jansen ate another spoon of fruit salad. Estela commented on what he said while also questioning him: "All right . . . I agree that the group that was less supported by their mothers could be more fearful than the group that was protected and sheltered. However, my doubt is if one of the groups developed better cognitive and behavioral aspects than the other group. What can you tell me about that?"

The doctor cleaned his lips using the napkin, before answering, "I can tell you that in the cases of the rats that had a connection with their mother, they would not only become more curious but would also be better at exploring the labyrinths, which reflected their intelligence. Furthermore, they were more friendly, less aggressive, and more self-controlled.

Oh! They were also healthier and would live longer."

"Can I make an observation?" asked Estela. "Isn't it possible that the difference is due to genetics? Maybe the rats who licked their offspring were already more intelligent than the other ones, thus passing that advantage to their descendants, which would mean that the connection was not a cause."

"Excellent observation!" exclaimed the doctor. "The scientists also tried to clarify that, changing the baby rats from one mother to another, and also changed their cages[xxix]. The result was the same: it was not about genetics! Those who were cared for and licked became more intelligent, braver, and calmer."

"All of that because of licking?"

"It was not because of licking. It was the bond; the connection changed something, under the skin, in a more profound manner, creating a huge difference." Michael smiled. "Anatomically, the brains of those rats ended up being different in regard to shape, size, and complexity, especially considering the brain portions that control stress. If you want to go even further, Meaney and his colleagues also managed to demonstrate that this display of affection controlled the genetic expression[xxx] by changing the DNA."

"What? You are speaking Greek to me."

"These scientists used genetic sequencing and concluded that licking and caring activated a genetic segment that controlled a part of the hippocampus. As a result, the rats would produce fewer stress hormones during adulthood."

"But that's what happens with little rats!" exclaimed Estela.

"In this case, it is possible to generalize and apply this knowledge to humans[xxxi]. Do you remember that gene that controlled part of the hippocampus and that was activated when the rats' mothers licked them and took care of them? Necropsies of people who committed suicide[xxxii] and were abused during childhood showed that they had that exact part of the gene turned off."

Estela felt a shiver down her spine.

"Tell me that it is not curious," said Dr. Jansen, opening his hands. "Licking and taking care has the opposite effect of abusing, turning on genes that otherwise would be turned off. DNA interacts, thus, with the environment, with caring, with stimulation, demonstrating that genetic expression is something dynamic, which is what we call *epigenetic*[xxxiii]. Remove a baby rat from his mother, and his growth hormone[xxxiv] levels will fall. If you anesthetize the rat's mother and place her next to him, the growth hormone will stay at low levels. Now, let her lick him, and instead of falling, the growth hormone level will rise."

"Still, that only happens with rats," Estela emphasized.

"No, Estela, not only with rats," the doctor highlighted. "I can quote another study, performed by Tiffany Field and Schanberg, from the University of Miami. They analyzed premature babies in neonatology units[xxxv]. There, they realized that if mothers touched premature babies for at least fifteen minutes, three times a day, caressing their bodies, moving their limbs, the babies would grow nearly fifty percent quicker, were more alert, would mature faster, and would get their hospital discharge almost one week earlier than the babies who were not touched."

"Impressive!" Estela was astonished.

"Thus, I repeat: more important than feeling love, is showing love. Stress is not something merely internal, which starts on the interior to express exteriorly. The lack of expressions of affection, of caring and empathy, can also result in stress, which represents an outside-inside dynamic. So, if you provide the effective ingredients of love to your baby daily, she will become more confident; she will be able to grow without emotional restrictions and will reach her potential. Otherwise, if she doesn't have that, she will become unsure and will have long-term problems. She will not be willing to explore, to test, to do what babies do best since they are mini-scientists by nature. If they do not test their environment, they will become less intelligent. Furthermore, they will have difficulties balancing emotions and calming down on their own. When they become adults, they will have more internal conflicts; they will be more anxious and depressed. Hence, there will be risks that they will face problems in their lasting relationships, like their marriage."

Estela barely blinked due to being so involved in Dr. Jansen's explanation. She was absorbing every word he pronounced.

"On the other hand, if the parents fulfill the baby's emotional needs, especially during the first phase, the child will become happier. Furthermore, obedience, which so many parents praise, will come from that feeling of connection and not through fear or punishment. The way you take care of your child's emotional life while she is just a kid will have a huge impact on her future."

"So according to your experience, parents need to pay more attention to and show more love for their children?"

"Certainly. I'm apprehensive about the times in which we are living, with all the world being connected to the Internet through their cell phones, tablets, and computers, while they are nearly disconnected from everyone around them. Some mothers and fathers are close in space but keep doing other things, not paying attention, looking at their Facebook accounts, and they barely look to their children when they call their parents. They are "anesthetized;" they are close but absent at the same time. Is it possible that, in humans, ordinary negligence leads to the same harmful effects in children that were observed in the rats that were removed from the care of their mothers?"

Despite being amused by the conversation, both of them listened to the sound of Sofia crying vigorously, which was coming from the adjacent room. Estela immediately stood up and after inviting Dr. Jansen to follow her, ran to answer her daughter's call.

"Calm down, little daughter, calm down," she said, using a soft voice when she was already holding the baby in her arms. "Mommy is here."

Gracefully, she opened her shirt buttons, removing her breast. The hairy baby grabbed it, starving as she was, and sucked vigorously. She still had the swollen eyelids of a new-born. She was wearing white overalls, and her delicate wrist showed a golden wristband.

Estela sat on the breastfeeding armchair while Michael noticed every gesture, every expression, nodding with a smile on his lips.

"Tell me, Doctor, how can someone not show love to such a defenseless being that is, at the same time, so loveable?"

"I don't know . . . with a baby, it is more straightforward. Besides the fact that babies are graceful, there is the oxytocin [xxxvi] hormone influencing the mother. It doesn't only stimulate milk production but also the feeling of maternity. Oxytocin goes away with time, and children grow."

Estela caressed the straight dark hair of her daughter.

"I want her to grow!"

"Enjoy each phase! Didn't I say that you are complying with the first step correctly?"

"I'm ready for the next step. Is it related to reading?"

Dr. Jansen showed the number three using his huge fingers of his right hand while saying: "That's the third step. Let's take it easy; we are still on the first step."

"Is there any element missing to fulfill that step?"

"A small detail: did you ever hear about mirror neurons?"

"Yes, vaguely."

"Mirror neurons receive the actions we see other people performing—not only actions but also the intentions and emotions associated with such actions. The interesting thing is that those neurons start acting when we are babies. That way, it is possible to infer that when we pay attention to our children, they also pay attention to us. Thus, they examine our actions and try to decipher our facial expressions, in an attempt to find some additional information that might not be transmitted through words. Mirror neurons make children learn through the actions performed by other people, especially the actions of their parents. This means that we are the tutors of our children, so we have to be very careful with everything we do and with everything we allow them to do. If we want to encourage reading, they have to see us reading. If we want to encourage a healthy life, we have to follow a healthy diet, practice sports, not smoke or drink. We must teach them not only with our words but also through our daily actions. Think about it."

Dr. Jansen walked toward the mother and daughter and gently caressed Estela's covered shoulder, saying: "I have to go now. I don't want to take any more precious time from the mother and, consequently, the daughter. I feel that you want the best for Sofia. I know you already are a good mother. I want you to think about what we talked today."

Estela stood up.

"No! Stay a little longer, Doctor. I'm enjoying this conversation so much!"

"Enjoy your little daughter! We could meet tomorrow morning, at nine o'clock, in the park near here. What do you think?"

"Of course. Deal! I'm eager to learn the second step . . . So early tomorrow we will meet in Aclimação Park, near the main entrance . . ."

"See you then!"

During the afternoon, Estela described Dr. Michael Jansen's visit to her mother and remembered the several points of the conversation.

Mrs. Sônia looked apprehensive somehow. Finally, she asked: "Did I connect with you, my daughter?"

"Of course, Mother. Am I not a perfectly capable person?"

"I think so . . . But you are going to write about this connection in your blog, aren't you?"

"Maybe. He spoke about so many things that . . ."

"You have to!" her mother ordered. "That needs to be shared, my daughter. Many people don't know it. They are ignorant on that matter. Since parents don't get a manual when their children are born, it is natural to share all this knowledge with his followers, who will, possibly, share with other people and ... If back in my days I knew this, I would have paid more attention to my actions, and I would have given more attention to my little girls ... "

"You did, Mother! I had everything. You were always a great mirror for us. In your eyes, I've seen much encouragement, I've always seen smiles. And your hands always caressed so much. They were always very kind ..."

"Even so . . . You have the responsibility of posting that information on your blog. Not everyone has access to an illustrious neuroscientist who comes to their home to share advice and step-by-step guides. Don't you understand? He wants you to write about it!"

In the afternoon, Sofia slept again. Estela typed on her blog: "The First Step for the Good Development of Children: Connection."

She started to write the text, initially with some reservations. However, the theme was so exciting, and at the same time, so close to her, that words started to flow automatically, draining everything she had learned with the doctor. Thus, not only did the writing happen by itself, but also it was enriched with the addition of links to scientific articles quoted by the doctor and to those that Estela found as she did her research, deepening the topic.

Soon, she got many comments and countless questions, including some regarding the second step.

CHAPTER 04 —
THE SECOND STEP:
COMMUNICATION

"The more we stimulate children and encourage communication, the better off we are going to be."

—*Linda Hurwitz*

E stela pushed the stroller down the uneven sidewalk when she saw Dr. Jansen, who was stretching near the gates of Aclimação Park[xxxvii]. He was wearing comfortable clothes: tennis shoes, black athletic pants, and a white T-shirt, and was in perfect physical form.

"Michael?" she greeted him waving while walking toward him.

"Hi, you two. What a beautiful day!" He bent down and looked into the stroller. "Oh, I see you are very active today, Sofia! Let's take a walk in the park." He looked to Estela. "Can I hold her?"

"Of course!"

Michael adjusted the baby in his arms skillfully. She was staring at him, with her eyes a little bit less swollen than the day before.

"Did you know you are graceful, Sofia? So active, pink, and healthy. You remind me a lot of my children when they were newborns. They were all strong and hairy."

"How many children do you have?" Estela took a chance with a personal question.

"Three. One son and two daughters, who gave me six grandchildren in total. I'm still waiting for a granddaughter, but I think it is not likely to happen." He caressed the hair of the little girl while observing closely with clinical eyes, which didn't neglect a thing.

Soon he gave Sofia to Estela, who was under the impression that the doctor was assessing the next move: if she would or would not hold her daughter. Due to considering the previous day lesson, she decided to keep her in her arms. Thus, Michael offered to push the stroller. While they talked about the newborn's daily life and their routine, Sofia opened and closed her little eyes, trying to stay awake; however, she was gradually defeated by tiredness. In the middle of the first lap around the lake, both Michael and Estela noticed she was already sleeping, and Estela put her in the stroller softly.

"So, Doctor, do you think I really am prepared for the second step?"

"Of course. I read what you wrote on your blog regarding our conversation yesterday. It was perfect! You wrote in a clear way; however, it was also deep. You are an expert in the first step."

"Thank you. My mother convinced me to post it immediately, before I forgot any information. I also added some data I found while doing some research about that matter. Now I'm curious about the second step. What is it about, specifically?"

"It is about the children's communication and language development. This step is so essential for Sofia's success that it isn't due to chance that we established it as the second principle. If we stop to think about it, we will understand that communication skills have a huge impact on the child's life. Communication is present everywhere: from being able to understand or not understand a simple conversation, to absorbing knowledge and being able to transmit it. When accompanied by a critical vision of the world, it positively influences the performance of individuals in their people-to-people relations. Those who are good communicators have amazing advantages!"

Before proceeding with the explanation of the second step, Michael continued: "However, contrarily to the unitary construction of the first step, where the focus is on the solid and deep connection between parents and children, the stimulus of communication is a mosaic, a puzzle. Therefore, it is assembled using several pieces, that, in the end, will provide us a beautiful figure. I will try to express myself better. However, please, interrupt me if you feel the need to."

Estela nodded. Michael kept walking with giant steps; however, his focus was on Estela's brown eyes.

"Not only through speaking do we communicate, since there are several other forms of promoting interaction: touching, smiling, a different look, winking . . . everything is communication. So, when you hold your daughter on your lap when you kiss her, when you look at her from far away, when you point. . . You are communicating with her."

Michael abruptly stopped walking.

"Did you see? I communicated with you."

Then he restarted walking, while he kept speaking.

"In the beginning, more and more, the baby starts babbling. Then there is a short conversation using a few words, and it is the bidirectionality, between the baby and the one with who the baby is communicating, that guides the communication. That two-way path is the base for all communication. Babies understand that pattern and call people; they cry; they ask for the attention of everyone around them. They also understand that when they stop breastfeeding, their mother looks at them. Over time and with the many interactions, these acts generalize, becoming instinctive. This way the baby shows affection for parents and caregivers, who give attention or milk to this baby, or even change the baby's diapers."

Michael momentously interrupted what he was saying to look at the movement of people in the park. Estela, due to being so interested in the topic, was not even aware of her surroundings, so she was happy when she heard his voice continuing what he had been sharing.

"Now, let's fast-forward a little bit more and visit the moment when the baby starts to babble. In that phase, if there is a *dialogic exchange*, an immediate correspondence between the mother and the child, soon the baby will understand that vocalizing is important, that it makes sense. In this way, the baby will make an effort to obtain the mother's attention and that of those around him or her, and quickly develop speech skills."

"So, the first step, the well-adjusted connection between parents and children, does it help develop speech?"

"Precisely!" Estela noticed a spark in Michael's eyes. "And that is the first piece of our puzzle: the correspondence between parents and their children, or, as we say in the clinic, the two-way path. Listen carefully; the parents or the caregivers are the ones who must pay attention to the baby, not the other way around. For example, the mother must notice when the baby looks at a flower and says 'ga.' She has to correspond to that attempt to speak, explaining: 'That is a flower.' Or even asking: 'Do you want the flower?' Then, she must wait for the baby to answer. It is necessary to have that continuing interaction: the baby speaks, the mother speaks. The mother doesn't need to answer by verbalizing; she can also touch him, or clap due to the baby's initiatives...The mother just can't leave him 'speaking alone.' If there is no contact, that babbling will stop making sense for the baby. Our goal is to encourage them, to wind them, not to stop that development."

"According to what you are saying," considered Estela, "the busy mother, who already has other children, who is living in an overpopulated house, will give less attention to the baby when he or she is babbling, and, in theory, that will delay the development of the baby's language. I always thought that the more people that lived in a house, the quicker the baby would develop speech."

"No," said Michael Jansen. "There are many studies that show that babies who live in overpopulated houses, with lots of people, may have a delay in their cognitive development. However, it is not due to the number of people that this process happens, because socializing with many people is, in fact, interesting for the child. The problem is the lack of responsiveness of the parents or caregivers. Children who are submitted to that situation thus have a less sophisticated, poorer vocabulary in the future."

"I've read somewhere that the mother has to talk with the child to encourage speech and that it also has an impact on the development of the child's intelligence. Is that true?"

Michael frowned while answering, "Speaking a lot[xxxviii] is also one of the pieces that constitute this second step. There was a study done a few decades ago in the 1980s that explains the importance of interaction through dialogic activity. In it, researchers Todd Risley and Betty Hart[xxxix] tried to answer a question that was intriguing them: why do children with fewer financial resources fail to achieve the expected results regarding language, even those who enter school very early? To try to answer the question, they selected forty-two families from Kansas City, which had babies who were seven to nine months old, and divided them into groups that corresponded to their social classes. Thirteen upper-class families; ten middle-class families; thirteen lower-class families; and six families that lived on welfare. Every month, they would go the families' houses and record one hour of the interactions between parents and children, for a period that lasted until children became three years old. While analyzing the data that resulted from that research, they found that almost every word used by children when they were three years old came from the parents' vocabulary. Not only that, but also the length of the conversation, the speech patterns, and the average of words used were also quite similar to the parents."

"Expectable," deduced Estela. "It's like what we spoke about yesterday: mirror neurons. Children mimic their parents..."

"Exactly!" reassured Michael. "Until this point, it is compatible with what we would expect. However, with the vastness of data they had, the scientists started to look for other variables. It was at that moment that they were faced with the real reason for school not producing the desired results in the poorer children's language."

"What was the reason?"

"When they analyzed the number of words spoken to children, there was a huge difference between social classes. Children whose parents depended on welfare heard 616 words per hour, while those whose parents were in the upper class heard 2,153 words per hour. It was such a huge difference that school could not bridge that gap."

"So," concluded Estela, "depending on the social class the child is in, she is exposed to language more or less frequently."

"Yes! But not only that. Children who were in the high socioeconomic class were subjected to more encouraging words than children from lower classes. More than that, poorer families rebuked children more—they used more negative reinforcement and criticism, such as, 'Don't do that!' 'Enough!' 'You are dumb!' Richer parents used, on average, six encouraging words for every reprimanding word. The working class had a proportion of 2:1, and the parents who relied on unemployment compensation inverted that proportion: an encouraging word for every two reprimanding words."

"Poor children! And then they don't understand why they have low self-esteem."

"Low self-esteem and low IQ[xl]! Because Hart and Risley realized that the biggest influence on IQ and vocabulary, for children up to three years old, is the number of words spoken by their parents; the more the parents communicate with their children, the bigger their vocabulary and the knowledge being transmitted. Children from the group that had parents working had a vocabulary of about 1,100 words when they were three years old, while children from parents who relied on welfare knew about 525 words, or in other words, less than half what their peers with working parents had."

"So, I have to start speaking a lot with Sofia from now on?"

"Yes," said Dr. Jansen, smiling. "You have to talk a lot. Initially, you need to enunciate words very clearly and simply while you speak. I've noticed that you communicate with Sofia correctly, using what we call 'motherese.[xlii]' Babies prefer that nearly sang rhythm and treble sound, that is also slower, with stretched vowels, which we use, almost without realizing it, when we get close to them. There is concrete evidence that motherese helps the baby understand what is being said and also helps during the first stages of learning phonemes since it is a way of speaking that clearly defines the sound of each vowel."

"I thought it was silly to speak that way, but since becoming a mother, I notice myself doing it all the time."

"Motherese isn't silly. It is the correct way to speak with babies and improve their speech skills. Since babies have a very narrow air stream, they can only reproduce a few sounds, especially the treble sounds. As a result, they mimic that way of speaking since it is easier to utter those sounds. Besides speaking a lot and using motherese, the person with who the baby interacts needs to promote word repetition. Babies like repetition because it gives them a sense of predictability and control. However, over time, the issuer—the parents, caregivers, relatives—must put simplicity aside and try to expand the child's vocabulary, bringing richness and sophistication to the child's ears."

"Hmm!" muttered Estela. "I understand."

"Furthermore, I have to alert you: when Sofia starts speaking, try not to amend her. Amending induces a negative message, that might delay and discourage her, especially in the beginning. She will be making such an effort to speak, to coordinate about eighty muscles of the vocal tract, that no one should worry about the sound she articulates and if it is the correct or the wrong way of speaking. The important thing is that she is attempting to communicate. The best way to amend grammatically is by giving suitable examples, speaking correctly."

"I'll remember that."

"Another important aspect is to observe our behavior when we name or label objects. Every parent does that: they point at a black swan and say, 'Do you see the swan? It's beautiful!' Even though it is a nearly spontaneous action, the best way to help the child learn the correlation between the significance and the meaning is waiting for the child to look at the swan before commenting on it. Therefore, parents should not intrude or direct the child's attention toward the object. Instead, they must wait for the opportunity to comment on what the child saw on his or her own. By waiting for their children to have initiative, parents allow them to create a better relationship between the object and the pronounced word. Parents who can adequately identify the name of the objects for their children help them develop their vocabulary faster. The exchange is, thus, essential. One must not speak without pausing occasionally. There must be interaction with the child. The child must contribute to the conversation! You, Estela, have to realize that Sofia understands you, or at least tries to understand you, that you are synched with her."

"And what if the baby is very young. How can I properly name the words?"

"There is a technique that consists of moving or rattling small objects in front of the child and synching that with motherese." He pulled the zipper to open the side pocket and picked up the car key, balancing it and slowly saying, using treble sounds: "Keeeeeyyy . . . Keeeeyyyyy . . ." "Moving the object attracts the attention of the baby. However, that technique only works until they are fifteen months old. From that moment on, it doesn't bring the same benefits.

"I will show Sofia many objects using that technique . . ."

"Don't overdo it! Your function as a mother is not to ram the British Encyclopedia down her throat. You have to create the foundation and inoculate the love for knowledge. Acquiring knowledge is a seamless process that comes in layers. Therefore, sedimentation is necessary so new layers can come, with small differences, and then a few more, and some more again..."

"It makes sense. Oh! Now I understand why there is no benefit in placing the child in front of the TV, even if the child is watching the Discovery Channel. Children don't have the foundation to understand it."

"Parents who do that might even harm their children. Do you know why? Small children need to interact with real people, flesh-and-bone people. Children need to see a person's face while they are speaking, to observe the lips moving. Depending on their age, children can't decipher sound; they don't know where a word starts and where it begins; everything is 'Greek' to them. Television won't speak motherese with children. On the other hand, babies can't interact with television: if the baby cries, nothing happens; if the baby produces a sound with the tongue or babbles, nothing happens. Reading the lips is important because children absorb how the word is formed and will understand it with higher accuracy. When you see the lips of the person that is speaking, it's as if the person's volume is increased by twenty decibels. You can test it. That increment makes all the difference for a newborn. And, let's face it, Estela, televisions should never work as babysitters!"

"I know. However, I have some friends who place their children in front of the TV to watch movies by Baby Einstein while they are cooking or preparing the baby food..."

"If you are their friend, you should warn them about the evils of that action. Let them know that in August 2007, the magazine *Pediatrics*[xlii] published a study from Washington University, in which the researchers concluded that children up to two years old who watched 'videos for babies' had a smaller vocabulary than children who didn't watch such videos. It is worth reminding them that children's vocabulary is directly proportional to their intelligence."

"Not only am I going to warn them, but I'll also warn mothers through my blog."

"Very good! Don't forget to highlight that the ideal is that children should not watch television until they are two years old[xliii]. After that age, TV should still be limited, [xliv]since it incites the child to hostile behavior and can create concentration problems. For each hour a child under the age of four sees television, there is a 10 percent higher chance that the child will participate in bullying in school."

Michael took a deep breath and categorically said, "The increase of attention deficit follows the same proportion. Not to mention the lack of physical activity watching television causes, leading to obesity and other serious medical problems that are so prevalent today."

"Direct interaction with people is the best formula for a good emotional, social, and cognitive development," Estela resumed.

"That's right! The more people, the better, mainly to allow the child to learn new words. A study from Iowa University[xlv] demonstrates that correlation. In that study, the researchers found that children who are fourteen months old generally can't learn new words if they are only pronounced by one person, even if the word is repeated several times. So, they presented the same word to the children but with more people saying it. The result was astonishing! Children immediately learned the words."

"But ... why?"

"Children had the chance to hear the same word in different accents, tones, and speeds. That is enough to facilitate learning."

Estela was going to comment, when she was disturbed by a noise coming from off of the path but immediately in front of her. Both she and Michael stopped walking and paid attention to what appeared to be a cat fight. It became clear it was just cats fighting when a gray cat jumped from the nearest bush to the asphalt; and then, another cat, a brown one, followed the first one. The gray cat stared at the other feline with an angry look, showing all its teeth and roaring loudly. However, the brown cat was not scared and kept going after the gray cat, running through both Estela and Michael, who were observing the scene in absolute silence.

Due to all the noise, Sofia woke up, scared.

"Calm down, my little one; Mommy is here," Estela promptly answered, holding the baby.

"From the way she is crying, she is also hungry," Dr. Jansen interpreted. "Let's stop at that bench."

They walked a few steps toward the concrete park bench, where they sat next to each other, with the image of a green lake in front of them. Sofia, alarmed by what had happened, quickly grabbed Estela's breast, who commented, smiling: "Phew! I'm glad I'm not pregnant anymore. I was always running away from cats. I was scared to death of getting toxoplasmosis."

"And you were right to be," said Dr. Jansen, focusing his fiery eyes on Estela. "Those cats reminded me of a fundamental matter, the fact that many people erroneously think that senses, intelligence, and development are completely innate. They act as if those are already placed inside of them to bloom over time, independently of circumstances. However, it doesn't work like that. There are delineated learning windows or critical periods[xlvi]. Did you know that if we pick up a newborn cat, stitch one of his eyelids shut, and leave it like that for a few months before opening it again, that eye will never be able to see again?"

"That's such cruelty against kittens!" censured Estela.

"Nowadays, thankfully, that experiment would not be possible. However, it was done in the '70s by David Hubel and Torsten Wiesel[xlvii], from Harvard, and they got a Nobel Prize with that research. The researchers noticed that the eye that had the eyelid stitched would represent an increasingly smaller area in the cat's brain. So, Estela, if there is no visual activation during that short time window (which varies from thirty to eighty days in kittens), that we call a *critical period*, it is too late for the development of vision. Hence, a 'healthy' eye will remain virtually blind for the rest of the kitten's life."

"But no one would close a baby's eyelid . . ."

"That's true. However, the baby might be born with a congenital cataract, which would produce the same damage as a closed eyelid. The absence of visual stimulus, due to the opacity of the lens, leads the visual cortex, which is the part of the brain that is responsible for vision, not to develop. It also allows another function, such as hearing, to use more space. If it is bilateral, the problem might result in total blindness, if the child is not submitted to surgery early. In Brazil, congenital cataract[xlviii] is one of the main causes of blindness in children. It can be potentially cured, and the blindness it causes is not a medical problem anymore; instead, it is a problem of neglect by the public policies in the country."

"I'm despondent to learn that children pay such a high price for not having access to a medical procedure," said Estela, saddened.

"There are also cases in which children are born with strabismus[xlix], a problem that makes eyes compete with each other for vision. If not cured, children will become visually-impaired, lose binocular vision, and can even lose the ability to see three dimensions.

Estela stared at her daughter and asked her: "Do you see me perfectly, my daughter?"

Sofia kept breastfeeding, without paying attention to her mother.

"A newborn sees the world through a narrow and opaque tunnel. Besides, she has a low sense of depth. If we compare it to adult acuity, her vision is just 1/40. In the beginning, babies pick up more movement than shape. Luckily, vision improves very quickly, and soon it will aggregate depth, acuity, color perception, and fine control of ocular movements. When a baby is one-year-old, his or her vision is similar to adult vision."

"Really?" inquired Estela, surprised.

"Yes, that's right. However, for vision to develop correctly, it needs to be used. Therefore, the stimulus must first pass through the eyes to go to the brain. The foundation of the critical period is the stimulus, the experience, the contact with things and events. That is what will leave a footprint for the future, or, in other words, the signs, the sensorial marks that will allow the development of perceptive skills through life. It's usually denominated "use it or lose it." More than 80 percent of the neuronal connections, called *synapses*, form after birth, and that process of cerebral expansion only stops after one is twenty years old; in men it continues for a longer period. The brain is like an unfinished painting, as it remains to perfect itself and mature. Even elderly people still have a certain degree of plasticity. Can you imagine it? The brain keeps transforming completely as it happens with children and babies."

"And that critical period is also valid for communication?"

"Of course. An example of that rule is the process of learning foreign languages. Human beings are born with the ability to speak any language, but that ability is not eternal. Patricia Kuhl [1]demonstrated that. She is a global authority in the field of language development, who tested Japanese people, both adults and children, to see if they could distinguish some basic phonemes that were important for the English language but rarely used in Japan, such as 'ra' and 'la.' She would play a tape to the Japanese adults, who were all proficient in English, with sounds like 'rake, rake, rake . . . lake, lake, lake,' for them to identify the phonemic differences. Meanwhile, no one was able to identify where *rake* ended and *lake* began. For adult's ears, or better, for their brains, everything was the same. So, she decided to repeat that research with children. Those who were exposed to those phonemes before they were seven months old could differentiate the "r" from the "l." They were what she designated as "citizens of the world," with the ability to learn any language. Those who were exposed after they were ten months old couldn't distinguish the phonemes. They were as "deaf" as adults regarding their ability to differentiate the "r" from the "l."

"Why does that happen?" asked Estela, raising an eyebrow.

"Apparently, the brain starts deleting everything that is not used at a very early stage, 'trimming' the connections that are not being used. It is not a necessarily bad process since children become 'experts' in their native language and strengthen the connections that already exist. Now, if you think about today's globalized world, it would be better to expose children to several languages at a very early stage, to avoid trimming abilities that could become hugely important in their future."

Michael Jansen noticed that Sofia stopped breastfeeding and was making faces.

"Can I hold her?"

He placed her on his shoulder and patted her on the back until he felt she was comfortable.

"Did she want to burp?" asked Estela.

"All babies swallow air while breastfeeding," he explained.

After bravely caressing little Sofia, he gave her back to her mother. Then he stood up and helped Estela stand up too.

"Do you see those willows near the lake?" he asked, pointing far away. "Do you hear those great kiskadee singing? Everything the baby sees, feels, hears, smells, tests will create new footprints, new circuits in his brain. The more those circuits are used, the more they will strengthen, becoming a permanent part of the neuronal net.

"That is why it's so important to expose her to several stimuli!"

"Certainly," Michael assured. "The diagram is constituted this way: when we live a new experience through any of our five senses, our brain stores the memory of that experience. For example, your daughter places a lemon on her mouth, and her palate detects bitterness, which she never tasted before. From that moment on, the signs of bitter lemon are stored in her brain. When she repeats a similar experience, such as tasting pineapple or even placing a fresh lemon on her mouth, those previous footprints will form a link with that new feeling, transforming the previous experience. Automatically, comparisons will arise—this lemon is more bitter than the other one . . . It's like reading a book. When you read it for the first time, you have a different experience than when you read it for the second time, for the third time . . . The same writing evolved because we evolve. Children's experiences also evolve with them. Thus, we have to expose them to the proper stimulus and enriched environments[li]."

"Enriched environments?"

"Yes, environments that have diversity, people, different things to see, feel, taste," answered the doctor, adding new information. "In the middle of the nineteenth century, Charles Darwin mentioned that domestic rabbits had brains with less volume than wild rabbits since they 'don't exercise their intellect, instinct, and feelings the same way that those who are free in nature do.' However, researchers only demonstrated that causal relation between an enriched environment and the brain morphologic differences after 1960[lii]. They divided thirty-six little rats into three groups of twelve: the first lived in an enriched environment; the second in a normal environment; and the third one in an environment that is poorer than normal."

"What would an enriched environment be like for a rat?" asked Estela.

"A big, collective cage, where the twelve animals lived. It had five to six objects they could explore, such as, for example, small labyrinths or things for them to climb, such as stairs or wheels. The objects were changed two or three times per week to improve the feeling of challenge and novelty."

"Interesting. And in the other two groups?"

"In the group with a normal environment, three rats would share a medium cage, without any object to entertain them. In the poorer environment, the little rat would be alone and without any toy. The result became evident during the necropsy. The thickness of the cerebral cortex of the group that was in the collective and enriched cage was much bigger than that of the rats that were in normal conditions. As expected, the thinner cortex belonged to the group that remained solitary."

"And how do we do that in practice?"

"We can't permit the environment to become monotonous

for the baby, or better, for any of us. The baby needs entertainment. We don't need to buy different toys every week, but we need to take them to new places, help them meet new people and experience different situations . . . Like today . . . By coming to the park, we are enriching Sofia's environment. She is watching people running; seeing butterflies flying, flowers with different colors, trees with different sizes; smelling unknown scents, hearing birds singing, and even seeing cats fighting. That is thickening her cerebral cortex, and consequently, increasing her intelligence. We are creating new footprints in her brain. The essence is diversification. Try to go to theaters, museums, notable places, toy stores . . ."

"Do you have other tips?"

"When she gets a little bigger, I would suggest that you place her on the floor, lying prone[liii] on a soft surface. The longer a baby lies prone[liv] on his or her own belly, the sooner he or she will develop the chest musculature, the arms, and the neck, since they are engaged in crawling. There you have the last piece of our puzzle: physical development and cognitive development are correlated. That can be confirmed through several studies that observed people who couldn't move their limbs due to some brain injury and people who suffered a cerebrovascular accident, both of which lost part of their verbal skills. That occurs because gestures and speech use similar neuronal circuits[lv]."

"Really?"

"Really. Verbal communication and non-verbal communication keep their roots even when they diversify in form. We also know that babies can't acquire more sophisticated vocabulary before they acquire more sophisticated motor control over their fingers."

Despite being very absorbed by the conversation, Dr. Jansen understood that they were near the entrance of the park and decided to stop there.

"The sun is getting too hot for Sofia," he warned. "Let's stop here. I've spoken too much today. However, I would like to recap the main points so you can understand them. What do you think?"

"Sure. Let's go," said Estela. "First piece: two-way path."

"Very good! Two-way path," Dr. Jansen repeated, pointing with his index finger. "Correspondence between parents and children. Parents have to listen to what children are saying, to notice a slight babbling and to encourage them. Do you remember the second piece?"

"Second piece: talking a lot with the baby. In the beginning, we must chant in motherese, with clarity and simplicity, repeating everything many times. Then we must attempt to bring richness and sophistication to the vocabulary. Hmm . . . the third piece is?"

"Social interaction," the doctor readily said. "Watching real people speaking, watching the lips, listening to the same word from different people. Zero television until they are two years old and after that, only in small doses. And the fourth piece?"

"I'm not sure if it is the fourth one, but I think it is the one regarding not losing our learning windows. Babies should listen to different languages until they are seven months old to create brain footprints."

"And the environment?"

"Enriched, with as much diversity as possible. And the last piece is the motor stimulation since speech is related to physical activity. Allowing the baby to lie prone to strengthen their muscular abilities and for them to develop crawling."

"Congratulations, Estela. You remember all the pieces, and I can take you home. First, do you want some coconut water? Breastfeeding makes you thirsty."

"No, thank you."

They walked until they reached the door of Estela's building, where they said goodbye.

"This morning was quite fruitful," said Estela. "Now tell me: when will we meet again to discuss the third step? It is about early reading. I'm very excited about it."

"Don't worry, Estela. These two first steps are actually more important for your baby. Focus on those for now. I will give a lecture about the topic at Awake Clinic in one month, and I will reveal a secret on which we have been working for almost one year. It will change the strategies for performing the third step.

"I can't wait!" exclaimed Estela, smiling and showing her dimples on both cheeks.

Estela followed him with her eyes, and while she watched him walking, she noticed that the first impression she had of him, a mix of sympathy and genius, now included a paternal and protective image. Suddenly, his figure vanished in the horizon. She got on the lift, thinking about how she would approach the second step to explain it to her readers.

CHAPTER 05 —
THE THIRD STEP:
READING

"Reading is a brain function."

—Glenn Doman

W hen Estela entered the amphitheater, one hour before the beginning of the lecture, she expected to be one of the first people arriving, but she was wrong. While she walked toward the stage, she felt the different scents of feminine perfumes and noticed that the front seats were all taken and that the other rows were filling quickly. She chose one of the few chairs that were still free in the fifth row and in a few minutes saw the amphitheater full. In the center of the stage, there was a big screen where the image of a brown baby, looking to a book that had "Stimulate your baby to read" written on it, was being projected.

Twenty minutes before the expected time, Dr. Jansen, with all his natural grace, appeared from the stage's curtains. He was wearing a bright, steel-gray suit, and his white hair glowed in the dark. Immediately after his entrance, the bustle in the auditorium became louder and gradually intensified until it became a resounding mass of noise. The woman next to Estela clapped excitedly and explained to her husband, "He is Dr. Jansen!"

Soon, the doctor's deep voice echoed through the speakers: "Good evening, everyone! It's a privilege to be here with you. I see that the firemen will have to evacuate the building tonight," he said, joking, to draw the attention of the emotional audience.

People laughed.

"Seriously! I have been giving this lecture for more than a decade, and I've never seen this amphitheater full. That's a good sign! It means we are doing something right . . ."

The low ceiling lights started to turn off completely, only leaving a light beam on, directed to the doctor's figure, which made his status even more evident while, at the same time, he also looked friendly, transmitting a sense of trust and authority.

"For those who don't know me, let me introduce myself: my name is Dr. Michael Jansen, and I'm the director of Awake Clinic. Here, we take care of children who have any difficulty developing. Today, however, the lecture is meant for parents who want their children to start reading earlier, whether or not they have a disability. I can ensure that, from today on, each one of you will have, in your own hands, the strategies needed to teach a baby to read."

A round of applause interrupted his speech.

"Before anything else, I will tell you my story, detailing how I was introduced to the topic of precocious reading."

At that moment, the noise in the auditorium stopped completely, signaling people were absorbed in hearing what the doctor was about to say.

"Once upon a time, there was a young doctor who had just left his neurology residence. Every day, he felt powerless when he saw children with severe brain disorders subjected to a medicine that did little to improve their situations. One day, at the beginning of the '70s, he went to a place called The Institutes for the Achievement of Human Potential[lvi], where the incredible Glenn Doman and his team taught very young children to read. Somebody had told him that the place could have the answer to some of the questions that bothered him so much. There, he witnessed something so remarkable that it changed his way of thinking forever. You must be asking yourselves, what did he see? I want to share that experience with you. Please, pay attention to this video."

Dr. Jansen pressed a button on the pointer he was holding, and on the screen behind him, a projection started with the image of a hairless baby and his mother. The mother was holding a white card with the word *hand* written on it, and the baby laughed and stretched his right hand, quickly opening and closing it, saying, "Ha . . . hand." The mother changed the card, now showing the word *foot*, and the baby kicked with his foot. Then she showed *tongue*, and the baby reacted by showing his tongue, gently pressing it between his fingers. To each action, the mother exclaimed enthusiastically: "That's it! Congratulations!"

Dr. Jansen paused the video and continued to speak in the center of the stage.

"Because of that, my vision about children completely changed. No one had told me babies could read. Even if somebody did, I wouldn't have believed it. I was ecstatic with what that little boy, who was only nine months old, could do. I understood that the baby was having fun, which enchanted me even more. When he saw the words, he would point and smile. That event was so significant that I became a neuroscientist, instead of being just a neurologist. You are here today because of that moment."

Dr. Jansen placed his hand on his chin as if immersed in his thoughts.

"Why hadn't I ever seen a baby reading until that very moment? Why have I never read anywhere that babies are capable of reading? Or was that baby unique, outstanding, extraordinary?" he questioned while gazing into the audience. "I will ask you one more question, and I want you to answer me with all the honesty in the world: Can babies read?"

The entire auditorium answered in unison, quickly and vigorously: "Yes!"

"Yes? It seems that no one doubts it, doesn't it?"

He unfroze the video, and the screen showed a woman showing the word *kiss* and the baby sent two big kisses with his hands.

The audience melted and sighed.

"This baby's name is Renato, one of our babies, at Awake Clinic. He was born with a small disability, and his mother brought him to us when he was just a few weeks old. The clinical team established a standard treatment considering his diagnosis, and it only took a short period for him to recover completely. In that video, he was only eleven months old. Today, he is seventeen years old and an intelligent, wise young man with great relationships.

"Yet, let's get back to my question . . . Why is it that we don't see babies reading in our daily lives? As you saw in the images, babies have that inherent ability, right? Despite that, I'm sure that for many of you that was your first time seeing a baby read. If everyone here acknowledges that babies can read, why don't we see it all the time? Anyone?"

Nobody risked an answer.

"I will give you a hint which will allow you all to remember why," said Dr. Jansen, taking a piece of paper from his jacket's internal pocket and unfolding it slowly.

"Can anyone read what is written here? I know the people in the farthest rows can't read it, but . . . what about you, in the first rows?"

The doctor walked toward the front of the stage and crouched with outstanding agility for someone who was more than seventy years old. He brought the paper closer to the people in the front seats.

"Someone? Nobody? Nobody at all?" he asked, motivating the audience to participate in the discussion.

A red-headed woman stood up, placed her face close to the

paper, and shook her head, showing that she couldn't read what was written on the paper.

"Here, in this paper, I wrote my tip. Why can't you read it?" he questioned them again, giving them a few seconds in an attempt to invite them to reflect on the question.

Then, he invited a woman who was sitting near the corridor to go to the stage.

"Laís, would you mind coming here and reading the sentence loudly to everyone?"

A woman with brown curly hair stood up from her chair and walked down the stairs toward the stage until she got close to Dr. Jansen.

"A round of applause for Laís, for being able to help us," cheered the doctor, continually trying to mediate the audience's participation.

A stage assistant quickly appeared and gave a wireless microphone to Laís. Dr. Jansen told her, "Now, Laís, you can kill everyone's curiosity! Can you read what is written on this paper?"

The woman took the paper, turned it, and answered while giving a forced smile: "I don't know!"

"Come on! Try! I think you are not really trying..."

"I'm serious. I can't see anything here, just a blur on this side."

Dr. Jansen took a magnifying glass from his suit. "What about now?"

The woman profoundly inhaled and read the sentence in one go. "For babies to be able to read, you need to increase the size of the letters."

"That's correct!" said an excited Dr. Jansen. "For babies to be able to read, you need to increase the size of the letters!" he slowly repeated the sentence. "That's our first lesson today. Due to its importance, I will project it on the big screen."

The words started to appear, one by one, slowly and visibly. Estela saw the woman next to her pick up a notepad and write down everything. Other people took photos of the big screen, using their cellphones.

A stir from the crowd started to dominate the place until the moment when Jansen's loud voice echoed, "Did anyone here ask themselves why we need to increase the size of the letters?"

Suddenly, the atmosphere was silent again, allowing the doctor to continue with his explanation.

"The need to increase the size of the letters is related to the fact that babies *learn* how to see. Their vision isn't immediate. It happens over time, like so many other marks of their development, such as being able to lift the head, sit, or walk. Babies are born with rudimentary vision and can't focus properly nor move their eyes accurately. Furthermore, the visual stimulus is a new sensation, and the information that arrives at the brain needs experience to be interpreted. For these reasons, we can't ask babies to read normal-sized letters. It is virtually impossible! Newborn babies can barely see the face of their mother when she is breastfeeding them. How can they identify small letters on a piece of paper full of hundreds of small letters? It's impossible!"

Dr. Jansen thanked the woman, who got off the stage with the help of the assistant.

"Back to my story . . . I can state that my paradigm changed that day." Dr. Jansen started walking with large strides around the stage as he kept describing, "Something clicked in my brain, and my mind was hammered with questions: Were other children being deprived of reading precociously? Could this deprivation limit their inherent potential? Or better, could teaching a baby to read earlier help them have a better future?"

His voice not only transmitted his enthusiasm regarding this topic, but also his credibility as a diligent and experienced researcher.

"After decades of research, work, and experience with little children, I can tell you that many of these questions were answered when I found that precocious reading allows babies to achieve reading proficiency levels that their parents never dared to dream of. How? Teaching babies to read helps their vision mature, which helps them gain control of eye movements and the coordination between both the eyes. In other words, the eyes learn how to cooperate earlier, not to mention focus better. When we stimulate a baby to read, showing them the words, we help them perfect their visual center and give them a significant advantage when compared to other babies of the same age. While the other babies just see shades, the early reader baby sees details. Is that an important benefit?"

The question hung in the air as parents were immersed in the topic and were only looking to obtain answers.

"Let's see: the brain is intensely affected by our experiences[lvii]. All the senses . . . hearing, vision, touch, smell, taste . . . Everything leaves a footprint in the brain circuits, and those footprints can be strengthened with new experiences. When children see better, they also see more things around them, such as interactions between people, objects, shapes, distances between things . . . All of these help children become more intelligent in the end. Knowing that, I want to ask you another question: what is the ideal age for babies to learn how to read?"

A man in the audience shouted: "The sooner, the better!"

"That's right! The sooner, the better. Before babies are one-year-old is the best time to start teaching them how to read, joining the smallest effort with the biggest benefits. It is what we call a *critical period*. Younger children progress quicker[lviii] during this time than during any other life stage. The young brain has nearly twice as many connections between neurons when compared to an adult brain[lix]. If we don't use certain connections that are opened, the brain closes. A process that we call *trimming*[lx] starts happening, which closes the connections that weren't used. The contrary is also true. By strengthening those connections with the stimulus, they will remain open for future use. That is why reading becomes harder later, and why it is so essential to hold that knowledge window, to not allow that critical period to pass."

Estela remembered that Dr. Jansen said something similar about communication when they were walking in Aclimação Park about a month ago.

A father raised his hand, and one of the assistants quickly

handed him a microphone.

"Dr. Jansen, my name is Pedro. I would like to know what happens if we let that critical period pass. My daughter is completing her fourth year of life in the next month," said the father, visibly worried.

"Good evening, Pedro," answered Dr. Jansen. "I believe that everyone here learned how to read after they were four years old ... or even five, six, or seven years old. Our effort was greater, but we achieved it anyway. Thus, no one here should feel guilty if your children have already passed that critical period. You don't need to get crazy about it. There is a Chinese saying that goes like this: 'The best time to plant a tree was twenty years ago. The second best is today.' Today! That is why, Pedro, you and everyone here wish to learn, to plant the seeds of success. If not with your children, with your grandchildren, nephews, neighbors ..."

Many sighs of relief echoed in the auditorium. It was clear that Dr. Jansen had the power to control the emotions of the audience, which was listening carefully.

"Another advantage I can see in early reading," Michael Jansen returned to the previous topic, "is the love for reading[lxi]. When you teach children how to read precociously, you are also stimulating that love for reading. We can't miss that opportunity[lxii]!"

The doctor pressed the remote control once again, and the big screen started to show an image of a neuronal tree growing, amplifying and quickly creating branches. The video, which was full of lights and colors, lasted about twenty seconds but left the audience ecstatic.

"The first months and years of life are the period during which the brain is the most fertile soil to plant any seed. The brain is in total expansion during this phase; it creates new circuits, multiplying itself. I know people who are afraid of teaching children how to read because they think they will lack the space in the brain for other more important knowledge forms. However, the space in our brain is virtually infinite. Therefore, it is exactly the opposite of what they think. The more we learn, the more connections we create, and those connections, if once again exposed to knowledge, will become stronger. In the brain, there is no empty field since everything there is a noble area. That 'field' can, as a result of this, become a house, a small building, or even a skyscraper. It all depends on how we occupy it, how we build on it. If we place a quality brick on top of another quality brick, our construction will be strong. We can also occupy that space with something useful, important, or our brain will give that space to another vital function."

The big screen showed another video of weeds growing, in high speed, on an empty field.

Dr. Jansen once again walked from one side of the stage to the other.

"Reading is a brain function, like speaking. If we plant a reading seed on fertile soil, which is the baby brain, with time, it will become an imposing tree. Can you imagine where a child with unlimited potential will go if we plant the right seeds from an early stage[lxiii]?"

Dr. Jansen put his arms up and said: "This child will be in the spotlight. What will happen with this child? Who of you have heard of the Matthew effect?"

The figure of a man with well-combed hair and wearing a suit, tie, and glasses appeared on the big screen, with the following caption: "Matthew effect—sociologist Robert Merton."

Then the voice of the doctor echoed, saying: "What is the Matthew effect?[lxiv] To explain it quickly, we could say the following: Opportunities are not equal for everyone. Those who are successful have more opportunities. Doesn't money generate more money? Isn't it true that a rich person will become richer more easily than a poor person? The child that stands out is the one teachers will be closer to, be fonder off, play more with, give more attention to, even if not consciously. We are human beings; we like people that enchant us, that are prettier, happier, more intelligent. Those qualities that make one appear fascinating to the eyes of another is what we designate as *cha-*

risma."

As the man kept speaking, the focus of the camera was closing on his face, which gave a feeling of proximity.

"We all desire to have qualities that make us, and especially our children, stand out. I, for example, want my grandchildren to be charismatic people. I want them to be successful, and I hope they can have an impact on this world. There is no better hour to plant the seed of success than now, while they are still very young and are not completely formed. Younger children are more malleable. They can learn new idioms quicker, without effort, just by listening and attempting to speak."

A person sitting in the center of the audience stood up and interrupted the lecture. Once again, a stage assistant quickly handed him a microphone.

"Good evening... My name is Edmilson, and I have a daughter who is two and a half years old. I'm afraid that if I teach my daughter how to read before school, she will be bored once she gets there. What do you have to say about that?"

"Good evening, Edmilson," Dr. Jansen greeted him with a smile on his face. "I was going to approach that aspect later. It is a great question and a very frequent one too. It comprises another myth. Let's see, today, here in this amphitheater, do you feel bored because you know how to read? If you are bored, that's not the reason, is it?"

"Of course not!" said Edmilson.

"School is not just about teaching children how to read. It also serves as a place for socialization, to interact with other children and adults, to meet different people, to make friends, and to learn racial, intellectual, and religious tolerance, since the children spend time with other children and adults who have different points of view than the child and his or her parents. For me, the ideal is for every child to already know how to read when they get to school, which would allow teachers to work on cognitive, affective, and psychomotor knowledge; that is what matters. As I said, for me, reading is a brain function, a tool. During all these years, as we stimulated thousands of children to read, we noticed that they were actually less bored, due to knowing how to read, as they could learn a lot more. Tedium only happens if what is being taught is uninteresting."

The man, not happy with the answer, presented a counter-argument: "And reading early wouldn't be prejudicial to her infancy?"

"No!" Michael Jansen answered. "Do you know why? Because I'm only asking for three to five minutes of her day. I only ask parents to pay exclusive attention to their children during those minutes. There can't be any other distraction, neither audible nor visual. It's just the child and the father or the mother. They can play, show figures, laugh, have fun . . . That's what children want the most: the real and complete attention of their parents. The people who criticize the method are precisely those who let their young children watch television and the atrocities in the news or on soap operas. What is more interesting for the baby's brain: ten minutes watching television or five minutes playing with their parents about little words, while at the same time, learning how to read? For me, there is no doubt. Because time is just one; it's not elastic. Either we use our time fruitfully to gather its fruits in the future, or our child will stay, when it comes to emotional and cognitive education, at an average level, although that same child had the potential to achieve more. There is nothing wrong with the average, but in the future, it might be more complicated. You know that it is true . . . Twenty years [lxv]from now, the prospect of having a job will be much less likely to be fulfilled than nowadays. We have professions that will be extinguished due to artificial intelligence[lxvi]. Either the baby starts the race ahead today, or the baby will have a bitter experience while becoming an adult."

Estela saw countless people shaking their head in agreement, absorbing everything Dr. Jansen said. She had read many times about artificial intelligence, but for the first time, she understood that it was closer than she imagined: her daughter invariably would be affected by it. Artificial intelligence wasn't something distant, in science fiction books. Instead, it was happening now. American citizens, with a degree in law[lxvii], were afraid to lose their jobs to Watson from IBM, which performs the work of hundreds of lawyers—without complaining or requesting extra hours or a more significant portion of the company's profits . . . She just needed to compare this reality with the transformation that, during the last few years, had happened in her profession, journalism. Once a stable profession, it was increasingly more unstable every day since the rise of the Internet and online newspapers, which delivered news in real time.

Estela was taken away from that sea of thought by the voice of Dr. Jansen, who continued explaining, "We adults must allow our children and grandchildren to have access to early reading. Don't take that opportunity away from your children! It is a small investment of energy, considering how great their destiny will be. From infancy, they will be driven forward, and thus, in the future, they will be in a more comfortable place than the average person, and they will be more confident. To do so, you must channel time and effort into what really will have an impact in the future: pay total attention to your children."

Like a good speaker, Jansen knew the value of fully explaining the topic, so he didn't save words and kept talking, exposing some strategies of early reading.

"In this way, my tip number two today is that you perform reading exercises at least three times per day. As I already said, you will use just a few minutes in total, but discipline is important. You have to show the words every day, and you must show them while speaking loudly, cheerfully, to motivate the baby. Once the session is concluded, hug the baby and kiss him a lot. Don't see that as an obligation but rather as an effective and cognitive investment. The energy of today will be highly valuable in the future. You won't need to pay for private tutors. You won't see your children struggling to perform a task or pass an exam. However, I repeat, for that to happen, your energy, consistency, and discipline are necessary."

Dr. Jansen walked over to a stool and picked up a cup of water, from which he drank a few sips before continuing.

"Now, I will take a moment to share a new fact in my presentation that I'm sure many of you will enjoy. Usually, at this point in the lecture, I present the technical part, regarding creating the little words. I share tips about which printing shop you should hire to cut the cardboard to the right size, which printers are the best to buy, what size letters are best during phase one, phase two, phase three . . . I would explain why you should opt for a determined font and the reason behind the red color, which grabs more attention from the baby than the color black. I acknowledge that my lecture would become much less interesting from this point onward if I were to speak about all that. However, luckily for you, I will not talk about it. If someone is interested in those specific points, I suggest you buy Glenn Doman's book *How to Teach Your Baby to Read*[lxviii]. It outlines all of this perfectly."

Dr. Jansen calmly told the audience, "We found out that parents' most significant difficulty was creating the words. That was the part during which most parents would lose their motivation. They start quite confident, full of energy and courage, starting to teach their babies how to read, but they get blocked by the little words and quit. First of all, I must say, it is expensive!"

The big screen showed two chests full of golden coins.

"Expensive! A color laser printer, cards cut in the print shop, paper rolls, and more paper rolls, contact paper to laminate the little words . . . I can tell you that it is quite expensive. I'm talking about a few thousand dollars."

Many people were awestruck with the enunciated value.

"I know, not everyone has financial resources to buy those materials . . ."

While the audience exchanged ideas about this new information, the big screen revealed an hourglass with its sand flowing quickly.

"Oh! Another important thing that we had to analyze was the time spent performing that work. Yes! Time, which is something parents of young children don't have."

"Other factors that are, perhaps, less important, also created friction and complicated the application of the method. One of those aspects was the observation that the cards with the small words occupied too much space in the house."

The big screen showed a small room full of educational materials, up to the roof.

"People need a chest to store the more than two thousand cards with small words and sentences, plus the little books. It is also worth mentioning another problem that may arise: the lack of a methodology that avoids the non-planned repetition of words to the baby. Many parents lost track of the progress and would end up complaining: 'Is it possible that I have already shown this little word fifteen times?' 'Is it already time for recapping the little words that I "removed" a month ago?'

A photo of a thoughtful man inside a labyrinth appeared to illustrate the stress of the situation.

"Last but not least, there was the lack of discipline. As I already told you, the method only works when there is engagement. We know that when we have many tasks to perform, like changing diapers, doing the shopping, bathing the baby, we end up forgetting about other tasks, which are relegated as not as important, due to not being necessary to survival. That's natural, and thus, discipline is a requisite that requires constant goodwill and effort from the parents. If those who are responsible for performing the tasks forget to do something once, twice, and then a third time . . . eventually, the opportunity of teaching your baby how to read will vanish . . ."

The image on the big screen was replaced by the figure of a super-busy woman, who was cleaning the house, cooking, holding a baby in the baby carrier, and holding a mobile phone to her ear.

Some women laughed once the image appeared.

"That's the reality. We can't pretend that we live in an ideal world. We are very good at making to-do lists and defining goals to be achieved, but in the end, we can't comply with those because our time is scarce. Suggesting an additional task in the daily life of parents that are already so overwhelmed might sound like an inappropriate proposal, no matter how important it is for the baby's future," considered Dr. Jansen, without stopping to value the method he was proposing.

"Due to all this, I concluded that our precocious reading proposal was not able to produce a large number of parents who are engaged in the method. As a result of this, we had to evolve, to find new paths that allow the active participation of parents in the process. If the method was failing here, we needed to find an alternative. We found it—a round of applause for my friend Gaurang, from Mumbai, India."

The audience vibrated with excitement while a short brown man wearing jeans, a black turtle-neck, and white tennis shoes stepped onto the stage. With large steps, he walked up to Dr. Jansen.

"Hi! Hello! Greetings." Gaurang timidly waved.

Dr Jansen continued, "Let me introduce you all to Gaurang. Gaurang is married to a Brazilian woman, Maria de Fátima. He works as a system programmer, which motivated us, about a year ago, to discuss an app that could solve the previously mentioned problems of the precocious reading program. With that intention in mind, we looked at the following factors that created issues for parents and delineated goals for overcoming them: (1) Cost: Make it available for everyone who wants to teach precocious reading to their children, including those who have less economic power, instead of aiming it at a few privileged people. 2) Time: Abolish the need to produce the material. The focus, thus, was creating an effective mechanism that was at hand and could be used anywhere. 3) Space: Store many words, without occupying physical space. 4) Organization: Provide a means for parents to organize their actuation strategy without getting lost with so many words, avoiding non-planned repetition. 5) Oblivion: Remind parents daily of the tasks to be performed at predetermined times.

After thoroughly listing all the aspirations, Michael revealed to the public that Gaurang had already created an app to do all this. In an attempt to involve his friend in the lecture, he asked him, "Gaurang, could you please give us the pleasure of seeing the app you designed?"

"Of course, Dr. Jansen," he said, his voice sounding a little jarred with his strong accent. However, the narrative didn't show how nervous the programmer was. "A year ago, we started to think about an app that was simple and global. After a lot of work, our app became something concrete and had a name: Tiny Readers[lxix]."

The big screen revealed the app icon. The Indian man, who was now calmer, spoke again. "You can download that app both from the App Store and the Google Play Store."

Instantaneously, nearly everyone took their mobile phone from their pocket or purse and started downloading the app.

The Indian man saw the immediate success of his speech and smiled at Dr. Jansen, and both of them waited for a few minutes. After that, the Indian man cleared his throat to call the attention of the audience and explained, using a low, yet clear and concise tone: "With that app, you parents will be able to mirror your mobile phones and tablets on the television. It's a simple solution since nearly everyone has a TV and a mobile phone. Therefore, this is not a strict app but rather a universal one."

Michael Jansen complemented, "By projecting it on the television, we don't have the problem of making a tiny word that babies won't be able to see. Naturally, older children, who are three or four years old, will be able to see the little words on the tablet without any problem and without the need to project those words. However, while the child's vision is not well adapted, it is better to show the word on the television."

After that brief explanation, he returned the floor to Gaurang, playfully telling him: "You may have a word now, Gaurang."

"Oh, of course, Doctor," he answered, smiling, before pressing the pointer, which switched the image in the big screen. "This initial screen is to register users."

Gaurang described the app functions and visited each item so the audience wouldn't get confused and could use it easily.

"I want everyone to be able to use the early reading method until the end," concluded Dr. Jansen. "I want all our children to experience great success. The app Gaurang developed will be helpful in making this happen."

A very excited parent stood up and started to applaud. Other people stood up and clapped too. Estela joined them. She thought about the impact the app could have in the lives of many families who never heard about the method. The older method required the parents to have a strong will to create the little word cards, but the new approach was convenient and required very little: just the commitment to showing the little words three times a day.

The Indian man and Michael Jansen thanked everyone and disappeared when the curtains closed. Now, Estela was in the dark. She knew the first three steps but had no idea about the next one, nor about when it would be revealed to her.

What would it be?

CHAPTER 06 —
THE FOURTH STEP:
CREATIVITY

"Imagination is more important than knowledge. For knowledge is limited, whereas imagination embraces the entire world, stimulating progress, giving birth to evolution."

—Albert Einstein

A few days after the lecture, Estela was returning from one of her walks with Sofia in Aclimação Park, when one of the doormen of her building handed her a pink and perfumed letter. It read, "If you are still interested in the fourth step, I invite you to come to Secret Garden School, Vila Mariana Unity, on Wednesday at 2:00 p.m. . . . I will wait for your confirmation."

Estela jumped with happiness; she reread the letter a few times and then picked up her phone from her purse to confirm her presence.

She was so absorbed by tasks like breastfeeding, changing the diapers, and doing professional and domestic activities that the time passed quickly. Suddenly, it was Wednesday . . .

At the scheduled time, Estela and Michael met at the door of the Secret Garden School. It was a big building, with a façade made of little orange bricks, and a garden full of trees and colorful flowers that danced with the wind.

"I asked you to meet me at this school, Estela," Michael Jansen started to explain, "because here I can properly exemplify the fourth step."

Estela's brown eyes opened even more.

"And what is the fourth step?"

"It's about stimulating the child's creativity. At the clinic, we often say: 'Let them be, let them play.'"

"Play?" Estela pressed her lips. "Seriously?"

"Quite seriously!" Michael Jansen's blue eyes sparkled. "Playing is the soul of creativity. For many people, creativity is like a vague and undefinable element. Yet, it isn't. It is the ability to invent or create new things, and playing is the easiest way to stimulate the development of creativity. Playing[lxx] prepares the child for a world that is constantly evolving. The future of humanity depends on the origination of innovative solutions. Playing is a bridge that leads to creativity. I chose this school because we have many different environments, with toy libraries, elastic beds, external parks . . . Everything to stimulate the autonomy and the creativity of children. Furthermore, one of my grandchildren studied here, and I became friends with the proprietary. Thus, I'm quite familiar with the school. Follow me, please!"

Michael waved to the entrance security guard, who let them in. The doctor guided Estela to an ample hall where nearly forty children were playing. Some were on the floor, forming a circle with their friends. Other children were playing inside a big structure with nets and physical challenges, and every time they managed to reach the top, they would come down using the blue slide. Some children were playing inside a ball pool.

Estela inquired, "Michael, isn't playing the norm for children? Something common? I always considered childhood the period during which children are free to have fun. Is there something different or new about this?"

"Estela, things are changing." The doctor sighed. "Back in my day, children were free. I was born in Birmingham, England, which is northeast of London. Despite the rigorous winter, we cycled, climbed the trees, played street football, raced . . . We played a lot outside, in the open field. I have vivid memories of the scent of the cedar trees, the pure and moist air around me . . . All of those things had a very positive effect on me. Nowadays, generations play less than their parents[lxxi]. Half of all children don't get outside daily[lxxii]. If we consider children who are a little bit older, it becomes even rarer. Less than 10 percent of American teenagers[lxxiii] play outside. The parks are empty, children enclose themselves in their houses, playing videogames and watching TV, videos, YouTube, or Netflix. That leads to the epidemics of obesity, diabetes, hypertension, depression, hyperactivity, and myopia[lxxiv]."

"Myopia?" asked Estela, showing her interest in learning more on the topic.

"Yes, there is an inverse correlation between myopia[lxxv] and time spent outside. In other words, the difficulty in seeing properly farther away increases when one spends less time outside. Children that spend a lot of time performing tasks that require forcing their vision to closer objects, such as reading and using cellphones and tablets, have a higher propensity to develop myopia. Staying in closed environments for a long period is also a risk factor[lxxvi]. Take a look at the number of young children who use glasses."

Estela looked around the room and saw that half a dozen children from three to five years old were using glasses of different shapes and colors. According to Dr. Jansen, this was a school where children played.

"Was it like this back in your day, Estela? Do you think that so many children had myopia? I bet it was different. Being exposed to solar light and trying to focus on the horizon, or in other words, to see farther away, are both antidotes to myopia. Every day I have to make it clear for parents that children were not made to be closed inside their homes. Personally, I can tell you that my daughter, when she was six years old, developed myopia. She devoured books, and my wife and I thought it was beneficial until myopia developed. So, we rethought about her dedicating so much time reading, and we tried to balance indoor activities with outdoor ones."

"I didn't even imagine," Estela commented.

"Many parents, whose infancy was free and laden with fun outside, are still reticent about allowing their children to do the same things they did. They are afraid. Afraid of violence, of the traffic, of everything around them. Fear paralyzes them and their children too."

"Well, I can't say they aren't somehow right. To be honest, I expected you to be averse to playing, and I imagined that after precocious reading the next step would be about teaching mathematics to your children, or something similar."

A broad grin formed on Dr. Jansen's face: "Me? Averse to playing? Not at all! I'm a passionate enthusiast[lxxvii]. While precocious reading is a tool for children, playing has several other advantages[lxxviii]. When we play, life becomes colorful; we feel satisfaction, we lose the sense of time and space and feel ecstatic, a state that the Hungarian psychologist Mihaly Csikszentmihalyi[lxxix] designated as 'flow.' Playing renews us, makes us more open to other perspectives, to new possibilities. Internally, playing changes our biology, our brain, making it more flexible, more adaptable[lxxx] to daily situations."

"I know that playing isn't an exclusive behavior of humans," concluded Estela.

"No, it isn't. Not at all. Birds play, dogs play, cats play . . . All animals play."

"And if playing is extremely widespread in the animal kingdom, there must be a reason for that, right? Otherwise, why would we spend time and energy with an activity that supposedly isn't productive, such as playing? I deduct that such a universal behavior that is so prevalent must have a fundamental value in survivorship. Otherwise, it would have been eliminated by natural selection."

"It has!" stated Michael. "An association between the size of the brain[lxxxi] and the act of playing was already identified in mammals in general. There is also a connection between playing and the ability of the pre-frontal cortex and the cerebellum to process information. Those brain areas are important for thinking, as well as for the ability to pay attention, for the sense of coordination and rhythm."

Estela analyzed Dr. Jansen's face. Meanwhile, her eyes' focus changed when Michael subtly pointed toward two girls that were playing, pretending to cook with plastic utensils.

"Children who socialize start doing it through parallel games. Each child stays in their corner, close to the other one but not interacting with one another. Over time, the games become more cooperative; they start sharing toys, smiling, and talking. From that point onward, they prefer to play in a group rather than alone. They pay attention to the extraneous contributions and start to understand their peers' point of view. That is what we call *empathy*[lxxxii], the ability to understand people from the outside to the inside, and apprehend what is going on in other people's minds. Children that develop empathy can benefit greatly because in a world where people are increasingly more self-focused and narcissistic, due to the internet and technology, they can be the differential."

The two children were surrounded by a universe of games. They stirred with the spoons inside the little pans and "tasted" the food in each one.

"Playing[lxxxiii] nourishes empathy[lxxxiv], supports social relationships and also expresses the individuality in each child. By playing, children find out that they are different and that being different is not a bad thing. They learn that giving and receiving with enthusiasm characterizes a healthy interaction. Through this, social conscience, cooperation, and altruism grow.

Estela looked around. All the children were playing with each other; all the teachers were paying attention.

"The child that plays is more attentive to her or his peers, thus having the chance to understand their feelings and perspectives, to read others' humor and mind. Those who, instead of socializing, spend too much time on the mobile phone, will find their social muscles atrophied since they only interact with themselves and with a machine, never getting genuinely involved with other people. That behavior shows that we need to socialize more again. We are social beings, and playing is a part of the tissue from which we all were cut."

A little boy was chasing another boy, while one of them was imitating the sound of a bicycle bell and the other was imitating the sound of a siren.

"And for children, contact with their peers is essential as it allows them to read each other's intentions and to improve their communication power. Do you remember the second step, about stimulating communication? The fourth step is also about stimulating communication[lxxxv] through the act of playing. The history of play during childhood influences adult life, shaping a person's life forever. Those who are denied play can do everything else as well as anyone else, but they can't socialize adequately. They won't be able to distinguish a friend from an enemy, they make mistakes regarding reading social signs, and they lose many emotional intelligence points. Playing helps children make more accurate judgments."

"More accurate judgments?" asked Estela.

"Yes. Children that play with each other can detect the difference between a joke and a provocation, even if the line between the two concepts is subtle."

"I believe those children will also acquire the ability of self-knowledge..."

"Exactly! Children will understand themselves much better.

They will discover innate abilities and hidden talents, which they can start developing from that moment on."

The two children with angel faces looked at the adults who were standing up, and apparently, they were bothered.

"Let's allow them to play," said Dr. Jansen, winking. "Can we go to the next room, Estela? I have other important aspects I would like to highlight..."

In another environment, the uniformed caretakers were giving lunch to a younger audience, made of babies who were about eight months old and who were using bibs.

"Such beautiful babies!" exclaimed Estela, getting closer to them.

"Babies also play a lot," continued Dr. Jansen. "They place objects in their mouths, stimulating their gums, they roll, crawl, clap..."

A baby, who was close to the two adults, clapped while eating baby food.

Estela smiled.

"Not only that, but they also throw the food to the floor and then repeat the act. They explore, learning. When their brain circuits become stronger, they become very skillful at manipulating objects, developing their skills as a result. If you closely observe babies and small children, they get pleasure from physical activities, such as running, hiding, assembling cubes, shooting a ball or just throwing it far away, to see it bouncing. Almost every child starts playing naturally. They find what they like to do, and then they start playing. In the cases in which there are some rules, like in football or chess, they will learn from each other, from their friends and teachers."

"I think we are interfering with them. They are quite focused on us and don't want to eat."

The babies were staring at the two adults, completely ignoring the caretakers.

"We are strangers here. They don't know us." With one hand, Dr. Jansen signaled it was time to go to another environment.

While walking through a large corridor, they heard a nursery rhyme coming from one of the rooms. The doctor followed the sound, opened a door, and looked at the interior, where two teachers and a dozen children clapped while some children danced near an audio speaker.

"Look at this," Dr. Jansen whispered. "They are dancing, having fun. They are not thinking: Oh my God, I look like a fool. When we play, we stop worrying, and we lose our sense of time. That's when the concept known as 'flow' happens, curing tedium. When we play, the brain is being tested and stimulated. We experience different situations, unexpected ones, and we make different emotional connections."

Estela carefully looked at Michael's face and saw his smiling expression changing, which scared her. Meanwhile, the following words explained the reason for the sudden seriousness.

"The world is becoming so competitive that parents forget that playing is important for the well-being[lxxxvi] of their child. They fill all the available time with cognitive activities, classes for this, classes for that ... And they seem to forget to save some time for playing. Playing is freedom!"

"I understand those parents," said Estela, frowning. "Our time is finite. We have to focus on the things that matter. Using some time to play seems like a discrepancy, considering the huge difficulties and demands of the modern world. We have a window for knowledge, don't we? Why would we allow the brain to rest if we can make it more intelligent?"

"That's where you are wrong, Estela! It isn't a mismatch to save some time to play because the brain becomes quite active while resting[lxxxvii], despite what the majority of people think. When you stop focusing on an external task, like studying, for example, the brain enters its default mode[lxxxviii]. It is during that moment that the unconscious works. The truth is that sometimes, being unconscious allows us to solve problems that we couldn't solve otherwise. Thus, people find solutions for problems when they aren't thinking about it. When the conscience fails, the unconscious state might succeed."

"How can that be?" asked Estela.

"Even while your attention is wandering, while looking through the window, without thinking at all or without playing, your brain is trying to find solutions for your problems. Right? A child psychology expert from the University of Southern California, Mary Helen Immordino-Yang[lxxxix], identified that children who present higher levels of connectivity during the default mode of the brain tend to have a better memory, higher intelligence, better reading skills, and, like I mentioned previously, a higher sense of empathy."

"Interesting..."

"And that's not all... When we ignore playing, we start having problems[xc]. Playing helps in maintaining our mental sanity. Children who don't develop their default mode have a greater tendency for psychopathy, exactly due to not being able to put themselves in others' shoes. In fact, there are studies about criminals in Texas' prisons[xci] that lead researchers to the conclusion that the absence of playing during childhood could predict the degree of these convicts."

"Gee!" Estela was awestruck.

"On the other hand, they also discovered that children with antisocial behaviors gradually become less antisocial just due to playing with other children. By sharing toys, playing house, dancing... their antisocial behaviors changed, becoming more tenuous. Furthermore, the humor improves, and the internal narrative starts changing from a sterile and sad version to a more colorful, richer, and more imaginative one. Playing reduces impulsivity and increases self-control, besides positively affecting other executive functions[xcii]. We human beings were made to play during all our lives. Is working important? Of course. Yet playing is important too. There is no conflict between studying and playing or playing and working. Those are integral aspects of life. It's like breathing in and then breathing out. Can you do that now?"

Estela filled her lungs and then emptied them.

"Breathing in and breathing out is cyclic and rhythmic. You can't keep breathing in, breathing in, breathing in, in, in... You breathe in—" Dr. Jansen raised his fingers "—and then you breathe out," he said, lowering his fingers followingly. "We were born to breathe in, which means working or studying, but also to breathe out, which is equivalent to playing. When you deny playing for a long time, you end up with less energy and a worse mood, and you become more pessimistic and incapable of feeling pleasure."

"Like what you experience when you don't sleep . . ."

"Exactly! When we draw a parallel between those two needs, we can state that playing is one of the most advanced ways nature invented to organize the brain, as well as sleeping. Both during sleep and play, we stabilize the nerves and strengthen memories. Playing and sleeping help us adapt to changes. When you sleep, Estela, you are consolidating the things you learned, recovering from physical damage, cleaning toxins, and dreaming, generating creativity."

The music suddenly stopped, also interrupting the conversation, and a teacher stood up from the floor, saying: "Alright! Class, it's time for today's story."

She walked to a shelf and picked up a thick book containing the best fairy tales from the Grimm Brothers.

"Who wants to hear 'Snow White'?" she asked aloud, looking at the young students while smiling.

Many hands raised in the air, especially those of girls.

Dr. Jansen continued: "The coherent narratives, with a beginning, a middle, and an end, are developed while we play. Telling stories isn't anything more than a narrative play which occupies the central role in our comprehension of the world. One of the functions of the left hemisphere of the brain is to create stories and explain the reasons behind things being done the way they are. Playing, therefore, makes our creative processes work. It's interesting to see how that happens, considering the theory of a famous English psychologist, Graham Wallas[xciii]. For him, the creative process follows four stages: the first is the preparation, during which a person finds a problem, thinks, details, and understands exactly what he or she is looking for.

The second stage is the incubation, during which the problem is interiorized, allowing it to ferment inside oneself while the unconscious mind works. The third phase is illumination, the stage during which the answer emerges from the unconscious. The last phase is the verification, the moment during which we test the answer to verify if it truly is right, making sure that the answer fits the problem perfectly.

"Memorizing and learning are processes that increase with playing. Many teachers know about this, so, they will tell little stories or use theaters or simulations to teach something harder or boring. Playing is a fertilizer for the brain. It's silly not to play."

"But . . . How is it possible to keep children playing? They have activities to perform, school tasks, sports . . ."

"That's exactly why I think this fourth step is so crucial. Children must be children. Pushing too hard[xciv] will generally break something, especially if it is something as fragile as a human. Children that only study and forget about playing, due to their parents thinking it is superfluous, don't experience feelings of competence or mastery regarding a subject. They feel the need to play. The excess of tasks impoverishes the land of those children. Remember to breath in and breath out. Having a chronic need for play is just wanting to breathe in, which represents an impossible dynamic. Thus, I think parents should not have a very rigid and inflexible vision about anything related to education. Children need the room for improving; they need to play with luck; they need space to maneuver."

Suddenly, a child passed by, running through the corridor before going into the bathroom. The dynamism of the school environment was contagious, making them feel more pleasure just by being there.

"When we play, we also rest, and without rest, there is no pro-activity or will to do something that requires focus. I don't know if you heard about it, but there is a study that became quite popular, developed by Anders Ericsson and his peers, about what differentiated the best violinists[xcv] from the average ones. Back then, the concept regarding the 'ten thousand hours' was quite commented on."

"Yes, I've heard about it."

"Well," Dr. Jansen continued, "a critical aspect in that study, which was not stressed in the following books and theses, was the fact that those violinists, with above-average abilities, rested more than others. They slept one more hour than the remaining violinists; they took a nap during the afternoon and spent more time doing activities that were pleasant to them. All of us need resources so we can focus on something. How do we get those resources? Resting, intermediating activities, breathing in, and breathing out. Therefore, resting, having fun, and playing are the main peers of working and dedication. I'm intrigued by the current tendency for people to focus only on working and forget about resting, about what they enjoy and what gives them pleasure. How can that be possible? They are avoiding doing the exact things that improve performance[xcvi]."

Meanwhile, due to being entertained by the topic, Estela and Jansen walked through the corridor that led to the preschool classroom, where children were sitting in colorful chairs, sharing square tables that were adequate for their age while coloring drawings with crayons and finger paint.

"Art classes," Estela noticed.

"And the act of playing is already its very own reward ... In other words, we must not reward things that children already enjoy doing," Michael told Estela abruptly, taking her out of the magical universe of the children to bring her back to the universe of ideas. "An interesting study[xcvii], which was replicated countless times with preschool children, can prove it. In that study, the researchers looked in classrooms for those children who loved to draw, children that spent their free time drawing and painting due to enjoying it. They divided those children into three groups[xcviii]. In the first group, they asked the children if they would like to paint something to win a beautiful diploma with their names on it. Those children who enjoyed painting accepted the challenge without having any

105

second thoughts. They did drawing and paintings, thus receiving the diploma at the end of the task. In the second group, the researchers didn't promise any reward for the children who enjoyed painting, only giving them the diploma after they finished the painting. In the third group, children didn't get any diploma, despite performing the proposed activities, and no reward of any kind was promised. Two weeks later, the researchers returned to the school."

"And what did they observe?"

"In the first group, the children who previously had their own will to paint, lost their interest in drawing and painting, since the researchers imposed conditions on them, telling them, if you do this, you will get that. Since the motivation[xcix] was not intrinsic anymore, becoming extrinsic, it backfired. Rewarding someone who already performs a task due to feeling pleasure while performing it, demotivates them. Playing, or in this case, painting, became work. In the other groups, since there was no imposition, painting was a natural act. We could perform that same experiment here, in this room, and we would see the same effect. So, I insist: do not reward children for what they already enjoy doing."

Michael and Estela walked to the outside area of the school, where there were some multi-sports courts, a sandbox, teeter-totters, and swings. The place was quite beautiful, with plenty of trees that softened the sun's rays with their branches.

They stopped near the green fence of a multi-sports complex where pre-adolescent boys were playing indoor soccer. They watched the first half of the game and were amazed by the skill of a frail little boy that could dribble past several opponents before powerfully shooting the ball close to the goalpost, scoring a fantastic goal.

One of the boys who was dribbled past, and who was stronger and taller, started pushing the smaller boy who scored the goal.

The teacher whistled and shouted, "Adrian, stop that! It was an amazing goal. Learn how to lose."

Estela was bothered by the aggressiveness of the scene and

immediately asked, "What about when children are mean to each other?"

"Even in those moments, playing is important," said Dr. Jansen, joining both hands in front of himself. "Everything indicates that that kind of play, though ruder, is also important for social skills. Pushing, being pushed, fighting . . . those are all experiences. Knowing how to control violent urges, even under adult supervision, is fundamental for a quality social coexistence. It is possible to improve some attitudes during childhood, thus not allowing those actions to happen again during adolescence or adulthood. We all learn from our mistakes. Aggressiveness is a natural behavior, in humans and animals, which can be employed to show dominance and competitiveness. So, in group activities, to promote healthy interactions between children, the adult must intervene in situations of conflict and demotivate more combative behaviors. When such behaviors happen, it is important to have an adult watching the children, for them to feel safe."

A noise of clapping invaded the place, impeding Michael from speaking. Estela looked to the teacher, who used the trick to get the attention of the children who were playing, absorbed, in the sandbox.

"Come on, boys and girls," she said. "It's time to pick up everything and get inside."

Michael was paying attention to everything that was happening around them and concluded, "Another important thing is time, especially for the older children. Children need to know that there are temporal limits for playing and that the local order has to be restored once the playing is over. In this way, they must not leave their toys wherever."

"Oh, please!" a little red-headed boy complained. "Just a little bit longer."

"Preschool children," the doctor continued, "might not want to stop playing and will also not want to put their toys in the right place. However, if they are told daily, on a determined schedule and in a benevolent manner, that it's time to stop playing and to tidy everything up, they will understand that it is reasonable and they will learn that behavior. Well . . . I hope I have convinced you about how important it is to play and have fun, not only for children but for everyone in general.

"You don't need to give me more reasons," Estela answered, smiling. "I already believe in you, Doctor. Can I ask you a question?"

Dr. Jansen nodded positively.

"Do you play?"

"Sure! We don't need to stop playing when we grow up or when we become teenagers, adults, or elders. We have to keep breathing in and out, finding hobbies, enjoying people around us, making new friends, enjoying finding new things."

"I see angry people who are extremely competitive, who spread unhappiness wherever they go. Did they forget to play?"

"Maybe they never played at all," he answered. "Some studies corroborate that those who have hobbies and are not exclusively dedicated to working have fewer cardiac problems[c] and are less prone to dementia in the future. Even if you are older, playing with young children can be as important in increasing longevity[ci] as a healthy diet and exercise. Take, for example, the centenarians of Okinawa, Japan. The elders in Japan take care of the children and the vegetable gardens, they gather with their peers, and they live together intensely. It is one of the secrets behind becoming a centenarian. I do as I teach. I practice physical exercise, I read my books, and, before lunch, I participate in a fun schedule that we have in the clinic. Once there, I sit with my children on the floor and assemble a puzzle, make houses with wooden blocks, sing, and dance. It's quite relaxing and fun. I permit myself to play every single day. The lack of playing must be handled as malnutrition: it represents a risk for health and the development of the body and mind. The world doesn't give us time; we have to find it and hold it. Saving some time to play in our routine, or a child's routine is an excellent strategy."

"You also travel a lot . . ."

"Yes, I enjoy sabbatical years every three years. I feel that they improve that balance between work and daily life. They increase my intimate connections and make me physically healthier. It's my time to pause, to dive headfirst into topics I want to investigate. I have time to think, to write, and to adapt myself to new environments. It's like a trampoline for new ideas, new life goals. I shield my relaxing time. And you should shield yours too."

"Can I ask you another question?" asked Estela, showing her dimples while smiling.

"Sure!" answered Dr. Jansen.

"The fifth step, what is it about?"

"Take it easy, my dear! Take it easy. Focus on this one. However, I know that you will enjoy the next step. It too is quite essential . . .

When Estela got home, Sofia, who was wearing purple clothes, was sleeping in her cradle, and Victor softly said, "She drank the milk you left in the fridge. Now she is sleeping. She is so sweet . . ."

Estela caressed her daughter's flushed cheek and stretched herself to kiss Sofia's forehead. "She has such beautiful hands! I'm in love with her."

Victor hugged Estela from behind. "So am I."

"She will play a lot; you hear me?"

"She must play!" Victor reaffirmed.

Later, in her bedroom, Estela sat on the armchair and quickly typed on her laptop: "Fourth step: creativity. You won't believe it. Let it be, let them play. That's it. Let them play. Playing is vital as it stimulates creativity."

While she was writing, she thought about what the doctor said regarding the fifth step. What would it be?

CHAPTER 07 — THE FIFTH STEP: SELF-CONTROL AND GROWTH MINDSET

"He who cannot obey himself will be commanded."

—*Friedrich Nietzsche*

O nce Estela posted the fourth step on her blog, the number of visitors increased exponentially. Furthermore, people kept requesting that she record videos regarding the steps and post them on YouTube. Estela was reluctant about it since she enjoyed writing and she wouldn't know how to behave in front of a camera. However, deep inside, the stronger reason was the fact that she wanted to have time to focus on Sofia. She really wanted to put the first step into practice, almost integrally dedicating herself to Sofia. Estela had a rule that stated she could only write and post on her blog while her daughter was sleeping. When Sofia was awake, they would walk and talk since Estela saw opportunities to teach her something everywhere.

"Look at this, Sofia!" she would say while shopping at the supermarket. "That's a Palmer mango . . . Feel the scent . . . Now pay attention to the red, smooth, and shining peel of that apple . . . Inside that yellow can, there is powdered milk, but I'm certain that you prefer Mommy's milk . . ."

At home, she would show Sofia words using the Tiny Readers app on a 65-inch television. It was a short, easy task, but since her daughter was so young, there were no evident results yet; however, Estela had faith that the results would appear soon.

She enjoyed breastfeeding, caressing the soft back of her daughter while changing her clothes, bathing her, massaging her little body with baby oil, and kissing her affectionately. Even changing her diapers was something she did with pleasure. Sofia was calm and slept all night, contrary to what Estela's friends said about their babies. Estela asked herself if it had something to do with the omega-3 supplements she had ingested during pregnancy or the massages, or if it was just her daughter's personality.

With the multitude of tasks that involved her, Estela didn't notice how fast time was flying by, nor did she notice the absence of any word from Dr. Jansen for several days. Since many people were leaving questions on her blog regarding the next step, she realized people were curious, and she felt the need to quench their curiosity. Therefore, she decided to send Dr. Jansen a message, asking him when he would have the opportunity to talk to her about the fifth step. She was quite curious herself.

A few hours later she received the news: "I'm taking my grandchildren to the zoo on Sunday morning. If you want to meet me there, we can talk. Oh! Bring Sofia and your husband."

Estela promised herself she wouldn't miss the opportunity of this meeting, even if Victor didn't want to go.

At nine o'clock in the morning, Victor parked the Volvo in the zoo[cii] parking lot. The sky was gray, but it still didn't look like it was going to rain. As a precaution, Estela placed the umbrella underneath her daughter's stroller.

In the entrance, Michael greeted them festively: "Good morning, Estela, Victor, and Sofia!" he said. "This is my wife, Ruth, and my grandson, Enzo."

Estela was not expecting to meet Dr. Jansen's wife, a friendly woman who removed her sunglasses to greet them, revealing her beautiful green eyes. She was carrying a camera on her neck, and her grandson, a pre-teen with long, thin legs, was also carrying a camera with a telescopic lens, using a shoulder strap.

"Pleased to meet you," said Victor while shaking Dr. Jansen's hand and lightly kissing Ruth's face. Then, he pointed at the camera Enzo was carrying and asked: "Can you take photos using that lens without shaking? Isn't it too heavy for you?"

"Of course I can!" answered Enzo, lifting the camera to his face with great dexterity. "This lens is a Sigma 150-600mm[ciii]. My grandma doesn't like using zoom, so she chose the 50mm[civ] 1.2."

"I like to take pictures of *people*," explained Ruth, using an arm to grab her grandson.

Victor commented: "I see that you prefer Canon. I have a Nikon, back at home. Today I just brought my favorite camera," he said while taking his mobile phone from the front pocket of his jeans. "My iPhone."

After trivial conversations, Ruth, Enzo, and Victor entered in a very animated and interactive conversation about photography. Since they all had a common interest, Michael gave them space to speak and focused on Estela.

"Sofia grew up a lot! She has gained weight too!" he exclaimed, looking inside the stroller.

"That's just mother's milk," Estela commented, smiling, showing her dimples.

"It's a pity she is sleeping," said the doctor, opening his hands. "I wanted to hold her."

A few meters away from the zoo entrance, the group stopped near the sea lions' space. They were fascinated by the animals and by the possibility of getting good photos, and Estela, Michael, and Sofia ended up getting behind.

Estela commented, "Like the readers of my blog, I'm very interested in the next step, Michael. Can you share it with me now?"

"Of course, my dear friend. It's great to know that people are showing interest in the subject. The fifth step works as the foundation for child development. It's about self-control and growth mentality."

Estela rubbed her hands together in front of her body. She knew today's conversation would result in precious information.

"Self-control? You've got me excited! Is there any kind of technique that can be used to improve self-control?"

Michael Jansen got quite close to her, and using a lower tone, said: "Self-control develops while we are children, and even as adults, we can improve it. Maybe you don't know this, but our emotions are regulated by two distinct parts of the brain: the limbic system[cv] and the pre-frontal cortex[cvi]. The limbic system is the one that reacts to any provocative stimulus."

Suddenly, he stopped, looked around as if he was searching for something or somebody, and said: "Look over there, Estela! Look at that girl who is jumping in pure joy due to getting her blue cotton candy. Imagine that, a few minutes before, she saw the vendor and asked her father to buy her that treat. It was her limbic system that made her wish for the cotton candy and is now making her eat it with so much pleasure. We are born with a limbic system working in full steam."

Estela picked up her mobile phone and created a note: "*limbic system.*" She needed to record as much information as possible to divulge it in her blog.

"The other part of that gear is the pre-frontal cortex," Michael continued. "It too is responsible for self-control. Remember the last time we spoke? On that day, coincidentally, I mentioned that by playing we strengthen our pre-frontal cortex. I think I told you that, didn't I?"

"Yes . . . Yes. At the Secret Garden school."

"Well, that's true. The pre-frontal cortex creates opposition to our limbic system, resists it, like if both parts of the brain were arm wrestling. If the pre-frontal cortex is under-developed, the limbic system will win the battle. Differently from the limbic system, the pre-frontal cortex is shaped during infancy. Therefore, a very young child, one who has not turned four years old yet, can't resist certain impulses. When in a supermarket, they will quickly pick up a treat in the checkout line. If you go to a toy store, they will want every single object they see. That's perfectly normal since children's pre-frontal cortexes don't yet have an efficient opposition to the limbic system. Over time, however, that region of the brain becomes more robust, managing to calm down, distract, and put out the fires of desire. Thus, children start making the right decisions. When we need to control ourselves, we depend on our pre-frontal cortex."

"Is the nonsense that certain teenagers perform related to inadequate development of that pre-frontal cortex?"

"Yes, partially. During the teenage[cvii] years, due to hormonal changes and a new wave of brain growth, the pre-frontal cortex becomes more vulnerable. In some cases, that vulnerability makes teens do unthinkable things, which they will regret in the future, such as binge drinking alcohol or experimenting with drugs."

"If I've interpreted what you said correctly, the limbic system is the accelerator, while the pre-frontal cortex is the brake for our internal desires."

"The pre-frontal cortex is our limbic system's sensor. It assesses the tempting stimulus and interferes with our will. It weighs the consequences, considering our objectives in relation to the tempting force and is responsible for the final judgment."

"Is self-control more genetically or environmentally influenced?"

"Both aspects influence it. However, environmental influences are clearly stronger[cviii]. The environment in which we live can shape our self-control-related skills. For example, if you live in a healthy environment, without considerable stress, with present parents and interesting friends, you will have a lower probability of messing up. The opposite[cix] is also true."

"How can we ensure that children will be able to resist daily temptations?"

Dr. Jansen placed his hand on his chin, considering the question a little longer before answering, "To answer such a question, I'm going to refer to a study from the '60s, that is quite famous, performed by Walter Mischel[cx]. It is known as the marshmallow experiment. In his research, Mischel used marshmallows as bait since they represent such a temptation for children, preschool children in particular in this study."

"Hmm . . . What strategy did he use?"

"He used a very interesting strategy that was quite tempting for children, of course. In each schoolroom, he sat one or sometimes two children at a table on which there was a tray with a delicious marshmallow. The researcher would speak with each child and present them two options: eat the treat immediately, or wait fifteen minutes to eat it and win another marshmallow as a bonus. After such an offer, the scientist would immediately leave the room and would only return fifteen minutes later."

"Some children couldn't resist the marshmallow, I'm sure . . ."

"Of course! Some children would eat the treat immediately. Other children would wait for some time but not the entire fifteen minutes. Thirty percent of the children would wait for the return of the researcher. In the face of such result, Mischel concluded that the group that didn't eat the marshmallow, leaving it completely untouched, was the one that demonstrated stronger self-control because they were able to wait for a bigger reward, suppressing the immediate instinct of eating the sweet in front of them."

"Why were they capable of waiting?" asked Estela.

"Generally, they were children who used a strategy to avoid giving in to temptation: they would distract themselves in order to wait for time to pass. Each one had their own tactic, which went from singing to hiding the sweet away from their own vision, closing their eyes, or even licking the marshmallow but still leaving it intact. You can view the experiment videos on YouTube if you want to."

"What was the result of the experiment? I mean, why did he become so famous in the world of psychology?"

"That simple experiment, my dear, demonstrated the correlation between *self-control during childhood* and *success in a later life stage.*"

"Oh! Interesting..." muttered Estela.

"Certainly! Children who succeeded in controlling themselves were more successful during adulthood. That 30 percent of preschool children who managed to rest their primitive instincts and not eat the marshmallow during the fifteen minutes were the same who got the best school grades and the best grades on their SAT. Furthermore, they were the more popular students, and had relationships that lasted longer, a lower probability of divorce, better social status, and a lower probability of experimenting with drugs or being imprisoned."

"In my opinion, if they managed to wait for fifteen minutes to win another marshmallow, they already had the skills necessary for self-control," Estela concluded.

"And that self-control remained a fundamental brain tool during adulthood, hence influencing every aspect of their life. Self-control is one of the keys for life success[cxi]."

"Self-control is one of the keys for life success," Estela repeated for herself.

Since she didn't want to forget the sentence, the journalist stopped for a few minutes beneath a tree that was on the side of their path and typed Michael's words on her mobile phone. She wanted to use it as a motto on her blog.

Dr. Jansen followed Estela and patiently waited until she raised her eyes. Then, he continued explaining, "In posterior studies, which already used functional magnetic resonance, other researchers noticed that children who passed the marshmallow test were the same people that had higher activation of the pre-frontal cortex during adulthood."

"I was already imagining that . . ."

"And those children who ate the treat immediately, as adults, presented a bigger activation of the striatum[cxii], one of the brain centers related to chemical dependencies."

Estela nodded her head positively before asking, "Is it possible to teach children how to achieve a higher ability to control themselves, to wait for winning the second marshmallow, or to say it better, to resist immediate rewards?"

"Certainly," consented a confident Dr. Jansen. "We have the obligation of teaching our children self-control strategies. In a posterior study, researchers taught children some distraction tactics before the marshmallow test. One of those strategies was to sing a song when their hand got close to the treat. When left alone with the marshmallow, children would remember what they had to do, and the majority of them were able to wait until they won a second treat."

"How could we teach such strategies in practice[cxiii]?"

"For older children, we can explain that not everything in life is as we wish, that patience is a virtue that almost always brings us better results. We live in a world with a *delayed return*. We can show them examples that exist in nature, such as the fact that normally we don't eat fruit until it is ripened; farmers first need to plant seeds and wait for favorable weather before harvesting . . . And so on and so on . . . I know that most children want instant gratification, but we must teach them that in practice *we must wait.*

"What about younger children?" Estela asked.

"Playing strengthens the pre-frontal cortex, as I told you previously. Furthermore, we can also teach them how to distract themselves in situations that are not so pleasant. We don't have to teach that by telling them: we can also show it through actions. A common example is when the mother is going to work and the child cries. The father can use a toy to distract the child during that moment of tension. Acting that way, he is teaching the child distraction and self-control techniques. Over time, the child will acquire those techniques and use them when necessary. However, if the father doesn't interact[cxiv] with his child and keeps using his mobile phone instead, he won't teach self-control strategies to his child, hence undermining the child's future."

Enzo came running to show his camera screen to Dr. Jansen. "Look, Grandpa! Look at the pose of this spider-monkey; it's so funny! I think he has a serious case of dandruff. If you zoom in, you can see all these white dots . . ."

"Very cool photo! Congratulations! It's properly framed . . . The ISO was perfect at 200, good choice, and the colors' balance is quite good too. I want to see the other photos later."

The boy left feeling confident and returned to where his grandmother was standing.

Estela commented, "He is so cute. It's obvious that you are using the steps with him. Nowadays, I see lots of children who want everything yesterday. They are too short-sighted and get frustrated easily, only desiring *instant gratification*."

"Parents must explain to their children that they can make their own decisions and that wrong choices might have disastrous consequences in the future. When children are quite young, they learn self-control by copying their parents. That's why it is so important for parents to act and react moderately and to spend time close to their children, giving them true love. Furthermore, it's important that parents give their children a certain degree of autonomy."

"What if parents are absent? What if, for example, the mother works all day long, in order to pay the bills, and the child never even met the father? How could such a child learn self-control?"

"Children that grow up in less protective environments often have more difficulties exercising their self-control. Usually, they are the same children who have a higher risk of becoming drug users, alcoholics, or convicts. Yet it is an avoidable situation. In the scenario you chose, the mother can nurture a good relationship with her child and teach the young child, by means of speaking and through actions, how to make the right choices. Parents, teachers, uncles, and grandparents can help them with that task, with strengthening the self-control muscles."

"I'm curious: I know people that behave properly in certain situations but don't have any self-control in other situations. Is this normal?"

"Yes. Self-control depends on the *situation* and *context*[cxv]. The pre-frontal cortex of someone who is obese or who has a sedentary lifestyle can consider that exercising is not important. That same person can demonstrate amazing self-control at work, always being on time, respecting his or her peers, and always being responsible. A person might show a lack of self-control in a situation, just to show an excess of self-control in other situations."

"Grandpa," said Enzo, who came running up once again, "I managed to take this photo of an alligator getting out of the water. See? How cool is that?"

Estela saw the camera display and was truly impressed, commenting, "What a beautiful photo! You are hugely talented, Enzo!"

The little boy blushed, thanked Estela, and left timidly.

Michael Jansen shared an observation with his friend. "That's not the best way of complimenting, Estela. Avoid complimenting talent; praise effort instead."

"I'm sorry," answered an embarrassed Estela.

"You have nothing to apologize for," said Dr. Jansen while touching Estela's arm fondly. "You came here because you wish to learn. I'm willing to share everything I know with you. Therefore, I'm going to use this occasion to tell you that our skills are not predetermined. Carol Dweck[cxvi], who taught at Stanford University, created a concept called *fixed mindset*, for people who judge that talent is an innate ability, for those who believe that either you are born talented or not. She also created a complementary concept, the *growth mindset*, for those who believe that talent is the continuous process of building abilities, in order to become good at something, depending on effort and dedication. People with a growth mindset keep growing, capacitating themselves during their entire lives. According to how they see things, their abilities are like an eternal building site, constantly transforming."

"That means," commented Estela with a relaxed posture, "that we are all born with the aptitude of becoming winners."

"Exactly!" exclaimed Michael with a broad grin. "People with a fixed mindset allow that erroneous thought to obstruct the progress of their abilities. They don't expand themselves. If they aren't able to achieve their goals, they see the problem in other people, instead of seeing it in the fact that they weren't capable of achieving such goals. For that group, skills are set in stone, hence, are immutable. The vision is, either you are born talented and intelligent or you are born incompetent and stupid and you will remain that way for the rest of your life. They absolutely value natural talent, but like I've been saying from the start, we can always improve ourselves; we can always grow. No one is born so talented that growing a little more is an impossibility."

"I know many people who have that mindset," said Estela, rubbing the back of her head.

"They judge themselves using that metric. Was I born talented enough? Will people notice that I'm not capable? Therefore, they have a need to show their skills every single time it is possible, or they hide."

"What if they fail?"

"A slip can show the world that they weren't born capable. They are more likely to cheat, to come up with excuses, to get rid of their interests when they aren't 'natural.' They don't think they can learn from mistakes because that process hurts them on the inside. A loss erases every success. That's the main problem: they restrict themselves, avoiding going a little bit beyond. Those with a fixed mindset wish for praise and to rest on their laurels. Yet, we know that to grow, we have to go a little bit beyond our current abilities. We need to look for new challenges, to risk a little bit more. They avoid doing that, as they fear falling from their pedestal. If they fall, if they make a mistake, they will be exposed, and people will find the truth: that they are not as good as they appear to be."

"And those with a growth mindset, how do they behave?"

"They have no difficulties trying, making mistakes, and wiping the slate clean to start over again. They understand that learning is a process during which making mistakes is a norm and not an exception. They know they need to learn from their mistakes to grow. Consequently, they stretch their arms a little bit further; they go a little bit beyond; they want to improve themselves. Maybe their parents taught them, not with words but with practical examples, that your intelligence today doesn't predict your intelligence and your abilities of tomorrow."

"They challenge themselves," summarized Estela, punching the air.

She asked herself which kind of mindset hers was, as she didn't want to have a fixed mindset at all.

Michael kept portraying those with a growth mindset: "They reconsider themselves and can drop strategies that were not successful because that won't hurt their egos. Their goal is to keep trying to improve themselves, fixing their own weaknesses. That encourages them because they feel the satisfaction of having the chance to learn a few more things. They have no difficulties accepting problems, and for them, no challenge is insurmountable. Instead, they see problems as goals that can be achieved if the necessary energy is applied along with new strategies."

"What if they fail?"

"The Japanese have a saying: 'Nana korobi ya oki.' Translated, it means, 'Fall seven times, stand up eight.' Failure is an opportunity to grow. They ask themselves: Why did I fail? Which lesson can I learn from my failure? Can I stand up again? In other words, they have the ability to react."

"Are their relationships different too?" questioned Estela, while observing, her husband animatedly talking with Ruth and

Enzo at a distance.

"Their relationships are different too, yes. Individuals with a growth mindset think they must get more involved in order for relationships to grow. They highlight the importance of teamwork and open communication channels. Others' opinions are welcomed, as they are more open and flexible. Those with a fixed mindset think relationships are immutable. They only believe in love at first sight, and they are not good at working with teams because they understate other people and try to become the stars of the project."

"Oh! I'm quite familiar with that attitude," Estela rambled.

"I think it is very important to explain to our children that they can grow and develop themselves," commented the doctor, "and that growth usually isn't constant. We grow a little bit and we improve ourselves, but there are times during which we stagnate or can even become worse versions of ourselves. It's not a linear path, and setbacks are a part of natural growth. Therefore, there are times of intense growth, times of stabilization, and times of doubt. In my opinion, it's important to stress that mistakes don't show that people are born without talents. No one is perfect and no one is immutable. Furthermore, many times, we have both mindsets: growth and fixed. What matters the most is that we tend toward the growth mindset."

"Shouldn't we aim for perfection?" she asked.

"We must try to improve ourselves," said the doctor. "Aiming for perfection results in frustration. People with a growth mindset know that the more they practice, the more they will improve. Hard work, dedication, and perseverance make the difference. They aren't intimidated by obstacles either. There is joy when one notices that an activity that represented an impossibility in the past can now happen successfully. As parents, we need to test the limits of our children, without asking for too much. We need to balance it; otherwise, children will feel discouraged."

"The dosage can make the difference between a remedy and poison," she added.

"That's right. So we must pay attention to them. Likewise, allowing a child to stagnate won't generate growth and can stimulate a fixed mindset. However, asking for too much and stretching a child's effort beyond their current abilities can make them lose their interest in an activity due to their lack of ability."

Sofia started groaning increasingly louder until the groan became intense crying. Estela quickly took her from the stroller and held her in her arms, comforting her with caresses on her soft, dark, little, bristly hair.

"Shh . . . Shh . . . Mom is here, my darling. Do you want to eat right now? Are you hungry?" said Estela while walking toward a place with wooden park benches and tables, designated for picnics.

Dr. Jansen slowly followed her, pushing the stroller. He wanted to give the mother and child time to get synchronized during such an important moment: breastfeeding. Sofia sucked eagerly as her mother looked at her daughter's face tenderly while sitting on one of the benches.

"Babies are born with a growth mindset," said Michael, sitting next to them. "They demonstrate a will to learn, are excellent scientists, touch everything they can, and test their parents and people around them. Each obstacle that appears in their way, they overcome. Everything they were not able to perform at first but, with time, managed to perform later, becomes something intrinsic to their lives. However, if parents keep judging their children or if any situation in their environment restricts them, children might adopt a fixed mindset. Likewise, if parents encourage them properly and teach them the pleasure of knowledge, they will improve their performance in some areas, assuming a growth mindset."

"What about you, Michael? Can you tell if someone has a fixed mindset or a growth mindset?"

"When babies are between one and three years old, anyone with experience can identify which kind of mindset the child leans toward the most. Even so, it's just a sketch, not the final product. Therefore, once again, parents have a fundamental role. I've heard mothers and fathers say that those with natural talent, like their children, don't have to work as hard as other children must. It's a pity because by thinking that way they won't encourage their children to work hard and dedicate themselves, and the talent of those children will atrophy over time."

"And parents don't listen to you?"

"No. They had a fixed mindset and their children also too, reflecting their parents."

"Speaking of parents . . . Teachers too have a great impact on the development of children's abilities. Don't you agree?"

"Of course! Teachers are important in helping children develop themselves. During daily school life, there are many moments when a student can't succeed on a test or in sports activities. If the teacher concludes that the student can't learn the contents, based on the test results and thus, will keep failing, that teacher seriously needs to think about changing his or her pedagogic posture. Since every single child can change, as they are still in the middle of their construction process; teachers must be more empathetic during such situations, always aiming at promoting dialogue with the student, in order to really understand what is motivating the failure in any given discipline."

"Dialogue is always the best path to solving problems," Estela added. "I think teachers must stimulate students' participation and compliment students as often as possible. Oh! Regarding compliments, is there a proper way to compliment children?"

Dr. Jansen placed his large hand on his forehead as if he had forgotten that topic.

"Carol Dweck [cxvii]and her colleagues thought about that question and decided to perform an experiment to see if they could instill children with both a fixed mindset and a growth mindset, using only compliments. They gave easy puzzles to several children who performed well in their task. As a motivational strategy, once the activity was done, the researchers complimented the children for completing the task. In some cases, they would compliment talent: "Oh my God! You managed to complete nine puzzles correctly! *You are very good at this!*" In other cases, the compliment was directed toward effort: "*Wow! You managed to correctly complete nine puzzles! I saw how much effort you put into this task.*"

"A subtle difference..."

"True! Both groups were quite similar regarding their success performing the task. So, let me ask you, Estela, do you think that a small difference in the kind of compliment could promote a difference between both groups' performance in the following puzzles?"

"Considering everything you already said, I believe it could."

"That's right ... Right after the compliment, the behaviors followed opposite paths. Children whose compliment was focused on 'talent,' rejected new challenges, as they didn't want to expose their failures. Furthermore, those who did accept another challenge had a bad performance, despite the fact that the following puzzles were as easy as the first ones."

"That's quite strange!" exclaimed Estela.

"In the case of the children whose compliments focused on effort, their performance actually improved. Those children attempted to complete harder puzzles, and despite failing in some moments, they kept learning from their mistakes. Then, they would return to the easier puzzles and would achieve much higher scores than in their first attempts. Some would even feel excited and say, 'I love challenges! I love working hard!'"

"In that case, we must know the right way of complimenting. I will compliment effort whenever possible!"

"And never label anyone."

"Neither positively or negatively?"

"Never. If you label a child positively, for example, saying, "You are great at math," the child might be afraid to lose that status and will certainly avoid performing harder tasks. If you use a negative label such as, "You have zero talent for math,"" the child will believe that the contempt is deserved and will rarely show you the opposite. Believing talents can be developed helps children achieve their potential and face difficulties, which will certainly appear sooner or later."

"I think we need to value more effort and less talent."

"And we need to stress that many people that are seen as innately talented, like Michael Jordan in basketball or Cristiano Ronaldo in football, are, actually, true examples of *dedication*. They got to their training sessions earlier and only stopped later than required, perfecting their dribbling and coordination..."

"That's true, but media love people with natural talent, even if they have to distort facts and minimize their effort."

"Meanwhile, parents, teachers, and coaches can explain that to children, stressing how athletes need to sweat in their jersey to achieve success."

Estela added, "We can't lose the chance to learn and to teach, right?"

The conversation was interrupted by Sofia, who stopped sucking and started making sounds that showed her satisfaction. Estela smiled and, staring at her daughter's lovely eyes, said: "I want you to feel pleasure in growing, in developing, in learning. Whenever I compliment you, my dear daughter, I will compliment your hard work and not your talent because I want you to keep trying to improve yourself, always aiming at getting better."

"Can I hold her in my arms?" asked her friend.

"Of course, Michael."

Estela observed the doctor analyzing her daughter and remembered she wanted his permission to create videos about the steps like many followers had suggested.

"People are asking me to share the steps in video format. What do you think about it? Would it be a good idea?" she asked.

"Not a good idea... it's a wonderful idea! It has a higher probability of divulging our message. The results will be even more intense and consistent."

"But I'm not sure how to start yet . . ."

"Remember about the growth mindset. Ask yourself how you could put this project into practice."

"I will think about it."

"At the clinic, we have equipment that we use to record the progress of our children . . . If you want me to, I can help you record the first three steps on one of those days. Who knows? Maybe during a weekend or a holiday . . ."

"After that I want you to tell me about the sixth step . . . I'm already anxious, but I know I need to learn how to wait . . ."

CHAPTER 08 — THE SIXTH STEP: FOCUS AND WELL-BEING

"True enjoyment comes from activity of the mind and exercise of the body; the two are ever united."

—*Wilhelm Von Humboldt*

E stela and Dr. Jansen scheduled a date for recording the videos for YouTube: ten o´clock on a Saturday. Sofia had just turned three months old, and the doctor insisted Estela bring her.

The journalist arrived before the scheduled time and was surprised by the fact that the Awake Clinic was as busy as during work days. Carrying her daughter in the baby carrier, carefully adjusted on her chest, Estela walked through the people at the clinic. Her baby appeared to be curious, observing, with her dark eyes, similar to olives, all the coming and going of babies, children, teenagers, and adults.

On the sixth floor, in the bright and aromatic entryway of the doctor's office, they found Michael Jansen lecturing an audience consisting of parents. The lecture's subject was child nutrition and addressed the benefits of fruits and vegetables for children. Estela, however, only managed to hear a few seconds of the lecture since the doctor was already thanking the audience for their presence.

While a big round of applause erupted in the room, the doctor invited parents to ask the first questions. Estela tried to sit among the group.

At that moment, Naomi, a timid Japanese mother, asked about the real advantages of organic food.

Dr. Jansen readily answered, holding the microphone. "Naomi, what matters the most is to eat vegetables and fruits. If you can buy organic food, even better. Organic vegetables produce defenses against plagues[cxviii], which means they contain a higher quantity[cxix] of phytochemicals, which helps to prevent diseases, such as cancer or the process of aging. However, if organic food is too expensive for your budget, you can buy conventional fruits and vegetables, wash them properly, and give them to your children without fearing anything. Despite the presence of pesticides, eating such food represents many more benefits than risks."

Countless other questions kept Michael in the same place, and when the audience finally dispersed, Estela walked toward the doctor.

"Estela . . . Sofia . . . It's such a pleasure to see you again!" said Michael Jansen, offering his honest smile while getting closer to Sofia. "Oh! It's good to see you, little princess. You are supporting your neck quite nicely! Are you allowing her to spend a lot of time on the floor, lying prone, Estela?"

"I try to do so, but she keeps complaining . . ."

"Remember how important it is to let her spend as much time as possible in the crawling position. As I told you, that simple act stimulates motor coordination and the muscles of the shoulders, chest, and neck, besides vision, of course. Talk to her, play with her . . . Place a little ball or a doll close to her so she gets used to spending time in that position. She will complain less that way."

"Okay! Did you hear Dr. Michael, Sofia? You have to spend more time on the carpet. It's for your own good!"

Michael Jansen laughed, and after lightly tapping Estela's back, he said, "Should we go to my office? I believe everything will be ready."

When entering the room, Estela remembered how comfortable that environment was, which made her think about the first interview with the doctor.

She was entirely focused on the motions of a young man who was adjusting the wires and testing the LED lights, located on the camera lateral.

"Almost ready to record, Doctor," said the cameraman, who was so focused that he barely looked at the three of them.

"This is Bruno, our cameraman," informed the doctor. "He also works as an assistant professor with some children. He has many skills. Did you know that he is an entertainer at Awake Clinic parties? He loves dressing as a clown to promote the happiness of our children, parents, and clinic staff."

Bruno, who was already used to being complimented by the doctor, didn't feel intimidated. He picked up a rectangular transmitter from the table and gently asked Estela for permission to place the microphone on the lapel of her coat and to adjust the antenna on her waist.

Bothered by Sofia's rumbling, who was demonstrating her discontentment with all the hustle, Estela asked, "What do you think? Should I release her from the baby carrier?"

"I think it would be better," consented Michael.

Bruno installed the doctor's microphone. Estela sat in front of Michael, staring at his eyes and holding Sofia in her arms.

Bruno used his hand to sign the camera was recording, and the journalist stared at the camera to say the text she had memorized: "Hi! I'm here with one of the biggest experts in child development in Brazil, maybe one of the biggest experts in the whole world, the neurologist and neuroscientist Dr. Michael Jansen.

He studied at Oxford University, in the United Kingdom, and has been practicing for almost fifty years, besides teaching in universities such as Yale, Harvard, and São Paulo. Today we are going to talk about the first step. This step comprises the topic of connection between parents and children. During the interview, we will talk about how parents should express love."

The connection between Estela and Michael helped them to explore the topic clearly and concisely. The doctor referred to types of parent control [cxx] as proposed by Baumrind and her colleagues, to didactically explain the different behaviors adopted by parents while educating their children. His voice sounded firm and convincing, as usual.

"The researchers classified the parents according to four distinct styles: negligent, permissive, authoritative, and authoritarian. While authoritative and authoritarian might sound similar, they represent different styles. Thus, please stay focused when I use such words and remember the concepts behind each word," said Michael, staring at the camera as if he could see the future audience of the videos behind it. "I will start my explanation by approaching the negligent parents, since they are generally less responsive and more emotionally absent regarding their children's requests. It is important to highlight that in this type of parenting, there is a clear lack of participation, an indifference regarding the child's education, which leads to the inexistence of rules at home."

"Dr. Jansen, could you please explain to us how that negligence will impact the future of those children?"

"Of course, Estela. I can say that this style of parenting is associated with children who develop more impulsive behaviors, with a higher risk of drug abuse or a bigger probability of being imprisoned or committing suicide[cxxi] later in life."

"I feel sad just imagining that ... Explain to us a little bit more about what differs between negligent and permissive parents."

"Permissive parents, contrarily to negligent parents, are responsive and affectionate, but they impose little to no rules at home. They are condescending, too tolerant, soft, and are much more likely to play the role of a friend than of a parent. That style is also associated with impulsive children with low social skills and problematic relationships who tend to be egocentric. Thus, we must pay attention to our educational actions and become authoritative parents. Why? Due to the simple fact that these kinds of parents assumes their roles as educators..."

"Explain clearly how that happens. What makes that type of parenting special?"

"Authoritative parents[cxxii] are affectionate, responsive, loving, and not only do they define the rules at home but also their child's objectives. Since they have a high expectation for their children's future, they value their child's independence. In other words, they don't suffocate them. That's the most effective parenting style, the style we should all adopt. Rigid but responsive. They expect great results, but they offer the necessary support to achieve such results. They offer support during the process and at its end. This parenting style is associated with children with better academic performance, which leads to higher self-esteem, better relationships, and good social skills. Besides, the delinquency rate and the rate of mental problems is quite lower in children parented this way than with any other kind of parenting."

"What about the authoritarian style?" asked Estela once the camera focused on her face.

"The authoritarian parenting style is problematic too, just like the negligent and the permissive styles. Parents who follow this style want to be authoritative but end up being hostile and irresponsive to the positive things their children do. They can only see flaws. They have strict rules and high expectations, but instead of supporting their children and allowing them to experience a certain degree of independence, they demand blind obedience. This leads to low academic performance, low self-esteem, lack of proper social skills, a higher probability of mental problems, such as depression and anxiety, a higher risk of drug and alcohol abuse, and a higher tendency to disobey laws and hierarchical superiors. I can't avoid highlighting that it is necessary to show love and empathy for our children, to be responsive and loving, and to provide the affective support they need so much. Thus, to promote good upbringing and to avoid the many problems I've mentioned, it is important to create a connection between parents and children."

After talking for nearly one hour, Michael Jansen and Estela stopped recording the first step. Estela was happy with the quality of the information provided by Jansen during the interview. Meanwhile, Bruno was notoriously nervous, which worried Estela.

"What's wrong, Bruno?" asked Dr. Jansen.

"I thought the video would be fifteen minutes long, maximum. I think it will be hard to record the three . . ."

"Don't worry," answered Dr. Jansen, standing up from the sofa and placing his long arm around the boy's shoulder. "I already spoke for too long today, and we will finish now. Thank you so much for staying and helping us."

Michael took a few bank notes from his pocket and paid Bruno for his extra work.

"Oh, thank you, Doctor!" said Bruno, who was happy to have the opportunity to apply his knowledge regarding video recording, acquired through an online course, and to earn some extra cash that would help his family.

Dr. Jansen removed the memory card from the side of the camera and handed it to Estela, who said, "It's worth gold!"

Sofia, who remained calm for the entire length of the recording, grumbled one, two, three times before starting to cry.

"Are you hungry, my love?" Estela asked her daughter.

"What about you, are you hungry?" repeated Dr. Jansen, this time asking Estela.

"A little bit."

"Can I invite you for lunch? At Ibirapuera, at the Modern Art Museum restaurant. Only if I'm not disturbing your plans."

"It would be an honor!" answered Estela. "It's always a pleasure to spend time with you."

"Thank you for accepting my invitation. Feel free to breastfeed little Sofia; meanwhile, I will change clothes. It's too hot outside to be wearing a suit."

Michael closed a sliding door made out of dark wood, which was in the middle of his office. A few minutes later he returned, wearing a light blue polo, shorts, and tennis shoes.

They walked to the restaurant, which was quite broad and beautifully decorated, besides being quite airy. They sat close to a glass wall with views over the Sculptures Garden. Dr. Jansen gently volunteered to take care of Sofia, who had already slept, so Estela could go to the buffet.

Estela returned with a plate full of colorful vegetables and grilled fish. Once she sat down at the table, she commented, "Your lecture earlier today inspired me. If I knew you were going to talk about nutrition, I would have arrived before, to hear it from start to end . . . Since I was not able to do so, I will ask you a question now." Estela pointed to the fish with her silver knife. "Should we not eat the fish skin? Or is that just a myth?"

"Fish, in itself, is an amazing food. However, pregnant women[cxxiii] would be better avoiding its skin, as it might contain mercury, pesticides, and PCB or polychlorinated biphenyl. The higher a fish is in the food chain, like sharks, dogfish, and tuna, the more likely it is that they have accumulated toxins in their fat, which is underneath the skin. I would advise you to choose smaller fish that can fit on a plate."

After finishing lunch, they left the restaurant and walked along the sidewalk, which was on the side of the running and cycling tracks. Dr. Jansen contemplated the trees and the buildings surrounding them, and afterward said, "Now that our glucose reserves are reestablished, would you like to talk about the sixth step?"

Estela's eyes opened widely as if asking, "Are you serious? The sixth step? Aren't you tired?"

"Not at all," he said. "I brought you here to talk about the sixth step. However, if you have other plans . . ."

"No . . . I have no plans, Michael. What is this step about?"

"It's about that," said Dr. Jansen while pointing at the back of a sweaty sportsman who had just passed by them like a rocket, wearing a black sleeveless shirt. "It's about physical exercise. Can we walk and talk?" he asked, looking at Estela's feet.

"Of course! I'm used to walking in high-heels."

"Can I help you with Sofia and with your purse?"

"Thank you so much," said Estela, handing him her white purse and Sofia.

Dr. Jansen returned to the topic. "Our ancestors moved around a lot. To give you an idea, during the Paleolithic era, humans walked about sixteen kilometers per day to find food. Some days they walked even longer. Generally, all animals were made to move. The complex engineering behind muscles, tendons, and joints is interconnected with the brain. Therefore, our brains were programmed to work better during physical activities."

Estela added, "Nowadays, we spend a lot of time sitting on our favorite chair in front of our office table, exercising our fingers on the keyboard and mobile phone and while using pens. From what I've read, the habit is as harmful as smoking . . ."

"Yes," he agreed. "Inactivity and sedentarism not only atrophy our muscles, but also our precious brains[cxxiv]. Progress brought us so many concessions . . . However, the sedentarism that came with it represents a retreat from the biological point of view since the lack of physical activity undermines human brain efficiency. The body needs movement for our mind to continue working properly and for our organism to remain healthy. We all know that if we go to the gym to do some aerobic exercise and to lift some weights, we will get stronger and more muscular. However, not all of us know that our brain also gets stronger with physical exercise."

"How does physical exercise positively affect the brain?" asked Estela, placing her hands over her own head.

"Physical activity has a deep impact on our memory, judgment, and reasoning[cxxv]. When the brain learns new activities, the connections between neurons, synapses, become stronger to process that information. So, physical activity strengthens those connections, even more, helping the brain to learn quicker."

"Through which mechanisms? How do they act?" Estela was gradually more curious and started to shoot questions to the doctor.

"To retain information, Estela, the brain needs the right quantity of neurotransmitters, like serotonin and dopamine. Those neurotransmitters improve our mood and motivation and help neuronal cells to connect. Furthermore, physical exercise also promotes changes in the brain cells."

"Great! What kind of changes?"

"When you move, your body produces proteins called *nerve growth factor*[cxxvi]. Those proteins travel to the brain, making our neurons more efficient in the formation of synapses. Furthermore, those growth factors are fundamental components in those connections. As you correctly said, we are too sedentary. The worst thing about it is that it doesn't apply only to adults. It's disheartening to know that American children spend more than five hours [cxxvii] per day in front of a screen: either a television, mobile phone, tablet, or videogame. This way, childhood and teenage years, that used to be times of intense physical activity, unfortunately became deserts of inactivity[cxxviii]."

"And how is inactivity affecting our children?"

"It affects them in several ways. Our children are losing the ability to focus. They are labeled as hyperactive or diagnosed with ADHD[cxxix] . . . Once they are three years old, parents start noticing that their children are more anxious than their peers; they are not able to sit for a long period, they run from one place to another . . . Next, they look for an expert, who medicates these children most of the time. Maybe that's why 6 percent of American children[cxxx] go through therapies that include medicine for short attention span and hyperactivity. Generally, they start taking medicines once they are seven years old. The most alarming thing is that during the last decade there has been an increase of nearly 50 percent[cxxxi] in short-attention-span cases. I work in the field, and I see that children's ability to focus truly has been worsening. Besides not being able to focus, they are more restless and impulsive."

"Is that related to the lack of physical exercise?"

"Partially, yes. It is also related to the smaller amount of time spent sleeping[cxxxii]. Since they spend a lot of time staring at screens, like mobile phones and televisions, they excite their brains beyond the norm. Furthermore, they don't play, or they spend little time playing with other children; they have restricted contact with nature, and most of them eat certain coloring agents[cxxxiii] and preservatives through industrialized food."

"Coloring agents and preservatives?" asked Estela, who was awestruck.

"It's true, and that is why I keep insisting parents of children with ADHD pay attention to their food intake. Sodas, cookies, yogurt, salty snacks, chocolate snacks, and several other products must be avoided, as they can worsen hyperactivity."

"Despite knowing a little bit about the hazards of many industrialized foods, I'm shocked to learn how hazardous such food is to children. Thus, I would like to ask you, do you advise parents feed their children greenery, fruits, grains, and white meat and avoid food additives, sugar, and caffeine? I managed to hear you saying that during your lecture today . . ."

"Exactly! Today's lecture was precisely for parents who have hyperactive children[cxxxiv]. Look, in this technological society we live in, many people intoxicate themselves with caffeine to remain focused or use stimulant drugs, such as Ritalin and similar drugs. Furthermore, there is a lack of sleep, lack of physical activity, and lack of leisure time . . ."

"Or the lack of everything together . . ." added Estela, smiling and revealing her dimples. "Not to mention stress, which is present everywhere."

"Of course. Our children feel stressed too, and stress destroys the connections[cxxxv] between neurons and might reduce the size of certain areas of the brain that are related to memory and focus."

"That is certainly deleterious..."

"It really is! It's a vicious cycle in which stress leads to the loss of memory and focus, thus resulting in poor school performance, which means bad grades, resulting in further stress. Physical exercise is the only factor that can break that cycle and revert the destructive effects of chronic stress. When we move our body, requiring our heart to pump harder, our brain also benefits. Physical activity acts on two different fronts against stress[cxxxvi]. From the physical perspective, it increases neurotransmitters and the nerve growth factor. Considering the emotional point of view, it provides the possibility of regaining control. Emotional control is a primary weapon against stress. Not to mention the fact that it increases our tolerance to negative situations; it fights the harmful effects of cortisol on the brain, and it reduces the body's resistance to insulin."

"So, to reduce stress, we don't need to drink a cup of wine, we just need to go to the gym?"

"Exactly! Furthermore, it is known that physical activity can make an adult more intelligent."

"Wow! Is that true?"

"Yes. Our brain is constantly changing and renewing itself; it is plastic, malleable, and shapeable. That doesn't happen only with babies and young children, but rather during our entire life. *Neurotrophins*, such as BDNF[cxxxvii]—a nerve growth factor derived from the brain—are created while we exercise and act as neuronal fertilizers. Neurotrophins create neurogenesis. In other words, they create new neurons. That fact alone proves that we need movement."

"In the past, we used to hear that while aging we lose neurons. It's a good thing that we have that 'brain plasticity[cxxxviii].'"

"It is . . . Right now, as we walk together, we are creating a neurogenesis process without even noticing it. Experiments performed with little rats, conducted by Cotman[cxxxix] and his peers, identified that the more physical activity a rat performs, the higher the activation of BDNF, especially in the hippocampus, which is related with memory. Therefore, I reaffirm that physical exercise helps condition the body and the mind."

"As a consequence, that neuronal growth makes people more intelligent. Is that right?"

"Certainly. An overwhelming example regarding that topic is the Zero Hour project. It was performed at Naperville School[cxl], in Illinois, in the USA. It is a big school, and academically, that school was average, until the physical education teachers formulated a project they called Zero Hour. The goal was to find out if performing physical activities before the beginning of classes would improve students' reading ability."

"Interesting," muttered Estela.

"The result was surprising . . . The school became one of the most athletic ones in the United States of America and achieved some of the best results in the intellectual field. Inclusively, they performed a test with the eighth grade to compare it with the world education level. In the science field, students achieved better scores than Singapore, which was number one that year. In mathematics, they achieved sixth place when compared to other countries. In other words, this school achieved scores that were quite better than the United States of America average."

"Impressive!"

"Yes, it is. Please note that these results were not easy to achieve. Naperville students gave their very best during training sessions, and their heart rate was monitored. During the process, teachers worshiped each one's effort, not talent. Furthermore, they stimulated cooperation, both regarding problem resolution and group activities. They would even attribute a bonus score to the students who, despite being out of shape, engaged the most with athletic activities. To add more benefits to physical exercise, teachers asked students to identify the discipline they had more difficulties learning right after Zero

Hour."

"Right after? Why? Why does it matter?"

"The state of clearness, focus, and quietness that physical exercise promotes lasts for about an hour or an hour and a half. That's the period during which you will have the best benefits. So, it's important to enjoy that period with quality activities."

"If we study while we perform physical activities, will we also get better results? Is that useful considering a cognitive perspective?"

"No! Acquiring knowledge is a process that must happen after the physical activity, just like they did in Naperville. We must not perform exercises while we study complex content that requires our focus. During physical activity, there is a certain leakage of blood from the pre-frontal cortex, which hampers our executive functions, including having complex thoughts. Do you remember about the pre-frontal cortex?"

"Of course! I wrote about it . . ."

"Very well. Physical exercise momentarily releases the pre-frontal cortex."

"How can that be an advantage?"

"Since physical movement releases the pre-frontal cortex handbrake, it also erases our thoughts' censor. That releasing process gives us a better ability to imagine and to dream. Thus, when we are walking, our imagination gets sharper, we think about many things. It is one of the many reasons why physical exercise can rescue a person from depression. By not having the pre-frontal cortex involved, it is possible to break the negativism cycle[cxli], during which we can only see negative things. Therefore, we start seeing the world from a better perspective, appreciating the good stuff and thinking about a happier future. It will give one the will to change!"

"I see now."

"Since right after exercise the pre-frontal cortex[cxlii] reassumes its function and is stronger and rested, that's the ideal moment to focus on a project, to study, or to work . . . If we practice intense physical exercise and right after that we go to study . . . Oh! How different it will be! Our focus will be sharpened, and our memory will absorb information like a sponge."

"It's good to know that . . . I'm sure there will be a bang once I publish that information on the blog. It will help many people enjoy the benefits of physical activity more. That includes my friends and me."

"It's worth saying that exercise acts as a natural antidepressant, reducing anxiety and cooling the nerves. It is crucial for children to perform physical activities to reduce anxiety. There is a risk that an anxious child will become an anxious and depressed adult since both pathologies go hand in hand."

A very gracious interruption made Michael change the subject.

"Your little princess woke up," he said, looking at Sofia, who woke up scared in his arms.

They stopped walking a little bit and showed Sofia the trees and the people who were skating or walking on the pedestrian crossing. When the baby calmed down, they replaced her in the baby carrier that was attached to Estela. The baby girl was quite alert, watching everything around her.

The journalist said, "You stopped talking when you were on the subject of improving depression with physical activities. I know depression is a severe problem and that it was even considered the number one problem of the twenty-first century by the World Health Organization."

"It really is a worrying problem since it is increasing gradually[cxliii]," confirmed Michael. "During chronic depression, the brain suffers structural changes. High levels of cortisol kill neurons in the hippocampus[cxliv], which, as I said, is related to memory. Some decades ago, when we started to better understand what depression was, we thought it was an imbalance in the neurotransmitters: it should be something related to low levels of serotonin, dopamine, or norepinephrine. Nowadays, however, we know that it is a more complex and deeper problem than that. People with low BDNF are more likely to get depressed and feel hostility and anxiety. However, there are ways to minimize or to end those processes. Physical exercise and antidepressants can increase both the levels of neurotransmitters and BDNF."

"So that is why physical exercise is an ally against depression."

"It's a great ally. A study called SMILE[cxlv], developed by Blumenthal and his colleagues, corroborates it. They divided more than 150 patients with depression into three groups, randomizing 50 people to each group. In the first group, people only used sertraline, which is a commonly prescribed antidepressant. The second group used sertraline and practiced exercise. And the third group performed only physical exercise. As a part of the study, those people had to perform exercises until their heart rate was around the submaximal, for at least thirty minutes, three times a week."

"What was the result of the study?" asked Estela.

"The people in three groups presented a significant improvement regarding depression. However, the most interesting aspect happened during the period after the test . . . Six months later, the group who performed physical activities but did not use any medicine was the one with the lowest depression rate, since more than 70 percent of the individuals no longer faced the pathology. The group that exercised and took the medicine had a worse result when compared to the group that only performed physical exercise."

Estela abruptly stopped, saying, "That's strange! How could the group that used antidepressants and exercised achieve worse results than the group who only exercised?"

"That's simple. Apparently, using medicine erases the feeling of being in control. During the study, the researchers observed that the depressive patient couldn't distinguish if improvements were a result of his or her actions, of practicing physical activities, or of using the medicine. Those who only performed physical activities had no doubts regarding regaining life control."

"What about postpartum depression?" asked Estela.

"Physical exercise can also improve that kind of depression[cxlvi]. We know that gestation makes pregnant women feel good due to the high levels of hormones such as estrogen and progesterone. Thus, the sudden decrease in those hormones after birth can alter the mothers' emotional state and result in postpartum depression. The good news is that studies show that women who recently gave birth can control their emotional state by performing physical activities for twenty-minutes, which also increases their well-being and provides better sleep quality, which helps new mothers recharge their energy . . . That's all mothers need."

"But . . ." Estela had a new doubt, "how can mothers go to the gym if they have a newborn and they feel depressed?"

"There's no need to go to the gym. Even now, we are walking, watching the trees and lakes, inhaling the scent of recently cut grass, and receiving our dose of BDNF, serotonin, and dopamine . . . Mothers don't need to feel guilty due to saving some time for themselves. If going for a walk is hard, mothers can also practice rope skipping or buy portable steppers with which to exercise at home, while their baby is sleeping. Mommies need to understand that the benefits of exercising go beyond physical appearance. It is a part of the cure for depression."

"I think that improving the physical appearance is also a part of the cure," Estela added.

"I don't disagree. Yet, feeling that you have more energy and being less tired is even more important. Vigor helps mothers focus on their children, their husbands, and everyone around them, resulting in healthier relationships. I always tell my patients' mothers, or better, everyone who passes through my office, "You have the right to exercise. You don't need to question yourself regarding how good of a mother you are just because you take some time to exercise. Don't start a conflict with yourself because when you take care of yourself, you are also taking care of your children and family. You will feel pleasure in life again, and that will reflect on all your relationships."

"It's interesting to hear you correlating exercise with emotional health. The importance of the state of mind and the family's well-being[cxlvii], in my opinion, is quite more relevant than physical beauty."

"Of course . . . If the focus is on physical appearance, the depression might worsen because some mothers are demotivated precisely due to their own body. Normally, they complain about the weight they gained during gestation, about not being in good shape, thus not being able to go to the gym because other people might think they look fat and their training clothes are too tight and—"

The sound of Estela's laughter interrupted Michael. His look was enough for her to notice he didn't understand her reaction.

"I'm so sorry! I couldn't help it. I kept imagining your reactions hearing all the feminine anguish."

"My dear friend, after so many years dealing with my patients' mothers, I have learned a lot about the feminine universe. I try to listen to them, and if possible, to help them. One way of doing this is to inform them that exercising increases their chances of getting in good shape again, which increases their self-esteem, and consequently, their motivation. In other words, they will create the virtuous cycle themselves."

"I see that the benefits of exercising go far beyond burning calories..."

"Body and mind," said Michael, putting his hands together, interlacing his long fingers, "are both parts of the same individual. Those parts fit perfectly. Those parts belong to each other."

"I already had some notions about the importance of getting physical activity. However, now I'm much more convinced about its real importance for our physical and mental well-being. So, I have this question: how important is exercising for children?"

"Well . . . I see exercising as an important stimulus for children to blossom and to become conscious of human values such as courtesy, solidarity, perseverance, responsibility and self-esteem . . . The fact that exercising improves memory, mood, discipline, focus, and the behavior of younger children, inside and outside the classroom, is enough to demonstrate its uses. Students who are also athletes usually don't want to be seen as troublesome but rather as leaders."

"Since I would rather see Sofia belonging to the group of leaders, instead of the troublesome group, I want to know which kind of physical exercises you recommend for children."

"Swimming . . . That's my favorite sport for young children. First, because they will learn a vital skill, one that will allow them not to drown. Second, it's a complete exercise. Regarding other physical activities, I also recommend martial arts, such as judo or karate, as those value discipline. There's also ballet, football . . . In fact, any sport is valid as long as children can adapt adequately to it, practice it regularly, enjoy practicing it, and can improve as a person. As I said, when we talk about the fifth step, we should value having a growth mindset more. Thus, parents must avoid immediate gratification to teach their children how to work for the longer term goal achieve "the second marshmallow.""

"There are a lot of people who say that martial arts increase aggressivity. Does that statement have any ground? How can martial arts help people to become more disciplined?"

"Quite the opposite[cxlviii]. People who practice martial arts follow the rules, hence they gain self-control and discipline. A study from Hofstra University[cxlix], in the United States of America, considered children who were from eight to eleven years old and who practiced martial arts twice a week. The study demonstrated that those children were disciplined and never lost track of their direction. In school, they always delivered their school assignments on time; they were less likely to break the rules, they were more prepared for classes, and consequently, their grades were higher."

"And what do you think about competition between children?"

"I think competition can be healthy. If children have an internal will to stand out in sports, they must be encouraged to compete in an honest manner, always respecting their opponents. Some people think that competing is wrong, and I can also understand their point of view. However, in my opinion, competing is a part of the creation of a child's character. We can't believe that daily life won't have competitional aspects. Thus, I think it's wrong to put our children in glass cages. During their social lives, unavoidably, children will be tested and compared to other children. We need to teach them how to stand out and how to do their best. If their best doesn't make them Olympic athletes, that's not a problem. However, not competing due to being afraid of feeling frustration and being compared to other children? Parents who suppress healthy competition are fooling themselves and their children. That attitude is a result of a fixed mindset! On the other hand, if a child wishes to compete, is stimulated by his or her family to achieve the desired victory, self-esteem and motivation will always follow. As a result of their achievements, they will interact with other people, who are on their level or quite close to their level. They also will get more technical support and emotional support from their peers, thus becoming more confident. Furthermore, they will learn that working hard and making it by the sweat of their brows aren't only figures of speech, as they will literally work hard and have sweat on their brows, and their muscles will be sore, shaking, and hurting."

Once at home, the first thing Estela did was take off her high heels. Her feet were pulsing. She was physically tired, but happy due to having acquired boundless new information, not only for her blog but also for herself. She was a woman that enjoyed acquiring new knowledge, and Michael was a walking encyclopedia.

"Do you want a relaxing foot massage, my love?" Victor solicitously asked.

"I can't reject your massage. It's invigorating!"

Victor picked up a body cream that smelled like strawberries with whipped cream and massaged Estela's feet.

"Your scars are very red," he said, referring to the accident she had during infancy that led to surgery on both her feet.

"My feet are hurting all over, and I can see they are quite red. Michael looked at my high heels and asked me if I was sure about walking . . . Since I never want to miss the chance of learning something new, I accepted the invitation to walk with him. I learned a lot today. Now I need to edit the video for YouTube and write about the sixth step. Would you help me with editing since you're such an expert at it?"

"Of course!" answered Victor, satisfied with Estela's comment. "I'm sure the video will be a success."

CHAPTER 09 — THE SEVENTH STEP: GRIT

"It does not matter how slowly you go as long as you do not stop."

—*Confucius*

"All our dreams can come true, if we have the courage to pursue them."

—*Walt Disney*

Victor, who was one of the best digital marketers in Brazil, created a YouTube page for Estela. Illuminated by the blue light coming from the screen of their computer, he explained everything he had done during an afternoon working: "I've decided to divide the first video, which lasted for about an hour, into several small clips to segment the topics. Many people don't have all that time to stop and watch the complete version of the video. For every one of them, I've created vibrant and eye-catching thumbnails and also I've inserted the maximum number of related keywords, to attract the audience that searches anything related to your content."

"But you still posted the complete video, right?" asked Estela with a more serious look.

"Of course, my love! It's right here. Look," answered Victor, passing the mouse over the video thumbnail. "From what I know, it is the main one. Long videos are strong on YouTube if they can catch people's attention."

"So you think it will work?" asked Estela, showing her dimples.

"In the beginning, we should avoid nourishing unrealistic expectations. Even though your blog is famous, your YouTube page is just starting and has just a few followers. However, the quality of the content and your ability to interact with the audience will certainly make it work."

Estela looked at him and once again noticed how irresistibly beautiful he was and smiled.

Victor had become a wonderful parent and a caring husband. He did all he could to perform the necessary daily activities to take care of Sofia. Victor would wake up during the night to help his daughter calm down. He read books about child development, and many times, he would show the words from the app to the young baby girl. Victor would also discuss with Estela the contents she posted on her blog, sharing useful tips with her to improve the posts. He also had just spent a long time enhancing her page and videos, making them look professional.

On the day of their wedding, Estela had some doubts about if Victor would be a good father. She thought he was too immature and unprepared to face the problems of marital life. However, with time, he became more mature, grew up with the challenges of being a husband and a father, and became a better person. He genuinely wanted to be a role model for Sofia. Estela was quite happy with Victor not only because he was a responsible father but also because he acted as her partner, friend, and lover.

She read the comments posted by other women who had young children, and contrarily to what was happening to her, they felt completely unsupported by their husbands. Many fathers were hostile, would complain about their children crying and about expenses, and wouldn't assume paternity, overburdening their wives. She was bothered by the fact the wives of these men didn't even have time to go to the bathroom. Now she could understand why so many marriages couldn't survive the first two years of the life of a child.

"Oh!" exclaimed Victor, standing up from his chair. "I have a present for Sofia." He went to the adjacent room and returned with a ramp made of wood that was more than two meters long. He stared at Estela and said, "Since Michael Jansen said we should let Sofia spend as much time as possible in the crawling position, I asked the woodworker to make Glenn Doman's ramp, just like he suggests in the book *How to Teach Your Baby to Be Physically Superb*[c1]. I even asked the woodworker to cover the sides with this smooth upholstery and the base with rubber outsoles, to protect her knees.

"That was an excellent idea!" said Estela excitedly while examining the multicolored ramp. "Thank you!" Then she hugged and kissed him.

Sofia was a few days away from turning four months old when she sat without any support for the first time. For some time now, she would stay in the crawling position without complaining. She could already raise her neck to look farther away, and she would roll from one side to another and would hold her feet in an attempt to put them in her mouth. Estela had noticed that Sofia did well sitting with some support, but it was a totally new thing to see her sitting with no support at all.

Estela's mother-in-law, Sílvia, who would come every day to visit her granddaughter, was impressed when she saw the young girl sitting cheerfully and banging her hands on the toy drums in front of her.

"Amazing!" exclaimed Sílvia, her face illuminated. "I'm impressed! She is such a smart girl! Victor could barely hold his head up when he was her age. He was so soft . . . But look at my granddaughter . . . Oh! My granddaughter is unbelievable!"

She got closer to Sofia and smelled her neck before kissing her pink cheeks.

"What are you giving her, Estela? Some vitamin?"

"No, Silvia," said Estela, smiling and looking at her mother-in-law. "I only give her breast milk."

However, Estela knew that most of Sofia's signs of progress were a result of the three kinds of stimulus she and Victor used: reading, showing her the words of the app and telling her stories every night; intensive communication, talking a lot with her and naming the objects that caught her attention; and motor activities, placing her in the crawling position in an enriched environment with many toys for her to observe and try to reach.

Despite the many difficulties of finding time between Estela's obligations of motherhood and Michael's always busy agenda, Estela managed to schedule a session with him to record the second step on a Thursday morning. Estela was happy and thought, "Who knows, maybe he will tell me something about the seventh step."

Since she wanted to go on her own to the Awake Clinic, she decided to leave Sofia at home, with her nanny, on the scheduled date. Bruno and the doctor were already in the office and ready to work, just waiting for her.

Estela sat close to the doctor to start the long-awaited interview about the second step. She smiled for the camera and obeyed the indicative sign Bruno made with his finger, beginning to talk: "Hi, everyone! Once again, I'm here with our dear Dr. Michael Jansen. Today we are going to talk about the second step, whose goal is for children to achieve success and happiness during their lives. The second step tries to analyze how we should stimulate our children with communication."

While Dr. Jansen spoke, Estela remembered the conversation she had with him about the topic of communication at Aclimação Park. This time, she knew more information about the subject since she had read and written about it. She asked many questions for the doctor because she wanted the audience to learn as much as possible.

At the end of the interview, Michael Jansen stressed the importance of the topic: "Speak as much as you can with your children, even while they are very young and although you might believe they don't understand a thing. Speaking is one of the stimulus for child development with lots of scientific evidence to support it. It is known that this simple stimulus increases children's final IQ . . . However, you also have to pay attention! Saying a lot of words is not enough. It is also necessary to note variety and tone. Furthermore, it is important to hear the baby's answers, even if they are just vocalizations and you can't understand them. That strengthens the connection between parents and children... Try to say encouraging and stimulating words, such as 'I'm proud of you,' and avoid expressions that diminish the child's self-esteem, or in other words, pessimistic or limiting words..."

After recording for about one hour, they finished the interview. Estela was happy with the final result and exclaimed, "We did an excellent job!"

"That's true! I also found the conversation to be quite productive," agreed Dr. Jansen while standing up.

Estela also stood up, placed her hands in her jacket's pockets, and cleared her throat before asking, "Can we talk about the seventh step today?"

Dr. Jansen hesitated for a little while, checked the wall clock, carefully looked at Estela's face, and answered, "I have a commitment at eleven o´clock at the Clinical Hospital. Can we schedule that conversation for another day so we can talk about it calmly? In about ten minutes, my driver will call me..."

"Can we talk while heading to the hospital? I could return by taxi or Uber."

"It's your option, Estela. If you want to, Antônio can bring you back. It wouldn't be a problem at all."

"You already know my answer, Doctor," said Estela, narrowing her eyes and smiling slyly.

Dr. Jansen nodded his head positively, returning her a radiant smile before saying, "I'm sure you will enjoy the seventh step. It's about grit, or to put it better, about stimulating children's effort and persistence."

"The title alone was enough to get my attention!" said Estela, taking her hands out of her pockets and rubbing them in front of her body. "Can it be applied to adults too, or is it just for children?"

"It can be used for all of us, just like every other step," answered Dr. Jansen. "However, I love teaching children to value their effort and perseverance since those are incredibly useful qualities for their progress. Media and society value talent excessively, to the detriment of effort. Normally they don't stress the fact that people, to achieve their planned goals, work hard and are consistent in what they do. Commitment and perseverance are qualities the psychologist Angela Duckworth[cli] denominates as *grit*[clii]."

"Can you explain to me the term more comprehensively, please?" requested Estela.

"Grit is the union of two characteristics," explained Dr. Jansen, joining his two index fingers, "passion for what you do and the perseverance[cliii] not to quit. It's the posture we assume to go after our dreams, despite all challenges, even if they are hard, or apparently impossible, to achieve."

"Then having grit is the same as being determined," concluded Estela.

"Yes. It's synonymous with being passionate and having a purpose. It is also about not being overwhelmed by difficulties. Tenacious people are, as I previously explained, those who have a growth mindset[cliv]."

"I see. How can we stimulate grit? How can we make it grow in a child or an adult? Or is it a characteristic with a more genetic tendency[clv]?"

"If you are asking me if it has a genetic component, I must answer: of course, like everything else in life. Meanwhile, genetics are only a small part of it. The great responsible for perseverance and determination is the environment or, in other words, a child's past, the things they learned in theory and practice."

"In short," said Estela while adjusting her hair, "it's necessary for children to be educated in an environment where those values are fundamental. A strong passion and outstanding perseverance determine grit. Is that right?"

"Yes. That passion needs to be truthful and not fleeting, not a momentary enthusiasm. It needs to be consistent across time. It's not about the intensity of the passion but rather about the determination with which a person dedicates to the passion, thus making one walk the right path, while constancy will help one achieve the desired goal. The path we draw from the starting point to the goal is different from persistence, the engine that doesn't allow us to stop in the middle of our way, not allowing us to quit and to take a step back despite the realization that the path is rougher and longer than we imagined."

The driver, wearing a complete uniform, knocked on the office door before his head appeared inside the room, saying, "It's time, Doctor."

"We are on our way, Antônio. But first, I want you to alert you about a new mission: you must bring this young lady here back to the clinic safe and sound once you leave me, all right?"

"At your service!" answered the driver, greeting the doctor with an informal and playful salute.

They walked to the underground parking lot, where Estela came across a luxurious silver Tesla Model X. The doors opened upward, similarly to seagulls' wings, and both of them got inside the car.

"You invested a lot in this vehicle, didn't you, Doctor?" commented Estela, noticing a divergence between the doctor's simplicity and this disproportional symbol of social status.

"Quite contrarily," answered Michael Jansen. "I received it as a gift from the father of one of my patients."

"Wha . . . What?" stuttered Estela. "What a present! He must be very wealthy."

"Yes, he is. He was so grateful for the complete recovery of his younger child that he offered me this vehicle," said Michael Jansen while softly touching on the light leather seat.

After a few moments, Estela returned to the previous conversation about grit: "You were saying passion and persistence are two cornerstones for grit . . ."

"Yes, while passion will determine which path will be followed, perseverance[clvi] is what helps us achieve the desired goal. Passion is a compass for success[clvii]. For example, if a child loves swimming during primary school and then sees Michael Phelps winning another gold medal in the Olympics, that passion for swimming will propel the child to be like Michael Phelps. Passion is the guide."

Estela nodded her head, agreeing with Michael Jansen, who continued: "Look over there, at the onboard computer." The doctor pointed at the enormous monitor near the driver. "I want to get to the Clinical Hospital, and the GPS indicates that I'm twenty-seven minutes away from my target. Passion is what guides me to achieve my goal, but it is Antônio's perseverance that will get us there. Passion and constancy are characteristics that complement each other."

"Let me see if I understand: if children like chess, for example, their passion for chess will make them want to improve, giving them the necessary enthusiasm to become a great chess player or a grandmaster. But that doesn't just require passion. Children need to persevere while facing the challenges necessary to improve their game. Passion and perseverance are, therefore, two sides of grit."

"Exactly! Grit is, as I see it, more important than talent[clviii]! There are studies with chess players that show that in a group of children, the one with a higher IQ will learn the game rules faster, as well as its tactics. In the beginning, that child will be seen as the most talented one on the team. However, if another child puts more effort into it and constantly attempts to improve his or her game, the initial difference between the two of them will disappear. If that second child continues his or her efforts to learn increasingly more, eventually that second child will become better than the child who was initially more talented, and become a chess champion. Therefore, I insist on saying that talent isn't enough to make a winner because effort and putting in the work is what achieves victory. According to what I think, the seventh step is critical. For that reason, during my lectures, I try to highlight that parents must teach their children from a very early age the value of work. One must always work hard and try to achieve the defined goals, even if at first, one lacks the ability. We can always improve ourselves."

"What if a person is initially good at something and talented? How can that person avoid being exceeded by someone who works harder?"

"If a person is gifted at something, double care is needed to keep that talent from lowering the person's guard, thus allowing others who initially weren't as talented, to become better. That person needs to work harder than the rest of the group. I say this bearing in mind that talented people are treated differently by their parents, teachers, or coaches. Since those persons carry other people's high expectations, their focus is often doubled. That extra focus isn't negative if they understand that it is possible to materialize expectations, as long as talent joins effort and dedication. If they don't understand that, a fixed mindset might overcome talent, and the result will be deception."

The persistent horn of a motorcycle that was crossing a red light took their attention away from the conversation. Estela and Michael watched the bike passing close to the car and getting to the other side of the avenue unharmed.

"How can one cultivate passion?" asked Estela, staring at the doctor's blue eyes.

"For many individuals, passion is like a flower. In the beginning, it is beautiful and vibrant. However, over time, the flower wilts and dries, until it dies. Passion, therefore, needs to be nourished to preserve its beauty and the vibrant look it had in the beginning. To cultivate and nourish passion, it is important that, firstly, people, whether children or adults, find things they really enjoy. It is necessary to test and to discover those things. During childhood, when we take children to different environments, when we stimulate them to play a lot, to listen to stories, to be curious, and to practice sports, those tests happen naturally. Those tests allow children to know themselves, permitting them to conclude, for example, if they enjoy playing volleyball or if they would rather play basketball. That child will know if drawing is more pleasurable than playing with toys. To help our children while they discover themselves, we, as parents, need to have the sensitivity to understand what excites them. Once an interest is found, parents must carry on fanning the flames to get the child closer to the passion. Enrolling the child in a drawing or ballet class might help. Furthermore, it is necessary to watch the adaptation closely. If the activity doesn't represent a true passion, the child will demonstrate it."

"What if the children change their mind?"

"That is common. Children with several options can feel passionate about countless activities. The most important thing is for parents to be attentive and to be open regarding changes. Children can change their interests several times before finding a genuine passion."

"In other words, we must follow our dreams."

The doctor agreed, "It's true. Contrarily, we won't be able to materialize our potential, and we won't have enough energy to persist and to complete the things we start. Benjamin Bloom[clix], an American psychologist who contributed hugely to the field of child development, stated that during the first years, parents should encourage their children to find something likely to become their field of interest. That way, parents can help their children's intrinsic motivations to flourish. They must provide their children with the autonomy and freedom necessary for them to enjoy and develop their interests and passions. Children need to try a lot. Try here, try there, until a major point of interest appears. Believe me, my dear friend, our goal as parents is to provide opportunities and diverse experiences to our children, so they can choose their way, instead of choosing for them. We must not instill our interests in them. Instead, we must help them discover for themselves the things they want to achieve, the things they really like. I must also tell you that this exploration process can take years. It is a period that must be allowed."

"And after that?"

"Well . . ." continued the doctor, "after that, we must only follow their progress on the projects they initiate. We must not allow them to turn their back on a commitment they assumed, once problems arise. We know that the consistency of effort will determine if a person will or will not achieve a final goal, or even if that person will go past that goal. Daily acts will add up and become high-level performance, or not. Children must know that what they do continuously and successively matters, and it matters a lot, for their final performance."

"Hearing you talking about this reminds me of my childhood. I remember that my mother always insisted I finished Kumon. She encouraged me to practice it every day, including holidays and birthdays. She wouldn't allow me to stop. I managed to complete the Mathematics program when I was thirteen years old. I remember the feeling of joy and self-love I felt. Now that I think about it, I didn't even have an initial talent for mathematics, but I kept developing my abilities until I became quite good. From that moment on, I learned how to enjoy doing the exercises, and I started to be admired by my teachers and peers. I'm sure Kumon helped me with that field, even if my real passion was reading and writing. Since I was a child, I always read a lot: Monteiro Lobato, the Vaga-Lume series, and then I started reading Agatha Christie, Sidney Sheldon, the classics of literature . . . My passion for reading made me the journalist I am today. During college, I even thought about studying engineering due to my ability with numbers, but I understood that I would be happier working in a humanistic field."

"Kumon[clx] is an excellent method," highlighted Dr. Jansen. "It helps children become disciplined, which is something I find very interesting. It is the discipline, the effort, of picking up the worksheets every day to do calculations, without giving up half-way, which helps children develop their mathematics abilities from a very young age. When someone does something regularly, and while putting some effort into it, the tendency is to improve increasingly more. However, if children stop and their effort reaches zero, consequently interrupting progress, they might even lose the ability they acquired over time."

"Assiduity and persistence matter a lot on the long term," concluded Estela.

"There's no doubt about it! Those are the characteristics of a gritty person. In the case of children, monitoring and encouraging are essential processes that parents must do for them to find joy in performing the activities to improve their capabilities. Sometimes it takes children longer to learn how to enjoy a determined activity. They need to adapt, to work on their foundation or the activity techniques. Since everything in a child's life is a learning process, there is a need for parents to be insistent and dedicate their effort during the experience. For example, during the stage when babies try foods, they need up to twelve attempts to adapt to the taste of new food. So, we must not give up too early."

"I thought about giving up mathematics many times. I remember that in the beginning, I would always complain about it. When I became more mature, I noticed that I enjoyed performing calculations and that I would complete the method."

"Having a clear objective and dedicating focus and effort to achieve it helps children fulfill their dreams. Small victories help them gain autonomy and feel safe since they achieve by going through several stages. It's a sum. Performing the exercises, day after day, following Kumon or any other similar method, becomes a habit so children won't question whether they will or will not perform the exercise. We are creatures of habit. If we need to think about performing or not performing an action daily, we waste our willpower, which is limited. If we transform any activity into a habit, we overcome barriers, the barriers of questioning, which saves our willpower for other occasions."

"It's not easy, but it is rewarding," remarked Estela.

"And perseverance is a rare quality that is not often found in the world of today, that is so short-sighted," insisted Dr. Jansen. "Perseverance is the second characteristic of those who are gritty, and it's responsible for solidifying our abilities. We develop that perseverance as we mature. Daily practice and effort lead to mastering a subject or an activity. Children, teenagers, and adults all feel more self-confidence once they master something. That feeling propels them forward. Meanwhile, if people feel no passion for what they do, it gets harder to keep doing it for a long period. Without perseverance, it becomes impossible to achieve authority or mastery on a subject or activity."

"That's why the previous steps are so important, like playing and practicing physical activities, because they allow us to find our passions," thought Estela, muttering to herself. "Once we feel passionate about something, we have the will to work hard. Passions inspire us to give our best."

Michael smiled lightly while listening to Estela's reflexive process, and continued, "Half of it is about passion, and the other half is about perseverance," he said, joining his hands.

Estela couldn't contain herself once she saw Michael's gesture, and interrupted him: "It's so interesting how you use your hands to conclude determined subjects!"

"I try to engage my listener not only through my voice and the subject but also with gestures. The body speaks too!" he explained. "Regarding grit, when properly nourished, it gives fruits: self-esteem and self-respect. When we win, we remember those situations that required persistence. I'm sure that children always remember that project on which they gave their best and got the perfect score. Teenagers remember hearing their coach clapping when they swam 100 meters freestyle in under one minute. Those are the victories that strengthen and encourage us, making us go beyond. Those moments show us that committing is worth it. That a goal, imposed by ourselves, can be achieved. That is, sweating a jersey and giving our best is a great thing."

"And that way we start feeling pleasure about working hard and engaging in our projects," commented Estela.

"We also won't expect instant gratification and will acquire the patience to wait for the delayed return," complemented Dr. Jansen. "It's convenient to forget that defeats and failures are also important. After all, it is through them that people grow up and become stronger. That's something parents need to teach their children. For many adults, failing is not a part of the learning process; it's just a bad thing. They don't understand that people can only become more skillful by trying to outdo themselves. To become a better version of oneself, a person needs space to fail many times, to fall several times during the process. Sacrifices, bruises, daily fights, effort … all of that becomes personal growth."

"How can one cultivate perseverance?" asked Estela with a curious look. "I know many people give up even before starting and others quit everything they start."

"That passion needs to be bigger, or to put it better, it needs to be a vocation. You, for example, enjoyed mathematics and writing. You tended toward journalism because you had a bigger purpose that drove you. What was that purpose?"

"I wanted to help other people. To inform," she answered without blinking.

"That was your vocation, your call. You are helping other people with your skills. That's exactly what you are doing now: recording your videos for YouTube, writing about the Steps on your blog. You are materializing that vocation, trying to help parents with young children. I'm sure you don't feel tedium or any regret due to choosing to pursue a career as a journalist, thinking that you should have become a civil engineer, or am I wrong?"

"Not at all," laughed Estela. "I feel fulfilled by what I do, and I feel excited just speaking with you right here, learning and trying to share your knowledge with other people."

"A vocation helps connect people's goals to an activity that motivates them and pleases them. You chose journalism because you like to read and to write, but you also wanted to help other people. Medicine was my calling. Therefore, while I was in college, I didn't think that studying hour after hour, sacrificing my leisure time, was a bad thing. I knew I needed that theoretical and practical mastery to help people in the future. In other words, knowing that effort is being directed toward a bigger purpose helps us keep focused and steady. Thus, it's always important to stop and think and to ask, is it true that the things I'm doing today can improve my future and the future of those around me? If the answer is positive, then we know we are on the right path. If the answer is negative ..."

"It's a good time to rethink our professional choice?"

"Maybe not. The answer might be negative because we are being driven by a feeling of pessimism, momentarily, or not. This is a point I want to stress: tenacious people are more optimistic[clxi] than the average."

"Optimistic?"

"Yes! Optimistic. Optimism makes us not want to quit the things we are doing. First, because we can see clearly that the future will be better if we keep trying hard. Second, soliloquies, or internal statements, are stronger in optimistic persons, who say things like: 'I will make it,' 'Don't give up,' 'Be stronger,' or 'Don't stop.' These statements are relevant because they work as fuel for persistency and allow us to keep focused and not quit."

"What if the person is pessimistic?"

"Pessimistic people can also learn how to practice their internal conversations more positively. If you can't achieve this on your own, you can ask an expert professional for help, like a psychologist, for example. Pessimistic people have internal conversations that draw them down. They normally think things like, 'I'm not good enough,' 'I will quit,' or 'I can't make it,' and they really can't. That thought about themselves will lead them to behaviors that confirm that negative conception."

"One of the quotes I like the most, and that fits this perfectly, is the one from Henry Ford: 'Whether you think you can, or you think you can't – you're right.'

"Optimistic people quit less frequently. Since they value their abilities, they try to persist. Even when they fail, they always return and try to correct their mistakes. Optimistic people don't feel discouraged for long periods."

"What if parents notice their children tend to be more pessimistic?" the journalist wanted to know.

"Those children need instruction. Parents must help their children believe in themselves. They can give support and teach their children a more positive monologue. It's important to train your children to encourage themselves internally. Besides, parents must listen more, ask more; they must understand what is happening in their children's lives and try to criticize less. Criticizing disturbs. Parents need to be responsive to their children's needs and to see their needs as paramount. Always remember that being affective, respectful, and supportive are all requisites of authoritative parents, which is the kind of parent we should aim to be."

"Are there any other ways to cultivate perseverance?"

"Yes. Everything we talked about up until now was a part of the intrinsic motivation: the positive internal conversation, the vocation, the passion for what we do. There are also external actions and extrinsic motivation. Parents and teachers who motivate children or adults to continue, to keep fighting, to give their very best, are examples of that. Another example is being a part of a group of people who have the same interests and work hard to achieve their purposes."

"Like a study group?"

"That's a possibility. Being part of a group in which everyone is committed to achieving their goals makes people want to improve themselves. I taught at Harvard, and I saw the attitude of those students: they were enrolled in one of the best universities in the world; each one of them was more dedicated than the next one; each of them held their heads high, and no one nurtured laziness. The same goes for high school classes. If a teenager is in a class where everyone studies intensively and enthusiastically, wakes up early, completes the workbook exercises, and sacrifices weekends and holidays to achieve their goals, the teenager will want to keep up with the class pace. We are humans, and we want to be equal to those who are close to us, or even better. When the people who are close to us work hard to achieve goals that are similar to ours, we too will feel motivated to work hard. If, on the other hand, people close to us are lazy, we will also become too comfortable and sluggish."

"Therefore, it's important to observe the environment where we live and those with who we live."

"Of course! People who are guided by positive values will push you up. The inverse is also real. I will talk about that in one of the next steps: the value of good influences."

Estela added, "Andrew Carnegie, who was the richest man of his time, said that he made his fortune by surrounding himself with people who were more intelligent than him. I have no doubt about it."

They arrived at the Clinical Hospital. The driver parked the car, removed the doctor's suitcase from the trunk, and waited for him to get out of the automobile.

Then, Dr. Jansen told Estela, "I hope you enjoyed our ride."

"It was quite fruitful."

"Antônio, please bring that young lady back as carefully as possible!" said Dr. Jansen once he got out of the car. He turned to Estela, saying, "Grit really makes the difference between becoming successful or not. Another important aspect I didn't mention is this: those who are gritty have a healthier emotional life[clxii][clxiii] and are happier[clxiv]."

"Passion for what you do, effort, constancy, optimism," recapitulated Estela aloud.

"Parents and teachers that encourage children," complemented Dr. Jansen, "being part of a team that is truly dedicated and works hard. All of that, as a whole, ensures that children are on the right path for success and that they are happier with their own lives."

"Thank you, Doctor," she said, hugging him tenderly.

"Have a good day, and once you have the opportunity, we will talk about the eighth step."

"I can't wait. I want to know about the eighth step as soon as possible."

CHAPTER 10 —
THE EIGHTH STEP:
SECOND LANGUAGE

"A new language, a new life."

—Persian proverb

E stela's YouTube page grew as Victor foresaw. It started slowly, with a few followers, and it seemed to stagnate once it reached two hundred subscriptions. However, once she published the videos related to the second step, it quickly surpassed one thousand followers. Then it took off and achieved ten thousand followers.

"Wow!" exclaimed Victor. "Less than a month after creating your page, you already have ten thousand followers! It's an absolute success!"

It was. Estela remembered the day not too long ago when one of the articles she had written for her blog surpassed ten thousand readers. Now, several posts had more than one hundred thousand readers. One hundred thousand! A medium-sized city read, or apparently read, her opinions and tips. She saw the internet as a way to disseminate information on a larger scale and understood the advantages it had: many people that she could reach now would have been virtually inaccessible in the not-so-distant past. Furthermore, the videos she posted on You-Tube opened another door for diffusion, which allowed her to reach people who didn't enjoy reading or who didn't have the time or disposition for such an activity but that could watch the videos. And who knows? Maybe it would share her and Dr. Jansen's vision regarding the approached topics.

Meanwhile, not everything was rosy. In no time, people started posting messages, demanding the publication of other steps.

"When are you going to post the other steps, or this is it?" a mother asked.

"Estela, are you alive? Why did you stop on the second step? Do you want to sell your book?"

Book? Estela laughed and shared the link for her blog, which already had seven of the steps instead of just two. While comparing the two media environments, she understood that people preferred video since only a much smaller group read her blog. It was like two distinct environments: YouTube was a niche for those who enjoyed learning through videos, and the blog was for those who enjoyed reading.

She needed to split into two to get all of the content out, not to mention handle her daily life with her daughter and husband. Once Sofia turned five months old, she was already crawling everywhere. Estela's friends, who already had children, thought Sofia had reached her developmental milestones absurdly early. Estela always answered them the same way: "The ramp, reading, spending a lot of time in the crawling position . . . all of that helped Sofia improve her vision and her motor development."

Sofia started by dragging herself across the floor, but soon she was crawling. With crawling came worries. Estela covered all the sockets with protectors, removed everything that could break, and started making sure her daughter couldn't reach objects she could choke on.

Another situation that worried Estela was returning to work. How would it be to be away from her daughter for long periods? Her professional life was intense. Who would take care of Sofia? The current nanny was only one of her domestic servants who helped her whenever she needed her. She would have to hire a professional who would only assume the function of being Sofia's nanny. Estela decided to look for one that would meet her criteria: someone who had previous experience with children and was friendly and loving.

She went to the babysitter's agency, which had an excellent reputation for selecting qualified people and checking references. Estela spoke with the owner and shared her criteria. The woman indicated five professionals and scheduled an appointment with the first candidate on Monday morning.

The interview was completely different from what Estela had imagined. Not only did the nanny not meet her criteria, but also she looked too juvenile, didn't give Estela a good feeling, and had a limited vocabulary. After a few minutes of conversation, Estela had already excluded her.

On Tuesday, a friendly, joyful, and willing twenty-something presented herself. She had just achieved her degree in pedagogy at São Paulo State University and had recently moved to São Paulo with her husband. Since she had not yet found a job in her field, due to the lack of vacancies and market competitivity, she decided to try to find work in an area where she already had experience: working as a nanny. Her name was Andrea. She was red-headed, tall, and always had a smile on her lips. Besides having a vast vocabulary and instruction, she had also finished a first aid course. Furthermore, she was amazed by Sofia's development. When Estela detailed what she had been teaching her daughter, the young woman became extremely interested in the Steps and told her she wanted to be her right arm.

She met Estela's expectations, so she canceled the remaining interviews and hired the girl.

◆ ◆ ◆

After several failed attempts to schedule something with Dr. Jansen, they finally managed to meet at the Awake Clinic.

"I must apologize to you, Estela," said the doctor, looking regretful. "We haven't recorded anything for nearly two months. I have been traveling and lecturing, but today I want to make up for the delay. I managed to free my entire morning for you. We can record two steps for your YouTube channel, the third and the fourth, besides talking about the eighth step. Deal?"

"Sounds good to me," said Estela, smiling.

"However, let's change up the scenery this time, okay? I asked Bruno to set our studio in one of the development rooms. Is that okay with you?"

"No problem at all!" Estela answered happily. "Nothing against recording in your office, but recording in another environment is quite riveting."

Dr. Jansen guided her to the room on the fourth floor of the clinic, where Bruno was already waiting for them. One of the walls had a painted world map, and another one had a bookcase full of children's books. In the center, there were three small tables with chairs, and two poufs that were spread on the floor were also part of the decor. They sat in two armchairs made of raw leather, next to each other, that had been arranged by Bruno to record the videos.

"We are going to talk about the third step," explained Dr. Jansen. "Afterward, I think it would be good if we take a small break for coffee before approaching the fourth step."

"Wonderful," said Estela, rubbing her hands. "Is everything ready, Bruno?"

"Ready to go. You just need to start talking."

"Hi, everyone!" Estela said joyfully. "Today, Dr. Jansen and me are here to talk about the third step, which is about stimulating precocious reading. We know that it is a controversial topic, so today we want to clarify many educational paradigms. As a mother who sees the positive impact of the third step through my own daughter's development, I support this idea, but imagine what Dr. Michael Jansen has to say, considering his forty years' technical experience ... Enjoy!"

"When the topic is literacy," Dr. Jansen went directly for the theme, "there is always discussion about the best methodology. With good arguments, it is possible to convince lay people of the superiority of a method to the prejudice of another one. However, my intention here is not to generate disagreement. Meanwhile, I recommend Glenn Doman's methodology since it is the best for babies and young children. Despite finding that the phonics methodology is valid, I don't think it is the best during this stage because we see no babies reading using this method. However, I always recommend it as a compliment to Doman's methodology, especially for parents who can spare a little of their time to conciliate both methods. I think this methodology is even valid for teaching children who are older than four years old."

Dr. Jansen stood up, and Bruno followed him with the camera.

"Here at Awake Clinic, we use the phonics method with the 'Happy House'[clxv] and puppets. There is the daddy, the mommy, the grandma, the grandpa ... The best methodology, in my opinion, is to use made-up stories to present the variants of each letter. This way, we can work the spelling variations, the complex syllables, and the grammatical rules, among other aspects."

Estela, getting close to Dr. Jansen, questioned, "What if the child of the person watching us on YouTube is already literate? What can they use from this third step?"

"It's quite simple," answered Dr. Jansen, smiling. "Reading can happen during any stage or age. Therefore, the third step is not meant only for babies and young children, but everyone. Since we need to create a new generation of readers in Brazil, it's necessary to start working with younger children. Parents need to read for their children, because, as the writer Emilie Buchwald said, 'Children are made readers on the laps of their parents.' So there is the need for a magic moment during reading, almost every day: the children in the parents' bed, snuggling under the bed sheets, listening carefully, and maybe even reading together the story of the day. . . Through reading, children develop empathy because they can relate to the story characters, understand their feelings, and establish parallelisms with their own experiences. Reading also multiplies imagination and creativity. When children read a text or someone reads for them, they can get inside the story, imagining the environment, the context, the characters, and the sequence of events of the plot. Furthermore, children can propose their version of a chain of events. Reading also allows them to aggregate more knowledge and exposes them to more vocabulary, which provides the development of the language and the comprehension of different topics. Children listen more carefully when parents read little stories together with them."

Dr. Jansen, who was interested in stressing the importance of reading, assumed an even more emphatic tone to say, "You parents now have the opportunity to make commentaries about the plot and to encourage your child to relate a determined passage to their own life experience. However, you can also close the book and explore other aspects, like by asking your child about what they think will happen next, about how a certain character might be feeling, if another character is sad or happy . . . Reading is also a way of relaxing; we must not forget that by reading jointly, we are strengthening our bond with our children. That moment, as we said, is essential for creating mentally healthy children."

Once they finished recording the video about the third step, they took a break for coffee at the ground floor cafeteria. Since they wanted to continue working, they quickly returned to the development room and started recording the video about the fourth step. To differentiate it from the third step, Estela and Dr. Jansen decided they would alternate their lines.

Estela started, commenting, "The fourth step is about playing and its importance in enhancing children's creativity. Playing contributes to cognitive development . . ."

After much explanation, Dr. Jansen concluded, "Playing is not superfluous. Playing is essential for children to become creative teenagers and adults who not only are physically competent but also emotionally."

After the end of the recording session, Michael and Estela said goodbye to Bruno and started walking through the clinic while talking. Estela saw the pool and the place where they performed motor physiotherapy using cutting-edge technology equipment.

In the middle of the corridor, an African American boy released his hand from his mother and ran into them screaming in English, "Dr. Michael!" and hugged one of the doctor's legs.

"Hi, Jorge!" said Dr. Jansen. "It's good to see you again. Tell me about your swimming classes!"

"I love them! I'm learning breast stroke now."

Then the mother came over apologizing for the situation. "I'm sorry for Jorge, Dr. Jansen, but he is always so happy when he sees you."

"The pleasure of seeing you two is all mine, Paula. I hope Hugo keeps progressing."

"Of course! He is doing great. Always improving! I just left him with Cláudia."

"He is in excellent company."

The mother slightly grabbed her son's hand, who released the doctor's leg, smiled widely, and then said goodbye. "Bye, Doctor."

"Bye, Jorge."

Once the mother and son entered the elevator, Estela asked, "Are they American?"

"No, Brazilian. The elder son, Hugo, has autism and has been with us for more than five years. The younger one, Jorge, is following the Steps. He is a competent young boy, and his parents have been playing an incredible role for him to achieve his full potential."

"That's wonderful!" stated Estela. "But . . . What about his impeccable English skills?"

"Oh . . . He is enrolled in the third year in an international school. That's what the eighth step is about: encouraging your child to learn a second language."

"A second language?" asked Estela. "Why do you define that as one of the steps? Are there advantages of speaking a second language other than the ones that are already known? I know that some professions . . ."

Dr. Jansen stopped walking and kept looking into Estela's eyes, saying, "A second language is essential for the cognitive[clxvi] and social development of a child. That way, we can't avoid referring its importance in the Steps. Currently, we live on a planet that is increasingly more globalized, and we are exposed to several cultures and different lifestyles. Bilingual children will become world citizens as teenagers and adults, as they will be more open to different traditions and to countless cultural practices, and they will have the psychological tools to live together with people who are different from them. Learning a second language challenges the brain, making it grow and remain active. Structurally, the brain changes in size and configuration[clxvii], showing a higher density of gray matter[clxviii]. So, when children learn a second language during childhood, they won't have the same difficulties as adults who didn't learn additional languages, because they practically acquire linguistical knowledge through osmosis. Starting the same process when we are older is much more complicated, though it is still possible."

"I know learning a second language during childhood is much less complicated," said Estela, raising the corners of her mouth. "You don't suffer as much while acquiring it."

"From what I read in your blog, I noticed you could speak English relatively well," commented Dr. Jansen. "How old were you when you started learning English?"

"I was lucky," explained Estela, her eyes sparkling. "I started learning English at a very young age. We lived in a building in Leme, Rio de Janeiro. My mother met Sheila, a seventeen-year-old girl who, back then, had just moved from the United States to the floor above ours. I guess I was about four years old when my mother hired Sheila to be my nanny."

"And she would speak in English with you?"

"Exclusively in English. Her Portuguese was quite rough. I think it was a genius move by my parents because my sisters and I learned English quite quickly and without any accent. Speaking English, for me, was quite natural, and that gave me extraordinary advantages. I always achieved the best scores on English tests in school. Furthermore, Sheila became a good friend of the family."

"Hmm..." muttered the doctor. "That's quite interesting!"

"Personally, I can say it was a good experience to grow up speaking two languages naturally. It was a happy coincidence that Sheila moved to our building and that she accepted the job. It was she who took us to the ballet and swimming classes; she would clock our tasks and would even play the role of our elder sister. Even to this day, I still keep in touch with her."

"Always in English?"

"Always! What about you, Michael, did you speak English with your children when they were young?"

"Of course! English is my mother tongue. When they were young children, I would speak in English and sing lullabies that I learned in England, and I would play with them in English. When they grew up, I kept speaking with them only in English, while my wife would only speak Portuguese. Naturally, during family meetings or meals, our chosen language was Portuguese. They became bilingual spontaneously. I also speak with some patients and students in English too, like Jorge. However, I only do so if the parents request it..."

"Jorge speaks perfect English, with no accent at all!" observed Estela.

"If you learn a language from a young age, you probably won't have an accent," said the doctor. "If you start learning at a very late stage, like in my case, you probably will have an accent. I started speaking Portuguese forty years ago, and I still have an accent because my first contact with the Portuguese language was when I was already thirty years old. Even if I try, I can't get rid of my accent completely. It has improved a lot, I admit, but I still have an accent."

"Yes, you do," said Estela, smiling. "Yet it is a beautiful accent. It gives you an imposing and distinguished appearance."

"When children speak without an accent, it helps them be more accepted by those who natively speak the language, compared to those who have a strong accent. It's an advantage, without any doubt."

"Having an accent can give the impression that the speaker is not very familiar with the language in question, even if the bilingual person knows more about the language than the native speakers," emphasized Estela.

"However, it is important to stress that having an accent will only rarely block communication," explained Dr. Jansen. "If you learned English with an Australian, an Indian, or even a British person, it would be the same English language, in theory, that you would learn with a North American. However, the accent will always be quite different. Likewise, it differs if you learn Portuguese with a Brazilian or a Portuguese person. The accent is usually the first thing that gets our attention when we speak with other people. Even in a country like Brazil, we can distinguish the linguistical variations due to the different accents, which change from region to region. There are subtle variations in local or regional dialects, like the noticeable differences between the people from the Northeast, the South, Rio de Janeiro, the interior . . . Things like how they pronounce the letters *r* or *e*. When a person is bilingual, it can become even more complicated. Depending on how old people are when they acquire a second language, bilinguals might have an accent. Nevertheless, having an accent doesn't make a person more or less bilingual."

Estela nodded her head positively. Since she was quite interested in the topic, she preferred not to interrupt Michael, allowing him to proceed with his exposition.

"I insist that parents expose their children to one or more languages early since besides learning the language without developing an accent, they also will intuitively understand the grammatical rules," explained the doctor. "Some sentence structure will 'hurt' your ear. However, the foreigner doesn't know it. Children who learn a second language from a young age can identify the transgressions of the standard language just by hearing. They feel the nuances that would be unnoticed if they would have learned the second language during teenage years or adulthood."

"And what language would you recommend? English?"

"Any language is valid for the benefits of bilingualism. However, personally, I think English is indispensable," said Michael, placing his right hand on his chest. "The world doesn't have a global language, but English is currently the closest thing to one. It brings additional benefits to bilinguals for several reasons. For example, if you work as a researcher in the sciences or computation, you know that most scientific articles are published in English. It is also the language of the internet. About 60 percent of web content is in English."

Estela remarked, "Furthermore, English is crucial for anyone who travels abroad, allowing one to communicate with confidence."

"Without a doubt!" exclaimed Dr. Jansen. "Being able to speak English gives us a privileged position since we can communicate with the highest number of people possible, therefore assuring our well-being in several parts of the world. A quarter of the world speaks English. Besides the United States of America, Canada, India, Australia, England, New Zealand, and other countries that have English as the official language, there are several European countries where English is practically a second language."

"There are also the financial advantages[clxix] speaking English brings," concluded Estela. "You can get better jobs; multinationals can hire you, and you will probably achieve a higher wage."

"Not to mention the universities. If your daughter wants to go to a prestigious university abroad, she will need to speak English fluently. Thinking a little bit beyond that ... If she wants to immigrate to the United States of America, or Australia ... She will need to pass a proficiency test in English. Since the world is globalized as never before, it's better not to close any doors for our children. Instead, we must aim at keeping all the doors open all the time."

"I agree!" approved Estela.

"English equals our children's opportunities in first-world countries. Steven Pinker argues in his book *Enlightenment Now*[clxx] that people with a mobile phone and internet access earn, virtually, a few more hundred dollars than those without, each month. Anyone who has a mobile phone and speaks English has access to much more first-hand information than a person who only speaks his or her native language. Bilinguals can enroll in free quality courses; they can download an infinite number of books for a few dollars using Kindle by Amazon; they can listen to audiobooks in English using Audible. The real value of that accessibility is simply immeasurable."

"What if a child already knows English? What other languages would you recommend?"

"That varies widely," explained Michael. "If they live in Brazil, I would indicate Spanish as a third language, due to its proximity with the Portuguese language regarding vocabulary and some grammatical structures. However, if they are American, I would recommend French, which will probably be the most widely spoken language in the world by 2050, or even Spanish, due to the huge number of Latin immigrants in North America. Mandarin would be next on the list due to the great commercial power China is becoming. However, each case is different. For example, if a child descends from Japanese parents, I would recommend Japanese as the top priority."

"What other advantages do you identify in bilingualism?"

"Nowadays, being bilingual is more relevant than it ever was before. One of the main advantages, in my opinion, is connected with the perspective that the interaction with the next one is indispensable. Bilinguals have their emotional intelligence[clxxi] more developed. That is due to a better comprehension of foreign cultures and perspectives since a bilingual opens new knowledge doors by communicating with different communities employing a common language. A bilingual child develops relationships more easily and can achieve higher social comprehension, becoming more tolerant and having a wider vision of the world. Bilingual children[clxxii] develop social sensitivity and learn how to observe the world, considering perspectives that differ from their own. They discover that other points of view are not necessarily better nor worse than their own because they understand that two different points of view are just two possibilities within an infinity of points of view. The identity of such children transcends the limits and borders of a country. In this way, bilingual people are less likely to hold preconceived perspectives of the world."

"That means," added Estela, "those bilingual children learn how to have more cordial relationships with other people, without any exclusion."

"Isn't that how the world should be?" asked Dr. Jansen. "Bilingualism gives us a foundation for better attitudes. However, naturally, that depends on each person. When you share a language with another person or a closed group, you identify with them more easily, which helps the interpersonal relationship. Thus, bilingualism doesn't only allow children to become better people, but it also allows the world to be a better place, more connected, hugged by its similarities, instead of separated by its differences. Bilingualism nourishes benevolence, mutual understanding, and the respect for other races, countries, and religions, which makes it one of the cornerstones of world peace."

"That's an excellent view!" cheered Estela.

"There are many other favorable factors as well. Bilinguals have superior memory and higher decision-making power; they can switch more easily between tasks, understand the language structure better, which many labels as *metalinguistic conscience*, and, furthermore, they have better phonological, syntactical, and vocabulary conscience. It's precisely the metalinguistic conscience that will help them while learning a third or even more languages, making them more efficient communicators. Oh! We still have the brain malleability aspect. Bilinguals are better with divergent thinking, which is an integral part of creativity, than monolinguals."

Dr. Jansen stopped walking and took a black pen from his shirt pocket. He got closer to Estela and said, "When I ask you about how many uses this pen has, you can activate divergent thinking[clxxiii], listing countless uses. Divergent thinking is assessed in three distinct ways, regarding the number of answers you are able to give; the originality of each answer; and, lastly, the level of detail of each answer. Studies demonstrate that bilinguals are better at doing precisely that, managing to be more creative and finding solutions for problems more easily."

"And I read an article saying that speaking a second language puts you at a lower risk for dementia."

"It delays dementia," corrected Dr. Jansen. "Ellen Bialystok[clxxiv] and her colleagues at New York University discovered that being bilingual can delay the decline of memory for about four years. Comparing the age at which the first dementia symptoms appeared, they found out that bilinguals started losing their memory when they were around seventy-five years old, while monoglots had the same symptoms when they were about seventy-one years old. That is what we call *cognitive reserve*[clxxv]. Other studies, conducted by Ana Ines Ansaldo[clxxvi] and her collaborators at the University of Montreal, demonstrate that bilingual elders solve problems using areas of the brain that are less vulnerable to the corrosion resulting from aging."

"You managed to convince me. Bilingualism should be one of the Steps. However, I still have one relevant question: how can people who are not so financially fortunate afford to learn a second language? How can I talk about bilingualism on my blog without sounding elitist?"

"That's an excellent question. Let's look at your case, first of all. I know that Sofia won't have problems accessing the best education possible. If I were you, I would enroll my daughter in a bilingual international school. It is just a suggestion, naturally. International schools teach a second language through immersion. In other words, children speak a second language with their peers and with their teachers all the time, and their tests are written with the second language. They are challenged daily. Many of those schools cherish the excellency of academic teaching. Therefore, they provide an experience of two worlds since children need to dive into the language and culture of the country of origin of that language. That way, students acquire a solid education and internalize a second language, which is knowledge no one can take from them. Now, in general, you are right: bilingual schools are, in fact, quite expensive for the vast majority of the population. I have a solution that might solve that problem: why don't you read the book *The Bilingual Revolution: The Future of Education Is in Two Languages*[clxxvii], written by Fabrice Jaumont?"

"What is the book title again?" asked Estela, removing her mobile phone from her purse.

Dr. Jansen repeated the title while Estela typed it.

"The author puts his expertise into action to help the French, Japanese, Italian, German, and Russian communities of New York to develop quality bilingual programs in local public schools."

"What does he teach in the book?" asked Estela.

"He says that parents, once again, have a fundamental role to transform the reality of the education their children get. They must know the extent of their real power, which is truly big. He says that by joining parents with ideas, schools, and the public administration, it is possible to provide children of families with few resources a second language with quality. In the book, he explains that the effort of some parents and people in the community changed the education of many American public schools. He suggests that the project must be executed in three phases: the first one is finding families in the community interested in organizing meetings; the second phase is trying to create a program to present to schools and municipalities; and the third phase is about implementing the plan. Following this advice, it is possible to have bilingual public schools or at least schools that teach quality English."

"Instead of the current joke Brazilian public schools are."

"You're right, that's not learning English. The basic thing about learning a second language is that you have to be able to express yourself using it. Including English in the curricular program and not having a significant number of children who can speak the language at the end of the course is, as you said, a bad joke. Thus, we can't be passive and inactive, simply accepting the things other people impose. That's why I insist on this step. We can't ignore the importance of acquiring a second or a third language. You must put that on your blog. Make the value of this lesson very clear. If parents want to implement it, it only depends on them."

"I didn't know many of the advantages you detailed ..."

Dr. Jansen continued, "If we are aware that a teacher who speaks fluent English can change the life of all the students in a classroom, we must go to the school and fight until we achieve it. If we provide solid English classes for free to our children, with a low cost for institutions, it will allow children to have access to more knowledge and opportunities. We would be opening doors for their future. They wouldn't be enclosed in one language and would know they can be world citizens. They would take more advantage of all the abundance of information the internet provides us; they could study or work abroad if they wished to. As you will read in the book, it isn't easy to create such a program, yet it is feasible. In New York, more than ten thousand children are enrolled in English-Spanish programs in more than forty-five public schools, from kindergarten to high school. With the commitment of teachers, parents, the community, and the government, everything is possible."

"We have to fight for that to happen here," Estela said.

"A fight that is worth it. Having access to quality education and learning a second language effectively should both be rights of every Brazilian child."

"Now I understand that we need to do much more . . . a revolution," commented Estela.

"Great revolutions focus on hard facts. The French Revolution wouldn't have happened if Danton hadn't seen the French people's disdain regarding the monarchy. In fifteen years, he managed to supersede the oldest and longest European kingship with the ideals of liberty, equality, and fraternity."

"That's true!" Estela exclaimed. "What stops us from choosing a teacher that only speaks English during classes?"

Michael continued, "We must argue in the administrative universe and convince school directors, administrators, and mayors that it is feasible and important for the future of our children and country. Did you ever think about how much Brazil would win in tourism and human potential if a big part of the people were to speak a second language? We have already had private international schools in Brazil for several decades. The British School, the French School, the Swiss School, the American School. Of course, implementing that knowledge in a public school would result in a big question mark, but it isn't impossible to achieve and is worth trying."

"What about now?" asked Estela. "What would you suggest to the parents who can't wait for a revolution with such impact?"

"Nowadays we have Skype, FaceTime, and WhatsApp, which allow us to speak with people from other countries, almost for free. We can look at the eyes and lip movements of people who are on the other side of the world. We need to use that technology and transform it to benefit us. Private schools could offer full scholarships to those who can't pay for language courses. Some schools already offer partial scholarships. Another suggestion is to take advantage of the internet, accessing language schools online or websites that allow exercising conversation with native people. However, we must realize that to reach the same development level in both languages, we must use both of them in practice too. Hence, an English school is not enough. To retain knowledge, children and adults need to talk with fluent speakers; they need to read texts, to hear music with that language, and to watch movies without subtitles. Like everything in life, we need to be consistent, and sometimes, we even need to insist. Bilingualism is an investment that will certainly return in the form of knowledge and more professional perspectives."

Dr. Jansen, smiling, implied he was leaving. They were at the Clinic entrance. Estela noticed it was getting late.

"I have to go," she said, hugging the doctor. "I want to learn about the ninth step as soon as possible."

"You will learn about it at the right time. Goodbye!"

CHAPTER 11 — THE NINTH STEP: GOOD INFLUENCES

"We tend to become like those whom we admire."

—*Thomas Monson*

A day before returning to work, Estela couldn't sleep. She imagined how her daughter would react to her absence and how they both would feel while being apart. In the dark, she pressed the pillow against her mouth to conceal the fact that she was crying and to avoid waking Victor, who was sleeping by her side. She got up earlier than she needed to, and for about an hour, she watched her daughter in her crib, illuminated by a dim light that passed through an open curtain. Sofia's thorax was going up and down. She was so calm, perfect, and beautiful.

Estela cried again.

Andrea arrived at 6:30 a.m. and noticing Estela's swollen

eyes, assured her there would be no problems:

"Sofia is used to me. We are friends already. You can go to work peacefully."

Estela tried not to feel like weeping because she knew there was nothing to worry about. The nanny she had chosen was great. Nevertheless, it would take her some time to get used to leaving Sofia.

Estela kissed her daughter and hugged her tightly, inhaling the fresh scent of her clothes and skin. She left her in Andrea's arms, and once she got to the door, she instinctively returned and repeated the kiss and the hug. Then she told the nanny,

"If you need me for any reason at all, just call me, and I will fly home!"

Andrea answered in a relaxed tone, "Don't worry! Sofia and I will have a lot of fun."

The journalist gave her some more instructions. "There's milk in the refrigerator. Vera knows how to prepare the baby food..."

"I know, Estela! You can go; there is no need to worry at all."

After leaving the apartment, Estela looked at herself in the elevator's mirror and got ready, in an attempt to ensure that her appearance wouldn't give away how emotionally unstable she felt.

Once she got to the publishing building, her distress started to dissipate. Her coworkers greeted her with a welcome party, which included colorful balloons, cakes, and snacks. Everyone participated.

"You look beautiful, my dear!" commented Karen. "You are lean, flushed, and look at your hair! When I had my babies, I nearly went bald."

"Really? You have so much hair!"

"I lost almost everything," her friend said. "I visited the best dermatologists in town, and they told me it was something called telogen effluvium. I had never heard the term before. But over time, my hair returned."

"Fortunately!"

"What about your YouTube channel?" asked Karen. "When I checked it last week, you already had about fifty thousand followers. Are you making money with it?"

"That's not my goal. However, any profits are welcome."

"What about your blog?" asked Josi, another one of her co-workers. "You know, I always read your posts. Marcos and I are trying to get pregnant; we want a second child. I already told him we would follow your Steps."

"I'm happy for you, Josi. It is a pleasure to be back to work and to see all of you again. You know, last night, I was thinking about giving up everything and becoming a housewife. Victor would ask for a divorce, but I wanted to do it anyway."

They laughed at her situation because they had gone through similar feelings.

"It's always like that," explained Karen. "The maternal instinct is something animalistic. It doesn't allow us to let our child go, not for a minute. I felt like that, Josi felt the same, and now it's your turn, darling. It's normal! Forget about those silly ideas. You have a career to cherish. How many people would love to be in your place?"

Even knowing how much she enjoyed being at her workplace, her maternal instinct didn't calm down.

Every time she said goodbye to Sofia to go to work, it was heart-rending. She would call ten times a day to ask Andrea how she was and where they were.

"We went for a walk at the park," she would answer. Or, "I just finished getting her dry. She had quite an enjoyable bath," or, "She is eating her delicious baby food."

The physical and emotional battle went on for Estela for quite some time, but over time, she got used to it. She knew she could trust her nanny, who proved to be fantastic.

Victor, who managed to have lunch at home every day, always complimented Andrea. "She is quite careful, my love. She stimulates Sofia all day long. She sits on the floor with her, playing, telling her children's stories, and always keeps her mobile phone quite far away from our baby, never taking it out of her purse. I really see the difference between her and Vera, who doesn't leave the phone for a minute. She is always talking with a relative or chatting with friends on WhatsApp. Andrea is always focused on Sofia."

Estela felt the same, and Andrea gave them even more reasons to feel that way when the family went to Guarujá for a weekend. Sofia had just turned seven months old, and they chose to celebrate at the beach. They were happy and relaxed, playing with their little girl inside a tent. A second of inattention was enough for Sofia to put a handful of wet sand in her mouth.

After spiting the sand out instinctively, and once Estela cleaned her mouth with mineral water, the baby crawled calmly toward Victor, as if nothing happened, and said, "Da-da."

Instantaneously feeling moved, Victor dropped the coconut he was holding to the ground, stood up from the beach chair, and picked up his daughter, saying, "Did you hear that, my love? She said 'daddy' before she said 'mommy'!"

"Da-da!" repeated Sofia. "Da-da!"

Estela, who was delighted, cheered her daughter.

"Hooray, my little daughter! Yet, I'm not sure she said 'daddy'! I think she is hungry," she concluded.

"Da-da!" said Sofia once again.

"'Daddy' was the first word our daughter said," assured Victor, quite pleased. "I already recorded it in my memory. No doubt about it!"

Estela had to admit it. However, a few hours later, when they were both lying in bed, Sofia crawled toward her, climbed over her shoulder, and said, "Ma-ma . . . Ma-ma . . ."

"Did you hear that?" Estela asked proudly. "She said 'mommy'!"

"Ma-ma!"

"Mommy is here, my love. Mommy is here!"

"Ma-ma!"

"Record this moment, please! The first day she said 'mommy'!"

Victor picked up his mobile phone from the bedside table, pointed it toward his daughter, who had her eyes open wide, and, luckily, she repeated, "Ma-ma...Ma-ma."

"Now say 'daddy,' my little daughter," asked Victor, exhilarated. "Can you say it, my daughter?"

"Ma-ma...Mamm...Da-da."

Victor smiled due to the sheer happiness he was feeling.

Estela said, "Now, say 'supercalifragilisticexpialidocious,' my little daughter."

They both laughed out loud.

A week later, back at the apartment in São Paulo, Victor was lying on the floor of the bedroom, which they dubbed the "chaos room," while his daughter was crawling from one side to another, on the colorful EVA mat. He picked up one of the dolls that was lying around, held it in front of him shaking it gently, and called Sofia.

His daughter raised her head and, intensely staring at the doll, used one of the toys nearby to stand up.

"Come here, my baby. Come get your doll," Victor encouraged calmly.

Sofia looked at him and then to the doll, released the toy, and suddenly, tried to walk, but after three daffy steps fell to the floor. Victor stood up from the floor immediately and started calling to Estela, who was in another room, "She walked! She walked!"

Estela appeared, drying her hair and saying, "What happened, Victor? She is just seven months and eight days old."

"I swear! She walked to get her doll, three little steps to get this doll."

"Really?" asked Estela, raising one of her eyebrows.

Her husband nodded positively.

Estela decided to test it. She placed Sofia next to the baby bouncer, which she often used as a support to stand up. Her daughter climbed up quickly, using both hands to support herself on the object that was a bit smaller than her. Suddenly, she released one of her hands.

Estela stepped back two steps, holding the doll that was in Victor's hands, and softly said, "Come get your doll, my love."

Sofia shouted happily and then released the second little hand.

"I will catch my baby," encouraged Estela. "I'm going to catch my baby."

Her daughter stared directly into her eyes and took a first big step. Slowly, she took a second one.

"Come here, come to Mommy!" Estela teased.

Her daughter took a third step, a fourth and a fifth step. Finally, she fell to the ground.

Estela picked up her daughter, hugged her, and exclaimed, "Oh my God, my beautiful daughter, you are walking!"

Ever since Estela went back to work, it became harder to meet with Dr. Michael Jansen. Thus, Estela proposed a meeting at her apartment, on a Saturday afternoon. The doctor took two days to answer her message before finally accepting the invitation.

On the day of the meeting, Sofia was almost eight months old and was walking swiftly, exploring the larger rooms.

"I'm impressed with her, Estela," said the doctor, observing the high degree of skill the young girl was demonstrating.

"If even you, Michael, are impressed," said Estela, "I think we really are doing something right."

"She is intellectually gifted, isn't she?" asked Victor, getting closer to the two of them with his eyes sparkling. "She started crawling when she was five months old, her first words happened when she was seven months old, and her first steps didn't take longer than seven months and eight days. I'm starting to see a pattern. Estela doesn't believe me, but that's what I think."

Estela stared at the doctor and noticed a light severity on his eyes as if someone was stepping on his foot. Estela immediately tried to fix her husband's speech. "I already told him that to avoid inducing a fixed mindset, we must not talk about her in such a way. The truth is that the sum of everything we have been doing promoted the development of her brain, muscles, and motor coordination. Am I right, doctor?"

"That's right! Today, we will approach that topic for the YouTube video: the fixed mindset versus the growth mindset. Where are we going to record it, Estela?"

"Follow me," answered Victor, guiding them to the "chaos room," which was now much tidier than usual. In it, there were two large serge armchairs, which were brought from another room and placed side by side. The camera was installed on a rugged tripod.

Victor crouched to turn the LED reflectors on. Then he handed Estela and Dr. Jansen lavalier microphones, saying, "I need to run a test to be sure everything is working perfectly."

After confirming the recording would go smoothly, he said goodbye to Estela and Michael Jansen, informing them, "I'm going to take Sofia to the mall. Vera will stay until six. If you need anything, just call me."

He kissed Estela and waved goodbye to Michael before closing the door.

Estela cleared her throat, adjusted the microphone, and once again, started talking,

"Hi, everyone! Today we will talk about the fifth step, which is about strengthening your children's self-control and assuring they develop a growth mindset."

Michael Jansen explained to the potential audience the actions of the limbic and pre-frontal cortex systems. Afterward, Estela translated the medical concepts into the language of the lay people. "The pre-frontal cortex acts as a break for our impulses, and the limbic system is an accelerator. They live constantly challenging each other due to daily temptations."

Michael Jansen talked about the marshmallow test and the

work developed by Carol Dweck regarding types of mindsets. Finally, he concluded, "You must compliment children correctly. Not long ago there was the harmful self-esteem movement[clxxviii]. People preached that we should compliment our children all the time so they could develop a solid ego, capable of facing any challenge. Children were fabulous, beautiful, perfect . . . In their opinion, everything we said needed to be positive to avoid damaging their self-esteem. It was a disaster. It backfired! Those children became shallow and futile, and we know why. Self-esteem is not supposed to grow from the outside to the inside. People create their self-esteem through their victories and then express it. Thus, it is a movement from the inside to the outside. So, as parents, we must avoid complimenting talents, physical attributes, or immutable aspects of our children. We must compliment effort! When we say something like, "Congratulations, my child, you really worked hard to achieve that A grade in physics," we are giving importance to the aspect that matters the most. In other words, we are stressing their actions and not their talent. We must value physical or intellectual work, training, the process that helps to achieve success. It will be worth it!"

Once the recording of the fifth step was over, Michael Jansen suggested a small break to relax and unwind.

They went to the spacious, luxurious kitchen, with stainless steel appliances. Vera peeled and served a mango for each of them. They ate the fruit sitting close to the window and smelling the fresh scent of coffee coming from the cloth filter.

Michael Jansen chose tea, and Estela blew on a cup of coffee, saying:

"Can we talk about the ninth step before we get back to recording?"

"I like that idea," answered the doctor.

"The steps are always a surprise for me. I'm never able to imagine what the next step will be."

"Do you remember your best friend during childhood?" asked Michael Jansen while placing a little green tea bag on his teacup and pouring some boiling water.

"Of course! How could I forget about her?" answered Estela, feeling quite nostalgic. "Her name is Ana Flor. Why are you asking me about her?"

"Are you still friends nowadays?" he asked carefully.

"Well, you know what distance does . . . She is my friend on Facebook. She has a degree in biology, lives in Bahia, has two children, and takes care of sea turtles. She is a good person. We followed different paths, but I still love her very much."

"The Ninth Step is about that, the power of friendships and good influences," complemented Michael Jansen. "Friends are fundamental to everyone, especially children[clxxix]. The bonds of childhood last our entire life, even if only in our memories, our unconscious. Many times, we adults underestimate the importance of our children's friendships, even though we see our childhood friendships as special. Parents must support children so they can nourish their friendships, encouraging them to take care of those relationships until they become adults. During kindergarten, friendships help develop social and emotional skills, increasing children's perception regarding belonging to a group."

"And that reduces the stress children feel," added Estela, drinking a sip of coffee.

"Without a doubt. Social support is important to everyone. Teenagers, adults, elders, and children too. The majority of the children who have behavior problems and are unproperly integrated don't have friends or show difficulty interacting with peers. When parents help them create friendships, their inadequate behaviors become less common."

"Of course! Interaction makes children happy. Together, they can have fun or get their school tasks done."

"The more a child grows, the bigger the influence of friendships and of the groups to which that child belongs. In 1998, a North American psychologist, Judith Rich Harris, wrote in her book *The Nurture Assumption*[clxxx], that parents didn't have much power regarding their children's future since they must share their success, or guilt, with genetics and the children's friends. She argues, 'The world children share with their peers is what shapes their behavior and modifies the characteristics they have since birth.' In other words, she delegates more power to friends than to parents."

"What? Is that real?" asked Estela, with her eyes open wide.

"It is a polemic idea," answered the doctor, gesturing with his hands to calm Estela down, "and it is contrary to my perspective since it takes a considerable portion of the responsibility away from parents. I also think she is right regarding the argument that friends play a determinant role in a child's future. I believe in this point."

"A man is known by the company he keeps," Estela said.

"Yes," Michael Jansen agreed, using a calm tone and drinking his tea. "Once children become nine years old, they want to fit in a closed group of friends. It is known that friendships exercise a powerful influence on children's performance, either for better or worse. In other words, children will become good students if they have friends who enjoy studying. If their friends are lazy and troublemakers, they might acquire transgressive behaviors. Not to mention that bad friends might pressure them to do things they would rather not do, making them feel guilty, scared, ashamed, or regretful."

Estela nodded.

Dr. Jansen continued, "The problem is that children want to feel accepted, even when they feel they don't fit in. Thus, if the group picks on you due to the way you dress or the style of your hair, you might resign and change to fit your friends' opinion."

"I saw that when I was a teenager," added Estela. "Bullying somebody to go get a tattoo, to get as thin as someone else, to achieve the perfect body, to try drugs or alcohol, to have sex ..."

"That's peer pressure," summarized Michael Jansen. "We are all subject to it. Therefore, as parents, we have the obligation of monitoring our children's activities and carefully observing the friends with whom they spend time. A person's character is formed during childhood, and it goes beyond conscience, engraved within our being. If we look carefully, we can infer if a person is mean, angry, spiteful, or has a bad temper. We can't take too long to discover that our child is a victim of bullying or that he or she is behaving poorly due to the influence of their peers. We need to know our children and their friends too. Friendships have a huge influence on kids, as well as their environment. Therefore, we need to be very attentive."

"And nowadays, we also have to pay attention to drugs and other addictions."

"This isn't just a current problem," answered the doctor. "During the '70s, two North American congressmen traveled to Vietnam and confirmed their suspicions regarding the number of American soldiers who were addicted to heroin: 15 to 20 percent. Once Nixon, who was then the president of the United States, learned about those numbers, he declared heroin addiction as the country's number one public health problem. Back then, they thought that people being addicted to heroin was something irreversible and that losses of war, which were already expensive enough, would be even harsher."

"I was thinking about marijuana . . ." Estela commented. "So what happened with those soldiers?"

"In Vietnam, the intense psychologic stress, the conducive environment, the ease of acquiring the drug, the absence of other recreational activities, the lack of friends' and parents' disapproval regarding the use of such drugs, and, especially, the local friendships with those who were already addicted to the drug all led to an explosion of chemical dependents. However, when they returned to the United States, something incredibly surprising happened."

"What?"

"Lee Robins[clxxxi], who taught at Washington University, showed that 88 percent of those heroin addicts kicked the addiction from one moment to another, without any specific help, and they did not relapse. As I said, the environment and friendships. Those soldiers, upon returning to their country, felt welcomed by their friends and relatives, who also monitored them. Furthermore, acquiring heroin was nearly impossible. Since the familiar environment included much less stress and was healthier, due to the existence of other recreational activities, and since using drugs was culturally inadmissible, getting away from heroin and returning to normal life was the easiest path to follow."

"Interesting... The friendships we have are, without a doubt, significant for how we live."

"And friendships can influence even our unconscious. To mention an example, a study was published by the *New England Journal of Medicine* in 2007[clxxxii]. The researchers followed more than twelve thousand individuals during thirty years and found out that a person was 57 percent more likely to become obese if a close friend became fat, even if that friend lived hundreds of kilometers away."

"Really? How is that possible?"

"Friends affect one's perception regarding what being obese means. When your friend gains some weight, you don't perceive it as a bad thing. Consequently, you relax regarding your shape."

"Oh, well," a worried Estela said, feeling her waist.

"And, if you specifically think about children, recent studies show that around eleven years old, the IQ of our best friends influences our intelligence degree for posteriority. Tell me, Estela, how was Ana Flor? Was she intelligent?"

Estela laughed and answered, "Ana Flor was a genius!"

"I'm serious about this," said Michael Jansen, smiling. "When we socialize with intelligent children during childhood, our IQ tends to increase during teenage years and adulthood. We are more likely to mimic and absorb the attitudes and diverse manners (of speaking, eating, studying) of those around us. The research developed by Ryan Meldrum[clxxxiii] and his peers at Florida International University demonstrates that. After a few years analyzing data, those scientists found out that the intelligence of our best friend when we are about eleven years old influences our IQ when we are fifteen years old. That means that if our best friend when we are eleven years old is intelligent, we too will tend to be intelligent once when we are fifteen years old."

"Don't you think that is because children choose to become friends with other children who are similar to them?" asked Estela.

"It's not just about that. By mimicking our friends, we also absorb much of their knowledge and skills, increasing our own intelligence. We tend to imitate their habits. 'He likes reading? I must read too.' The more we like someone, the more we tend to look like that person, and that depends hugely on empathy and the activity of mirror neurons. When we see someone doing something, those neurons are activated so we imagine how things would be if we were performing the same action. We absorb the humor of the person we live with, and we reflect them through similar postures. However, I have to make it quite clear that Sofia must not choose friends according to their IQ. Instead, she must choose friends who are interesting, who participate in the same activities, who like the same things, and who help nourish the best in her."

"She should also avoid some friendships. What if her peers pressure her?"

"She must learn how to protect herself. She needs to learn how to say no, calmly. That will make other people in the group respect her. It is also important to understand that friends don't need to agree with everything. However, it is easier to avoid the pressure of people who are not doing her any good and to try to find a group where the desired behavior is the norm. For example, if she wants to become an A student, she must look for friends who enjoy studying, because by surrounding herself with people who behave like that normally, it will be easier to follow the same path. People around us show us what is acceptable and what is not. If she wants to become a professional swimmer, she must join a group of strong swimmers as that will motivate her to practice correctly, allowing her to become as good as her peers, or even better."

Vera served them a tray with warm cheese bread. Estela grabbed one, while Michael Jansen continued, after drinking a small portion of tea, "Children must become friends with people with good character, and they must have someone who works as a mirror. Children of successful parents have higher chances of becoming successful too, due to having a model to follow. Our parents are our biggest sources of inspiration while we are children."

"What if children don't have someone to follow?" asked Estela, biting her cheese bread. "What if children are needy, live in a violent environment, and are not loved and supported by their parents? How can we help kids in such cases?"

"It is a little bit more complicated. Anyway, it is still possible to help. Everything depends on who their role model is, their source of inspiration. It can be a teacher, the hard-working father, the mother, the older brother, or even a sports player. On the other hand, it can also be a drug dealer."

"I see . . ."

"Many people feel imprisoned by the environment in which they live, their parents, their flaws, or their defeats. Actually, we are all a result of our choices, just like Viktor Frankl taught us. It's important that children understand that clearly. Many times, we give up internally, even before we have lost. We must keep seeing a better future for ourselves, we need a personal mission that allows us to achieve extraordinary goals, like helping others or becoming an important person who is capable of contributing to the progress of humanity."

"We must take control of our destiny through our attitude."

"Correct! Children must not be made to feel they are a victim of circumstance. Instead, they must be encouraged to understand that their attitudes matter and that they can change any situation. Sometimes, children can't improve their lives due to the lack of a more solid reference, someone to look at or to be inspired by. A way of soothing the situation is reading biographies of historical figures who changed the world where we live. To do so, children who lack a reference will need someone to encourage them to read. The public library, their school, and social projects can help make reading more accessible to such children. Reading biographies can open a window which will bring the light of knowledge and possibly the hope for a better future."

"Okay! Reading biographies . . ." said Estela, recapitulating.

"Biographies might lead you to what the psychologist Abraham Maslow denominated as a peak experience[clxxxiv], which refers to those moments when we escape from the problems of a heavy day and we understand that there is something much bigger and sublime around us. A feeling of supreme freedom, a life with three dimensions. Empowerment! The opposite of accepting our current life situation and allowing it to define us, especially when you are born with a disadvantage."

"Oh! I got it!"

The doctor further explained, "Reading about the lives of those we admire allows needy children to find a perspective they never had before. It allows them to understand that all the heroes were, or are, real human beings with lives filled with mistakes and victories, which brings those heroes closer to us. This process is important so children understand that everything their heroes achieved is explainable and that those explanations don't diminish their achievements. They will learn that no one is born with phenomenal skills: not Mozart, Einstein, or Newton. No one! By reading the biographies of those who tried to make this world a better place, children can escape from their harsh realities. That kind of reading is especially important for children who live in a tough environment."

"Which biographies would you recommend?"

"There are so many! Viktor Frankl's *Man's Search for Meaning*[clxxxv] is a good start. He was a Jew who survived Auschwitz and Dachau, the Nazi concentration camps. He lost everything—family, friends, job, health, goods—everything except 'the last of the human freedoms—to choose one's attitude in any given set of circumstances.'"

"I read the book during my university years."

"There are plenty of other biographies that can be interesting as well: Thomas Edison, who I consider the best autodidact who ever lived; Tesla; Albert Einstein; Mozart; Marie Curie; Lincoln; the Wright Brothers; Da Vinci; Anne Frank . . . For small children, the book collection Dead Famous or Who Was[clxxxvi] talks about many compelling characters."

"Hmm," mumbled Estela, chewing another piece of cheese bread.

"What matters the most is the inspiration biographies pass on. Children and teenagers feel extraneous lives and plant the seed of change within themselves. They have exclusive access to the internal voices of each one of those historical figures who, despite their different styles, are all magnificent. Thus, they will not feel the need for admiring the drug dealer because they can be better and happier than that while trying to make a difference in this world. Visualizing a better future, having a goal, and doing good for other people will drive them forward. Do you know the story of Ben Carson?"

"Oh, the neurosurgeon of the excellent movie *Gifted Hands*?"

"Yes, exactly. His mother took care of two children by herself because their father left them. She was a housekeeper, semi-analphabet, and worked three jobs. Ben Carsen was one of the worst students in his classroom, if not the worst. His peers made fun of him and considered him to be stupid. Then, his mother had an insight: she insisted that her two children to stop watching television and start reading books and writing small summaries about them, which they would read to her later, at night. It was through reading books that Ben acquired his taste for knowledge . . ."

Estela completed, "His academical change happened when his science teacher asked the classroom if anyone knew the name of a dark-colored stone. No one knew, except for him, because he had read a book about rocks."

"Obsidian," added Michael Jansen. "From that moment on,

that teacher helped him, and his self-esteem grew gradually until he became a model student. Ben Carson graduated first at Yale and then at the University of Michigan, where he studied medicine. He became the first African American neurosurgery resident at Johns Hopkins Hospital, where he performed thousands of neurosurgeries, saving countless lives. That's another biography I would certainly recommend! The books *You Have a Brain*[clxxxvii] and *Think Big*[clxxxviii] tell his story perfectly and send a message about the possibility of changing one's destiny and releasing one's potential through the right attitudes."

"What about watching biographical movies, does that help?"

"Yes. However, reading is a more powerful experience. How long does it take to watch a movie? One and a half, two hours . . . Reading a book makes you spend more time with the characters, deeply visualizing each one and allowing you to identify with some of them. Furthermore, books give you access to the characters' minds, bringing you more details about their obstacles and humor. Besides, you can also imagine the environment where they lived. Those actions positively affect your brain, allowing people to reach their conclusions, which are much richer than what you get through the filter of the filmmaker's vision. Are there any good movies? Certainly. *Gifted Hands*[clxxxix] is one of many! However, reading injects us with a much deeper uplifting feeling. It expands our horizon and possibilities, teaching us many valuable lessons, which are often neglected in movies but that can still be useful during our lives."

"Besides the fact that movies are rarely better than their respective original books."

"That's another aspect. When a little boy reads *The Story of My Life*[cxc], by Hellen Keller, he immediately understands that his problems are quite small when compared to hers, as she became deaf, mute, and blind before she was two years old. Nevertheless, with the fundamental help of Anne Sullivan, who was her teacher, she managed to transform herself from an undisciplined and angry little girl, into a person of influence, an idealist who fought for the rights of other people. By reading the biography written about Winston Churchill, *The Last Lion*[cxci], people can see the countless failures and defeats this public man suffered. However, it also allows people to see his transformation. That change resulted in inflammatory speeches, which were an inspiration for the British people to escape Hitler's hands. We have many leaders who can inspire us. We need to look for inspiration in the right personalities, instead of worshiping the wrong idols, as many people do."

"Wrong idols?"

"Yes. For example, singers and actors, who are worshiped as martyrs, who died due to their addictions and excesses," said Dr. Jansen, frowning. "Their attitudes were insane, but the cinematographic industry sells an image of genius and freedom, which doesn't match the truth. Deep down, they wasted their potential, throwing it into a garbage can. Trying to link the use of drugs or their mad attitudes to creativity is a huge fallacy. Drugs, promiscuity, and excess only leads to the destruction of creative power."

"I feel sad whenever I see wasted talent," said Estela.

"I do too. It's important to know that to perform a work that produces an impact in the world of arts, science, or in life in general, it is necessary to have huge doses of emotional stability, discipline, and self-control. I consider the self-destructive attitude of those persons, who had it all, as a way of devaluing human capacity. Children and teenagers, while watching those movies, might be dominated by the desire to repeat the same crazy actions or lifestyles. It is important that parents and teachers encourage them to critically analyze the content of movies, media, music, and books, as well as the content of every speech. Having said that, what I propose is that we get inspired by people like Mahatma Gandhi, Steve Jobs, Louis Pasteur, and Benjamin Franklin. Thus, I insist on this ninth step: surround yourself with interesting friends, who force you to grow. And learn how to choose your influences, your idols."

When they returned, Estela started to record again, saying: "The sixth step is about encouraging your child to perform physical activities."

They both talked about the topic, with Dr. Jansen summarizing at the end, "When parents allow their children to spend too much time living a sedentary lifestyle, in front of the television or the computer, they allow them to damage not only their bodies but also their brain and mental health. The body and the mind are one. Moving improves your memory, logical thinking, and focus and reduces the risk of anxiety and depression, not to mention the diseases that are typically associated with physical inactivity, like diabetes, hypertension, and dyslipidemia. When we are sweating and exercising, the levels of neurotransmitters like serotonin and dopamine on the brain rise, making us feel happier and more motivated.

Furthermore, it makes our body produce neuronal growth factors, like BDNF, which acts as a neuronal fertilizer, helping the formation of new neurons and assisting us in remembering the things we learn more easily. Physical activity is essential for children to be both physically and psychologically healthy. Make sure your child is more physically active; make your child leave the computer chair and play actively. Later, in the future, he or she will undoubtedly thank you."

When they were saying goodbye to each other, Michael Jansen commented, "The next step, which is the tenth, is one of my favorites. I'm thinking about when and where I will share it with you.

Estela hugged him and said, "If it is one of your favorites, it must certainly be magical ..."

CHAPTER 12 —
THE TENTH STEP:
DELIBERATE
PRACTICE

"Without effort, your talent is nothing more than unmet potential. Without effort, your skill is nothing more than what you could have done but didn't."

—Angela Duckworth

"Y ou are famous on YouTube!" commented Helena, the chief executive publisher, turning herself in the swivel chair. "More than one-hundred-thousand followers and counting..."

"And to think that all of that was your fault! Do you remember that article about education in Brazil? Probably not. It was then that I found Dr. Jansen, who introduced me to the Steps, and, well, the rest is history!"

Helena nodded her head slowly and positively.

Estela continued, "If I told you that back then I could see how the Steps would become so popular, I would be lying. Since I'm sharing my knowledge with a specific audience, comprised of parents of young children or those planning to conceive, I was surprised that it produced such a huge impact."

"Brazil is massive," explained Helena. "You also have to add the other Portuguese-speaking countries. I'm sure you will hit the one-million-follower milestone soon."

"One million?" Estela asked, surprised. "I think that's a little bit unrealistic. Only popular YouTubers reach a million followers, and they post videos daily. I might achieve a quarter of a million subscribers, which is still a lot."

"Read my lips," said Helena while standing up from her chair. She grabbed Estela's shoulders and shook them lightly. "One million. I will only ask you one thing: don't leave me! I need you here! With all that success, we are going to sell magazines like never before!

Estela felt much calmer at work. Meanwhile, at home, Sofia was already walking from one place to another, better each day. It was rare that she ever crawled quickly across the floor anymore. Estela saw the satisfaction her little girl felt while standing "tall" on her feet, so she always encouraged Sofia.

When they went shopping, several people would be surprised when they saw a baby pushing a stroller, instead of being inside of it. However, not all of them saw Sofia's progress positively. One day, an elderly lady got closer to them and asked, "How old is she?"

When Estela answered she had just turned eight months old, the old lady opened her eyes wide, laid her hand on her mouth, and screamed at Estela, "Pure evil! You should be ashamed! She is going to have problems in her legs. Eight months old is no age for a child to walk."

"What should I have done if she started walking when she was seven months old?" asked Estela, slightly annoyed. "Should I lock her legs with plaster?"

On another occasion, a different woman stopped her to ask how old Sofia was.

"Eight months old," answered Estela, expecting another reprimand.

"She is so cute! My son, who is a judge nowadays, started walking when he was nine months old, and I thought it was quite early. But eight months old? She is very gifted! Wait and see."

On a particular Monday morning, in the middle of all the buzz at work, Estela got a phone call from Michael. "Estela, I saw that there is an exhibition about Leonardo da Vinci at Oca, in Ibirapuera Park. I want to invite you to record the next two steps of the sequence, next Saturday morning, and after that, we could see that exhibition. What do you think?"

"I say it is a great idea! I need to take Sofia with me. Is that okay? I'm getting to spend so little time with her, always working late."

"Of course! Bring her too."

After a week full of work at the publisher, the weekend finally came, and with it, Estela's meeting with Michael. At nine o'clock, Saturday morning, Estela and Sofia were already at the Awake Clinic. As always, the Clinic was full of people, and many patients' parents stopped the doctor, greeting him or asking him something regarding the development of their children. Michael answered them happily.

After a few minutes, Michael called Estela with a hand gesture, and they walked together toward the development room. They were in a hurry to start recording as soon as possible. Meanwhile, when they started the video about the seventh step, Sofia, who was in Estela's arms, started crying. She didn't want to eat, didn't need to change her diaper, nor she was feeling too hot. The journalist thought the little girl was just annoyed due to being stuck in that place and tried to calm her, holding her while walking and rocking her. However, she understood that the little girl would not last an entire session without complaining. She had decided to give up recording, when Bruno interceded, saying: "Estela, we have a toy library on this very floor that is always full of young children. There are several instructors and things Sofia could do there. Do you want to see it?"

"Of course! Let's go!"

"I will go with you. Don't worry, Estela! I'm sure she will love it," promised Michael.

The toy library was at the end of the corridor, so they only had to walk a couple of meters before entering a quite cozy room, which was similar to a nursery. There were about ten children having fun in the room, an alligator made of fabric, and several toys all over the place. Three adults were monitoring their children through the glass, from the outside.

"We are going to leave her here a short while," Estela told one of the instructors, handing her Sofia, who was wearing a little red dress and a hair tie in the middle of her dark hair. She gave a white handbag to the other instructor, which contained diapers and a pair of clothes.

"Take good care of her, Bianca," requested Michael. "We will be right there, in the development room."

The three of them returned to the improvised studio, and Estela, as usual, introduced the topic, "Hi, everyone! To continue with the Steps, today, we will talk about the seventh step, which is about grit."

"Grit is the junction of two characteristics we can observe in successful people," proceeded Dr. Jansen, calmly explaining his point of view, "passion for what you do and perseverance not to give up. Being passionate about what you do will work as a map that excites you, thus giving you the necessary strength to keep fighting. Persistency, or perseverance, is about the daily discipline, the consistency of our actions. Those who are tenacious are always focused too. That happens because when you are passionate about something and disciplined enough, you just keep following the right path. That leads you to achieve your goals and maintain a high level of performance over a long period. However, to maintain your performance consistently, it is necessary to stipulate an effort zone, with a specific minimum and maximum. That effort zone can't be placed too high, so that you can achieve that level even on a busy or hard day. Yet it can't be too low either, to make sure you keep working and stay focused."

Estela concluded, "So, children must find which activity they love, their true passion, instead of a fugacious interest. On the other hand, we all need daily challenges and optimism to achieve our pre-established goals."

Forty-five minutes later, they finished the seventh step and decided to visit Sofia. The little girl was distractedly playing with wood cubes and didn't notice them. They felt reassured and returned to the development room to record the eighth step.

After exposing a logical argument about the need for people to learn a second language, Michael concluded by proposing an analysis of the best stage to start learning it. "The sooner[cxcii] we expose a child to a second language, the easier they will learn it," he explained. "Many say the critical period to acquire a new language and to develop it to a native level, without a foreign accent, ends by the age of six or seven. Though other people insist that it stops during puberty, around twelve years old. In my opinion, there is no precise critical period[cxciii]. However, there is no doubt that the sooner one learns a new language, the easier it will be to become proficient at it. On the other hand, we must be careful, so the child doesn't lose the new language. Especially during younger ages, our brain 'trims' the synapses that are not being used. Even though children can learn a second language much faster than adults, the trimming process can erase or inactivate their memory more quickly. Thus, if children learn English as a second language and manage to communicate correctly in English but stop using it around the age of four, when they become fifteen years old, they might need to start all over again."

Oca[cxciv] is a circular, white pavilion, projected by Oscar Niemeyer[cxcv], with an architectural language that is similar to what can be observed in Brasília[cxcvi]. Michael and Estela walked calmly from the clinic to the pavilion's entrance. Sofia, who was exhausted after playing in the toy library, was peacefully sleeping in her stroller.

"It's a pity she got so tired," said Estela while she handed their tickets to reception. "I'm sure she would be happy to visit this wide and beautiful place. It's a shame! She won't have contact with Leonardo da Vinci's genius."

"That's okay. She will have plenty of opportunities,", declared Michael. "I like Leonardo too. He is one of my greatest idols. I read everything I can about him. His biography by Walter Isaacson[cxcvii] is particularly well written and highly detailed."

"I've read it! Well . . . I heard it, on Audible[cxcviii]," commented Estela. "I thought it was extraordinary! Seeing some of his inventions, right here, even if they are just replicas, makes everything I heard in the audiobook even more tangible. Leonardo da Vinci truly was one of the greatest minds who walked the earth."

"Did you ever ask yourself why some people are so good at something that they leave us baffled? Think about Leonardo da Vinci, for example. How could he become excellent in both arts and science?" he asked. When Michael was excited, his mind was an authentic turmoil of information. His motivation was expressed through the way he spoke. "In physics, he described some principles more than a century before Newton. In engineering, Leonardo did sketches of helicopters. In architecture, he built cathedrals. In the military defense field, he invented weapons, cannons, and catapults. How could he do all of those things until he was sixty-seven years old?"

"Well, I'm sure he was born with many talents . . ."

"Do you really believe that?" asked Michael, placing one of his hands on his forehead. "I've been telling you that talent only matters at the beginning of an activity. However, if it is not driven adequately, it can even become prejudicial. Nevertheless, you are telling me that it was Da Vinci's talents that made the difference?"

"Yes! I still think some people are born much more talented than other people, despite you insisting that talent is over-rated."

"The majority of people overrate talent, that's right. Anyway, I think Leonardo da Vinci managed to be an exceptional person who we should honor."

"Don't you think some people are born more talented and intelligent than other people?"

"I do not doubt that there are differences between talents, intelligence, beauty, empathy . . . However, that is not the only reason behind someone becoming a true genius."

"What is the biggest differentiating factor?"

"Should we recapitulate his biography? Leonardo was born as the illegitimate son of a respectable notary, Mr. Piero da Vinci. That was to his favor because bastard children were not allowed to perpetuate their parents' profession. When he was fourteen years old, he became an apprentice of Verrocchio, in Florence. Then, Leonardo, the artist, was shaped, practicing day after day to develop his abilities. His main talent was his constant search for self-improvement, always looking for solutions for problems he faced, observing the world around him to collect principles from what he saw." At this point, a painting got Michael's attention, and he decided to share the pleasure of that contemplation with Estela: "Look, Estela! Here is the replica of the famous painting *The Baptism of Christ*."

Estela turned to see the painting that was placed behind her.

"Did you know that Verrocchio, his master, painted a big part of this painting, while Leonardo only painted the angel on the left?" asked Michael.

"Notice the difference between the two. It seems that no lines were used to draw the angel's contour. Leonardo baptized that technique as *sfumato*."

"I didn't know that," answered Estela, analyzing the painting details. "Leonardo's angel seems to have true hair instead of a wig."

Michael Jansen laughed and then continued.

"After much training, learning about perspective, geometry, and shapes, Leonardo, by the age of twenty, became a better painter than his master Verrocchio. He became a master painter. There are histories about Verrocchio stopping painting once he saw that one of his apprentices became better than him, breaking his brushes in front of everyone at his atelier."

"What about this next portrait?"

"*Ginevra de' Benci*?" The original painting is, nowadays, at the National Gallery of Art, in Washington, DC. Even though it is one of his unfinished works, we can observe the painter's psychology expressed artistically. One of Leonardo's best skills was his ability to observe. He used both the eyes of the scientist and the artist to study nature, men, women, horses, birds. Then he would detail everything in his notebooks."

"Milan," read Estela on a sign above her head.

"In Milan," continued Michael Jansen, "he explored many of his passions and was funded by Ludovico Sforza, the duke of Milan. There, he applied his knowledge about nature, architecture, and engineering. He idealized cities with sewage and clean water and still managed to entertain the Sforza court with his theater plays."

"In other words," completed Estela, "he was a Renaissance Man."

"You know, he never stopped learning. Although he was good in geometry, he lacked the skills in other fields of mathematics. Thus, he got closer to the mathematician Luca Pacioli, who helped him improve his arithmetic skills. He also would enter debates about many fields of knowledge with like-minded friends like Donato Bramante and Francesco di Giorgio, who are renowned architects. The result of the many debates and his obsession regarding the proportions of the human anatomy was this painting here: *The Vitruvian Man.*

Estela observed the yellow and iconic figure, which demonstrated the balance and harmony of the human body's proportions, and she soon noticed that the doctor was standing in front of another piece of artwork.

"This painting here is the *Lady with an Ermine*, which is as beautiful as it is mysterious. If we compare it to *Ginevra de' Benci*, it becomes quite evident that Leonardo had been working on his sfumato technique."

"It is said that Leonardo loved animals," said Estela, looking at the ermine, which despite being strange to her, reminded her of a rodent. "He would free caged birds, and he became a vegetarian to avoid imposing any more suffering upon them."

"And it is true," said Dr. Jansen, who was already walking toward a big painting, about nine meters wide and four foot five inches tall. "Here is *The Last Supper*, a fresco painted by Leonardo for the refectory of the Santa Maria delle Grazie church, in Milan. Look at it carefully. Leonardo shows all of his observation power. Besides mixing his knowledge about optics, perspective, and human psychology in the composition of the painting, the painter also attempts to reproduce the moment when Jesus announced his apostles that someone had betrayed him, dramatizing the emotions each of them felt."

"Magnificent!" exclaimed Estela.

"Let's stop for a little while before continuing. In this exhibition, we saw the change that occurred over the years, in Leonardo da Vinci's artistical expression. Thus, I can say that his 'talent' did not appear from one day to another. He was not born ready and done. His success was the sum of small efforts, repeated day after day. Do you agree?"

"I'm almost convinced," she answered.

"The same applies to all of us: if we keep working toward learning and improving ourselves, we will become better people. What we saw today is the joint work of motivation, compromise, discipline, patience, and self-control. When we see someone who truly is exceptional, whose skills are unattainable for common people, that's not about magic ... That's the product of effort and training over the years."

The journalist asked, "What about Mozart? Was he born a prodigy?"

"The same formula applies to Mozart. Who was he? He was the son of Leopold Mozart, a not-so-bright musician who decided to inflict all of his frustrations upon his children. Leopold was one of the first music teachers who had the idea of starting to teach children as soon as possible. He even wrote a book about it. He started teaching his doctrine to Maria Anna, his elder daughter; however, it was with Wolfgang that he insisted the most, seeing that he could go further than any of his children."

"Yet people often say that Wolfgang Amadeus Mozart had absolute pitch, which only happens with 0.01 percent of the population..."

"Let's go slowly, Estela. Think with me. Could the first exposition to music, through his father, mother, and sister, and the access to several instruments and sounds in his home help him achieve above-average hearing skills?"

"Of course."

"That's what people define as *absolute pitch*. That's a skill that can be learned if we start working on it from an early age. I'm going to mention a study developed by Sakakibara[cxcix] so you can see how everything is about learning and working hard. That researcher developed an experiment involving twenty-four children ages two to six who were previously tested and did not have absolute pitch. During a year, they followed a training method she called *string identification*. Out of a total of twenty-four children, twenty-two managed to develop perfect pitch, which means only two children were not able to acquire that virtue as a result of having stopped with their training.

This means Sakakibara managed to practice those children's ears. That is a very relevant fact since absolute pitch is only identified in one in every ten thousand people. With training, that index became higher than 90 percent. So, in the case of Mozart, the early exposition to music certainly made all the difference. Furthermore, he also had his father as his mentor. Being exposed to different things and situations was also an essential aspect of Leonardo da Vinci's genius. He was the first great Renaissance Man who had access to printed books because Gutenberg invented the printing press[cc] about the time he was born..."

"Interesting," she commented. "We must raise our children by exposing them to experiences that might allow them to find their passions. That's why you insist on the importance of playing, sports, and acquiring a second language. Without access to those aspects, improving your skills will be difficult."

"Correct!" celebrated Dr. Jansen. "We are all born with a flexible brain, with the potential to become geniuses. That doesn't happen only when we are born. Our brain preserves a certain degree of flexibility and plasticity until the end. For us to achieve excellence, we need not only opportunities, exposition, diversity, and motivation but also persistence, hard work, and everything else we mentioned while talking about grit before. However, we must make sure our persistence is not pointless and aimless. We must guide it with training. We also need to add several other factors to become an above-average person like Leonardo. Correct practice leads to excellence. In other words, we become the product of our hard work. Anders Ericsson, the greatest expert in the fields of expertise and human performance, created a concept he called *deliberate practice*[cci]. He believes ingeniousness doesn't come by birth or chance. Instead, it is the fruit of years of intense practice and dedicated guidance."

"Like Verrocchio and Leonardo da Vinci."

"Of course! Training modifies the brain, strengthens synapses, and creates new neurons. The gift that follows those experts, those geniuses, is not related to being born gifted but about making use of the brain's flexibility to shape it according to their will through training. They knew how to take advantage of their natural characteristics like few others. This means they were not awarded in the genetic lottery: they fought for everything they achieved."

"Now, I can completely agree with you when you say talent is overrated."

"Good. Well, saying that Leonardo was born with multiple talents is the same as stealing all the merit for his effort, denying all the daily sweat and hard work, his observations, his continuous training. He worked hard to achieve what he achieved. When you look at a work like this," Dr. Jansen said, pointing at *The Last Supper*, "you can't forget all the dedication and effort that were necessary to create it. Remember, Leonardo was an apprentice, he became an expert, and he never stopped working on himself, observing the world around him and trying to identify the essence of things."

"To see the man behind the artwork?" asked Estela, looking again to all the paintings around her.

"Yes. To see that we can always improve our abilities in any field we choose. However, we must be passionate about it. Leonardo was passionate about nature; he had a wide range of interests and an insatiable curiosity. Those who think abilities are rigid are wrong. Abilities are like balloons, and the more we inflate them, the more they expand. The best thing is that, in many fields, the limits are not known yet. Every year we hear about new records, findings, and creations and news about several knowledge fields. Therefore, it is important to know this ninth step and to guide our practice to achieve excellence."

"So, it's not just about practicing, practicing, and practicing? Desire and hard work. Or, like Nike advertises: 'Just doing it?'"

"No, you have to work hard, and you have to practice correctly, through deliberate practice. It will take time, normally years or decades, but that's the only way you will be able to become the best in your field, a genius like Leonardo da Vinci."

"Ten thousand hours," concluded Estela.

"Actually, there's no magic number," protested Michael Jansen. "Malcolm Gladwell said that number in his book, called *Outliers*[ccii], because it is a round figure, easy to memorize, and big enough to transmit a good notion of how much a person must dedicate herself, the many hours of one's life that are necessary to achieve excellence on a world level. However, some fields require less than that, like two thousand or three thousand hours. Others require twenty thousand or more hours. It depends on the person we are considering and the area of action. If you practice correctly, after two hundred hours of deliberate practice, you won't look like an amateur anymore. But to become a real expert, you have to improve your training technique, find the best coach, and dedicate many more hours. Only then will you have the chance to compete as an equal with the best experts of a field."

"How can I give my daughter a competitive margin in a field that she chooses?"

"Anders Ericsson found the principles of deliberate practice by studying the best experts in several fields. If we follow those principles, we can help Sofia become the best in a field she enjoys."

"What are the principles?" asked Estela, quite interested.

Dr. Jansen was suddenly silent, placed a hand on his chin, and asked Estela, "How do we learn a new skill? For example, you decide you are going to learn how to skate. You buy the equipment, choose the clothes, learn the basics on your own or by asking a friend who is good at skating for help. You fall, you stand up . . . you fall, you stand up . . . and gradually you have practiced enough that you feel skilled at sliding using those little wheels. Suddenly, skating becomes an automatic action, allowing you to exercise in Ibirapuera Park every Sunday, wearing sports clothes and with your headphones on. Correct?"

"Correct."

"Years later, after skating for three hours every Sunday, you are now watching the Pan-American Games on TV, and you come across quick and exceptionally skillful skaters. My question is, would you be able to skate as well as they do? Could you perform the same stunts, pirouettes, and reach the same speed they did?"

"In theory, yes, but probably not."

"Why not? I can assure you that it is because you are not practicing the right way. When you felt satisfied with your performance while skating, when you stopped falling so frequently, you also stopped training, you were not interested in improving yourself any longer. Suddenly, you were just repeating the things you already learned. Thus, even if you skated three hours a day every day, you wouldn't achieve the same performance level as the athletes in the Pan-American Games. Those additional hours wouldn't count as practice because they became automatic. At that point you no longer need to think about skating. The same happens when we learn how to drive. After a few hours of practice, driving becomes automatic for us. You no longer think about if you should shift up, accelerate, or stop. Meanwhile, if you want to improve your driving skills even further, in order to become an F1 driver, for example, you need to go beyond your own limits."

"Go beyond your limits," Estela repeated the concept.

"During deliberate practice, you need a long-term goal and to strive toward it. In the example that I mentioned before, if you saw the skaters on TV and thought, 'This is my calling, I want to participate in the Pan-American games too,' you would behave differently. You would define specific plans, like beating your best time in x seconds or learning how to perform a different stunt. You would look at your performance from a different perspective and think about the aspects you could improve and how to improve them."

She commented, "There's no use for generic plans."

"That's right. You need a specific plan. Deliberate practice is focused on the things you want to improve. It's intentional! Deliberate practice involves feedback. So it is fundamental to have a mentor. You need to know which things you are doing right and which ones you are not. That knowledge will allow you to improve yourself by specifically training to correct the aspects you are not mastering."

"The goal of feedback is to lead you to understand the things you are doing wrong so you can fix them."

"Exactly! Without that process, there is no improvement. Deliberate practice takes us out of our comfort zone, allowing us to see our mistakes so we can fix them. Not to mention the countless hours you need to spend training, which looks like an infinite process. You need to work hard to grow, and often, practicing becomes painful. That might be the reason not very many people become exceptional. Since they feel they are good enough at doing something, they stagnate, weigh the pros and cons, and quit."

"The good is the enemy of the great."

The doctor added, "If people don't try to overcome their limits, to go beyond their achievements, they start repeating the same actions, failing in the same points, always avoiding the process of improving themselves and fixing their mistakes. Meanwhile, if they focus on improving their mistakes, they can raise their level a little bit. That way, little by little, they become above average."

Dr. Jansen and Estela noticed that many other people were behind them in the pavilion because they were obstructing their passage, standing in the way.

"Let's go!" said Dr. Jansen, making a gesture with his hand.

Estela restarted pushing the stroller with Sofia in it, and together they walked until they reached one of the exhibition wards that had a sign saying Borgia.

Estela and Dr. Jansen observed the scale models based on the drawings. There were cannons, weapons like a crossbow, machine guns, war tanks, and catapults.

"In 1499 the French troops occupied Milan, and Leonardo was protected by Cesare Borgia. He met Niccolò Machiavelli, the author of *The Prince*, and traveled through Italy, which was damaged by several wars, to recommend the best way of building a bridge, a fortress, or even weaponry. That way, he achieved one of his dreams: to become a military engineer."

"That's interesting!" Estela was thrilled.

"Look at this map, of the city of Ímola, from 1502. Imagine Leonardo's great sense of proportion. Imagine his cartographic techniques. Try to visualize how he drew the territory, the houses, the valley, and the river to scale and with such accuracy. It's impressive! Without using drones or satellites, only relying on the power of his brain. Imagine the years of practice and his sharp observation skills. Pay attention to his artwork, and you will see that he never allowed himself to stay in a comfort zone, always attempting to do new things. He wouldn't stop a moment, always trying to further his knowledge. Therefore, he would study obsessively, was resilient, and acted as one can conclude from one of his famous quotes: "I have been impressed with the urgency of doing. Knowing is not enough; we must apply. Being willing is not enough; we must do."

"And he did so many things!"

"He was amazing! Let me quote him once more: 'He who loves practice without theory is like the sailor who boards a ship without a rudder and compass and never knows where he may cast. In other words, you must practice the right way! Working hard outside our comfort zone is not enough; we must also define clear goals, with a plan that allows measuring progress. Naturally, we must keep our motivation high because we only genuinely lose when we give up. It is the commitment, pushing ourselves beyond our current skills, that modifies our brain," concluded Michael. "Have you ever been to London?"

"London?" Estela asked, feeling surprised and looking at the map of Ímola. "Never. Why?"

"London's streets are like a labyrinth, and the taxi drivers in London are very skilled. For you to become a taxi driver, you must pass a tough test, which requires years of theoretical and practical knowledge. Therefore, Maguire[cciii] and his peers decided to develop a study based on London taxi drivers. After analyzing the data carefully, they noticed that after years of practice, the posterior part of their hippocampus increased in size, which didn't happen in the control group, which was composed by those who did not pass the test or by bus drivers who always followed predetermined routes."

"So only the taxi drivers who made an effort to transport their clients as quickly as possible from point A to point B showed those brain modifications?"

"Yes. The same happens with skating. Those who only play have a different brain than those who can perform stunts and who practice winning a competition. In order for the modifications to keep happening, you must raise the bar, make it a little bit more difficult, or to put it better, you must always stay a little bit outside your comfort zone, pushing your brain and body further to adapt to a new homeostasis. Nowadays, we know that children's and teenager's brains are more susceptible to being shaped by training, allowing even more significant changes. Thus, Leopold, Mozart's father, was right about his theory, and that's how he created a genius like Wolfgang."

"That means that if we stay in our comfort zone, we won't become extraordinary."

"It's unlikely. It's not about an innate lack of skills but rather about feeling happy and satisfied with our current level. As I said, practicing the right way requires dedication. There are not many people who want to dedicate themselves thousands of hours to become the best in the world in a given field. However, it's important to make it clear that this is a real option. If children want to become as skillful as Leonardo or Mozart, they must understand that there's the need to work as hard as they did."

"There are no shortcuts, are there?"

"No, there are no shortcuts. Thus, it's important to keep someone qualified close to us!" Dr. Jansen said vehemently. "We can learn from the experience of other people. We need accurate feedback. We must know when we are wrong so we can fix it. We need to sharpen our skills to improve ourselves continuously. Bringing each move, each act closer to perfection.

Sometimes, it is even necessary to change our coach to learn something new, as many professional athletes do."

"How do you find the right coach? Is there any criteria?"

"It depends on the stage in which a child is. The best teacher during a very early stage is he who introduces a topic in the most pleasant manner possible. That piano teacher, who, for example, always gives candy to her students, who is cheerful, who interacts with each child, and who, despite her love for music, might not be the biggest expert. During that stage, that teacher will help keep the apprentice's interest, sharing her enthusiasm and love for music. That teacher will motivate students, allowing the passion to grow inside them."

"During that stage, learning must be a playful process," highlighted Estela.

"In the second stage, the typically nice and cheerful teacher might not be the ideal solution. There is a need for a more energetic training method, and it is necessary to fix posture and to teach students how to read music. So, the second coach must be a little bit more rigid regarding demanding the student to commit to the activity. Furthermore, this teacher must also be an expert on the topic to provide children with the necessary support for them to acquire the desired competency."

"I remember some teachers that belonged to that group," she observed. "Some were quite meaningful in my life."

"I think we all had a teacher or coach who had a positive impact on our lives. At the third stage, the child can overcome the master. During this stage, there is the need to find an extremely skillful coach or teacher, the best ones in the field, so students can aim toward higher levels, higher than their master ever achieved."

"What if you don't have enough money to hire a coach?"

"You can try to improve your technique using the internet. It is not an ideal solution because you need to know where you are failing to improve your performance, but it's better than nothing. In such cases, there is the need for a sharp critical sense so you can analyze yourself, identify your mistakes, and progress as if someone else were telling you them. You need to identify your weaknesses and practice until you minimize them."

"What about when the process of improving ourselves stops?"

"Normally, it means you are not acquiring new skills. When you learn a different activity, like skating, initially, your progress is quite quick. However, eventually, you will hit an obstacle and reach a plateau. Wrongly, many people think that happens because they reached the limit of their potential, and then, they accept it as a fact."

That's when we stop improving ourselves."

"Exactly. Thus, we should not accept that plateau as our limit. Instead, we should challenge our body and mind to overcome it. Otherwise, that specific barrier will prevent our progress. When we break a barrier, we feel proud, and that encourages us to go further, making us believe that we can be successful. In his book called *Peak*[cciv], Anders Ericsson tells a story about Steve Faloon, a psychology student he recruited to perform some tests about the limit of short-term memory. It is worth mentioning that Steve was an athlete too. On the first days of the trial, Steve's results were average: he could memorize seven to eight digits which were dictated by the researchers a second apart; for example, 5 ... 6 ... 8 ... 4 ... 6 ... 0 ... 1 ... 3 ... Back then, there were stories about people who practiced until they could memorize fifteen digits. With tests and tenacity, always attempting to find new memory techniques, Steve managed to memorize ten digits, which, apparently, was his plateau. However, after sixty sessions, Steve achieved twenty digits, a level that was comparable to the world record. Several plateaus after, precisely two years after the beginning of the experiment, Steve Faloon managed to memorize eighty-two random digits, which is many times more than his initial seven or eight numbers."

"Impressive!"

"So I must stress that we can't see our first plateau as our limit. No! We need to do something different. We must use our brain or body to overcome any obstacle." Dr. Jansen pointed to some paintings ahead of them and said, "Should we proceed? Leonardo got tired from all the war and the atrocities Cesare Borgia committed and returned to Florence, where Michelangelo had already become the new city star. The two artists were not comfortable with the presence of each other, and Leonardo da Vinci left this fresco, of the Battle of Anghiari, which he was painting at Pallazo Vecchio, incomplete. That artwork doesn't exist anymore; it was covered with a mural by Vasari."

"What a crime," said Estela, looking to the horses and soldiers that were fighting.

Dr. Jansen kept walking until Estela, who had stopped, asked him, "What about the human body replicas?" she said, looking inside glass showcases with skulls and illustrations from Leonardo's notebooks.

"Oh, right! Once he left Florence, he went to Pavia to dissect bodies and to study anatomy, always aiming at improving his drawing skills even further. It was during that time that Leonardo dissected the corpse of a centenarian and identified, for the first time in history, the process of atherosclerosis, which is the narrowing of the human blood vessels due to high cholesterol and calcium."

"What about this heart made of glass?" questioned the journalist.

"His studies were based on hypotheses and tests, just like modern science. Here, he represented the heart and the circulatory system. More than a century before William Harvey, Leonardo correctly threw light upon a mystery, when he described the role of the heart as working as a pump that made the blood circulate through the blood vessels. He filled the heart of a corpse with wax and created a cast of the heart that allowed him to observe the movements of the fluids internally."

"Fantastic!"

They walked a little longer and passed by a scale model which was nearly one-meter-tall and represented da Vinci's helicopter. There was a sign next to it, reading, Aerial Helical

Screw—1493."

"In 1507, Leonardo returned to Milan and dedicated himself to studying the air, water, and geology, observing birds and fishes, and improving his conceptions regarding flying machines. Afterward, he passed by Rome quickly and, finally, went to France, under the patronage of King Francisco I. A few years later, he had a stroke that left him partially paralyzed. Nevertheless, he managed to complete some of his most famous artworks, which are now represented there and can be seen at the Louvre Museum: *Saint John the Baptist*, *The Virgin and Child with Saint Anne*," and, lastly, *Mona Lisa*.

The three of them walked past the paintings, mesmerized by the artworks of the great master, while *La Gioconda* mysteriously smiled at them.

They left the place in silence.

Only when they exited the museum, did the doctor say: "Leonardo didn't want fame or glory, but he was moved by a great curiosity about the world and representing it faithfully. In 1519, a few days after turning sixty-seven years old, he died. However, his genius was immortalized in his body of work."

Estela nodded her head, agreeing with Michael. Afterward, she said: "Thank you for this great class about history and neuroscience. To tell the truth, I could never find a better teacher or mentor than mine. I'm fortunate to have met you. I know you don't appreciate being complimented this way, but I have to tell you that you are an exceptional, unique person, Michael."

She kissed him on the cheek, and the doctor blushed lightly.

"There are only two steps left now," commented Dr. Jansen.

"What a pity! I'm having so much fun!"

CHAPTER 13 — THE ELEVENTH STEP: VALUES

*"We live in an age when unnecessary things
are our only necessities."*

—Oscar Wilde

U sually, after snack time, Andrea would sit on the living room sofa, place Sofia on her lap, and show her the little words on the television. During one of those moments, when the little girl was about ten months old, Andrea heard a low sound: Sofia's voice, saying, "Foot!"

The nanny was impressed. She looked down, trying to see if Sofia would move her lips to read the next word, but nothing happened. Instead of enunciating the words that appeared on the screen, Andrea remained silent, staring at the little girl because she wanted to make sure Sofia had read for the first time.

She thought to herself that it was all a mere product of her imagination. She laughed at Sofia fondly and continued with the reading activity.

At the end of the session, Andrea was still doubting if she had heard Sofia pronouncing the word "foot," thus she went to the office. In the room, there was a little corner covered with EVA mats, where Andrea left the little girl sitting next to several children's books.

With excitement, she opened and closed the drawers of some shelves until she found a ream of paper and a red marker. She took two paper sheets and wrote the word *foot* on one of them and *hand* on another one.

"What did I write here, my little princess?" the nanny leaned down and showed the first word she had written. "You can tell me. I know you can."

"Foot!" answered Sofia, touching in one of her little shoes.

Andrea was awestruck. She had never seen a baby reading. She sighed deeply before saying: "Really? Are you reading already? I'm so proud of you!"

Afterward, she placed the two paper sheets on the floor, a little ways away from the little girl, and said, "Pick up the word *foot* for me."

Sofia stood up and calmly walked to the paper sheets, bent her little knees, picked up the word *foot*, and handed it to Andrea. She stared at her nanny and smiled, exposing her four front teeth.

Andrea was initially paralyzed but managed to react to the momentary numbness, ran to the living room to find her purse, and immediately returned to the office. Clumsily, she scavenged the bottom of her bag, searching for her mobile phone. When she finally found it, she took a deep breath and called Estela.

"Did something happen?" The voice of the journalist sounded slightly alarmed when she answered the phone.

"You are not going to believe me, Estela. Sofia read! She read!"

Estela inhaled relieved and said, "Calm down, Andrea. Tell me everything!"

"I'm going to call you on FaceTime to show you. It's unusual!

She is only ten months old! Ten months!"

Estela's face appeared on Andrea's mobile phone screen.

"Tell me, little princess, what is written here?" the nanny asked the little girl.

Andrea shook the paper sheet again to get Sofia's attention. She was quick to answer, "Foot! Foot! Foot!"

Estela was thrilled to see her baby girl had acquired another skill. She congratulated Andrea for her dedication and care.

A few hours later, when entering the apartment, Estela noticed the excitement of her mother-in-law and Victor, who were sitting on a fluffy mat in the middle of the living room playing with the baby.

"Estela! Estela!" her mother-in-law called loudly. "Your method really works! My sweetheart can already read the words *foot*, *daddy*, and *mommy*. I always thought it was a waste of time, all those reading exercises. I never imagined that babies could read. Now I must admit it. You were right the whole time. Imagine what my friends will say when I tell them that my granddaughter, who is not even one-year-old, is already reading. I'm sure they will think I'm lying!"

"You better not say it, Sílvia," advised Estela, kissing her husband and then her daughter.

"Jinx!" Sílvia nodded, pointing the finger at her daughter-in-law. "True, best not to talk. Jinx is terrible. The granddaughter of Inês is almost two years old and can't even walk!"

"If your friend's granddaughter spends a lot of time on her lap and is not stimulated often, she will take longer to start walking. That's it. There is nothing wrong with her."

"Oh! Well, I think there is something wrong," ensured her mother-in-law. The little girl is too quiet if you ask me. I don't think she's normal."

"That's probably just your imagination. Anyway, you can tell Inês to take her to Awake Clinic. Once there, Dr. Jansen and his team will assess her."

"Speaking of Dr. Jansen," said Victor, standing up. "Did he answer? When are you going to record the next videos? People are demanding them!"

"Not yet, but I can understand why. There are so many people trying to speak with him, and he also needs to manage the clinic, take care of his clients and his personal life . . . And he still finds the time to do us this favor."

"What do you think about calling him right now?" suggested Victor, winking. "You tell him that Sofia read her first words and then say something about the videos. I don't think it will be too invasive or a hassle."

Estela checked her wristwatch and said, "Eight o'clock . . . Well, it's not too late yet."

She got her cellphone, looked for Dr. Jansen's number, and called right away.

The deep and warm voice of the doctor answered on the other end of the line. "Good night, Estela! I'm sorry for not being able to find enough time to record the next steps. I've rechecked my schedule, and don't have any free time until next Saturday. However, I was thinking, are you free on Sunday, early morning?"

"Yes, I'm free. Why?"

"We could talk about the eleventh step for your blog. What do you think? Is it a good idea?"

"Of course! I would love to! I was calling you today because I wanted to ask you about the next recording day, but I have news for you too. Sofia is already reading little words! Your app works!"

"Oh! That's wonderful! I knew it wouldn't take long. However, don't test her, okay? Testing tends to make children feel stressed. You don't want to increase her anxiety, right? Remember, you must be loving and compassionate. The most important thing is that you keep communicating with her all the time."

"Oh, yes! Don't worry. We are not testing her," said Estela, looking at the mountain of paper sheets spread all over the carpet with words from *tooth* to *whale*. "It was spontaneous."

"Excellent! Over time, you will notice she has learned many

other new words. You don't need to test her. She will show it naturally. About Sunday, are you vaccinated against yellow fever?"

"Yes, I am. Why?"

"I was thinking about it, and maybe we could meet at the State Park of Cantareira, at eight in the morning, which is when it opens for visitors. Do you know where the Park is?"

"No. It would be an excellent opportunity to get to know it."

"I must warn you not to bring Sofia this time because of the mosquitos and the climb, which might tire her. If you don't want to leave her with Victor, we can schedule our meeting for another place and time . . ."

"No problem, I can go alone. Victor will stay with her. Normally, he has the weekend free to dedicate even more time to our daughter and us."

"Excellent. See you Sunday at eight o'clock."

It was still dark when Estela woke up that Sunday. She saw the sunrise on her terrace while she drank her morning coffee.

After traveling for forty-five minutes, she reached her destination: the State Park of Cantareira[ccv]. She saw Dr. Jansen stretching in front of his car.

"It's a beautiful day, isn't it, Doctor?" asked Estela, hugging him.

"This wonderful blue sky makes us feel energized. We arrived early, the best time of the day to enjoy the park. Have you never been here before? It's one of the biggest native urban forests on the planet, a stronghold of the Atlantic Forest, quite close to us."

"I don't know why you brought me here, but I'm eager to visit it."

"You are going to understand soon. The eleventh step is completely related to the environment. It's about teaching values to our children, instructing them to save our resources, whether they are financial or natural. Currently, we live in a world where everything is disposable. Relationships are disposable, the things we buy are disposable, and if you want to play with the idea, you could also say that even human life is disposable."

With slow steps, they started walking to the park entrance. Estela knew the doctor didn't like to waste time, so she listened carefully to what he said.

"We have many options. Everything is too easy. As a consequence, we don't value the things that matter. That mentality needs to change. The purpose of the Steps is not only to stimulate people to become more skillful and useful for the world, but also to give them wisdom. The goal of this step is to teach our children to build a conscience that values social well-being. Our current problems are also theirs. Like Abraham Lincoln said, "You cannot escape the responsibility of tomorrow by evading it today."

"Are you talking about global warmth, deforestation, and pollution?"

"Yes, that too," said Dr. Jansen, raising his chin. "Look, over there, Estela! They are opening the park."

They walked to the ticket office, paid for the passes, and went through the green spinning gate, before stopping near the park map, where Dr. Jansen identified the itinerary they were going to follow. "We are going here, Pedra Grande[ccvii]," said Michael, indicating the route with his long finger. "It's one of the most beautiful views in the city and is less than five kilometers away."

"And five kilometers back… No problem, let's go!" answered Estela, putting her tennis shoes to work.

The path was paved and surrounded by wild plants of several sizes and shapes, which blocked the sun's rays, resulting in a fresh, moist environment and leaving the air impregnated with the unique scent of the forest.

Estela filled her lungs and said, "I love the smell of pure air."

The doctor said, "I try to visit Cantareira every two weeks. In Japanese, it's called 'Shinrinyoku,' meaning a short and pleasurable walk in the forest, which in practice has an effect similar to natural aromatherapy. That happens due to the trees, which exhale phytoncides[ccvii], which help to regulate stress, reduce the risk of depression, and strengthen the immune system, increasing the natural killers, which are essential cells in fighting cancers."

"Interesting. I always knew that walking through a forest would produce a helpful effect; I just didn't know exactly what it was."

"In my opinion, nature is the source of so much knowledge. Like Leonardo da Vinci, I love observing it. Nowadays, children have little contact with trees, the soil . . . It's a pity because they too could feel the amazement of being surrounded by a wonderful landscape like this."

"Yes, society is different," agreed Estela. "Besides one's relationship with nature, values are important too, like you said. There is a lack of respect for the knowledge gained by those who have dedicated years of study to a determined field. Everyone thinks they are an expert. They ask themselves, 'Why does an expert's opinion matter more than mine?' They choose to base their knowledge on common sense and the media, to the detriment of the opinions of professionals who are quite qualified in their fields."

"Technology gives us the wrong idea that we can acquire high-quality information with little effort," argued Dr. Jansen. "While surfing the internet, nobody thinks they need those thousand hours to become an expert, to internalize a skill and become proficient in it. People seem to think that at the snap of a finger, anyone can become an expert, just by watching a YouTube video. Sweating, reading countless books . . . What's all that for?"

"I agree with you," commented Estela.

"Thus, we have the obligation of transmitting values to our children."

"How do children learn values?" asked Estela.

"Through a process similar to any other related to acquiring knowledge. In other words, by observing and mimicking other people's actions, reading, studying theories, and practicing. In the case of children, parents are the main educators. It's not enough to propose positive actions if they do the opposite."

"And there are also friends, who influence each other significantly," Estela added. "She will see herself in her friends too."

"Without a doubt, friendships influence the learning processes of our children. Especially when the subject is about values, so I insist that we must identify which are healthy relationships and which ones are not. To do so, it's important to strengthen the bonds between parents and children. Parents must also be friends, guardians, advisors. Many studies indicate that the stronger a relationship between parents and their children, the more likely those children are to follow the values their parents transmitted to them."

"I agree with the data from that research."

"Me too. That's why my proposal for this step is marked by the idea that not only must we understand our values, but we must also be aware that they influence our children's, in one way or another. We need to show them that the values that guided our life are relevant in their world. For example, they must be honest, which is an implicit idea since they would get away from false people to avoid condoning dishonesty and corruption. They must respect their peers because they would not like to be disrespected. We can explain our values by talking with them about everyday life, instead of looking for a specific moment to talk about it. Once our children grow older, we can start working on more general questions, such as, 'Why should we be generous?' 'What are our obligations toward those who are less fortunate than us?' or even, 'What is the right thing to do in this situation?' We must explain the reason behind the way we behave."

"I understand," said Estela, under her breath, trying her best to keep up with the doctor's pace.

"We, as parents, must teach our children the values we consider important. It's our duty. We can't let media or friends take that role from us. I was born in a post-war period; I wore old clothes my cousins gave me, and my mother cut my hair. We didn't waste anything in my home. Each child had the right to half a steak, three times a week. That happened because my parents were part of the lower middle class, and they felt the heavy hand of scarcity. Everything mattered, every penny was saved on glass jars in the kitchen. The current generation was born with many comforts and luxuries. They ask for designer clothing, know a lot about their rights and little about their duties. Like we said previously, they don't respect their elders' experience and knowledge, not even their parents' or grandparents'."

"They question, disobey, lie, scream, and talk to their parents anyway they want," said Estela. "I see a generation of spoiled kids, who are on the decline. Isn't there anything we can do about it?"

"Yes, there is, Estela!" answered Dr. Jansen, slightly smiling. "We must acknowledge that there are many common characteristics across this 'spoiled' generation. First of all, they don't do domestic chores. For example, they don't do the dishes, don't make their beds, don't clean the house, and don't even take out the trash. Second, they have a lack of rules, or the rules are not very clear at home. Third, they have an excess of material goods, like toys and clothes, which parents work hard to buy. Most of the time, this is because their parents didn't have the chance to have those material goods."

"What do you suggest?" asked Estela, listening carefully.

"Sometimes, the simpler things can make a difference. Making your bed every day is one of them. American Admiral William H. McRaven, who is now retired, argues that if you want to change the world, you can start by making your bed[ccviii]. In his book, he says that SEALs, which are an elite group of the North American Navy, learn how to make their bed correctly as a part of their basic training. If on any given day they forget to make their bed, they will be punished with what they call a 'sugar cookie,' which means they have to jump into the Pacific Ocean and then roll on the hot beach sand. To become a SEAL, you must make your bed every day, no matter what."

"Why does something so ordinary seem so important to

them?"

"It's simple. Making your bed every day, right after waking up, is what we call a small victory. In other words, performing a daily task every day is the trigger for perform a second task, a slightly harder one. Furthermore, making your bed can work as a house rule. With that simple action, children are a few steps further from becoming pampered."

"You're right, I must make my own bed before asking Sofia to make hers," concluded Estela with a forced laugh.

"That's obvious," highlighted Dr. Jansen. "Another strategy that can work well with children is educating them regarding finances. When children are instructed to use money correctly, they learn how to save money and acquire positive character- istics, like patience, moderation, and parsimony. Parents must show children their bills so children start learning how much things cost and that the air-conditioner and the water in the shower are not free. Giving children an allowance is also an excellent way to teach them how to spend their own money wisely. This shows children that money is not infinite and that they will only get more money each pay day. So, they start to think twice before spending too much. It's also important to stress that we must not associate the allowance with domestic chores. Children must understand that domestic chores are part of their responsibility and not a way of getting money. Allow- ance must be detached, and children should be able to spend it as they want."

"What if parents are wealthy? How can such parents avoid raising children that don't care about money? Do you think giv- ing allowance will work for them as well?"

"We can mimic Warren Buffett," suggested Dr. Jansen.

"The billionaire? The same Warren Buffett who was once the richest man in the entire world?"

"Yes, precisely," answered the doctor. "Warren Buffett has lived in the same higher-middle-class house since 1958. Ac- cording to him, his house was one of the best investments he made. It has five bedrooms and three bathrooms. Nowadays, his fortune is estimated at $83 billion. His daughter, Susan Buffett, only found out that her father was rich through the *Wall Street Journal*, which published a story about him when she was more than twenty-two years old. Imagine, a multimillionaire father managed to hide his richness from his children. Not only did he hide it, but he also was able to share the values he found mattered the most."

"How did he do it?" asked Estela.

"By not squandering his money and acting correctly, which was also the key to his success. During those days, he was not famous. He would leave his house every day, early in the morning, and go to work, and he would only return at the beginning of the evening, to have dinner at home. After getting home, interacted with his family, and before going to sleep, he read a lot. His routine was similar to the routines of the parents of his daughter's friends. In other words, his lifestyle was like anyone else's. Because of this, Susan learned how to manage money without excesses. She internalized values related to work ethic, frugality, coherence, and philanthropy. Warren Buffett is a great role model for those who think that money in the bank allows them to underestimate other people—which happens in cases of people whose money is not more than a grain of sand when compared to Warren Buffett's fortune."

Michael's passion for the topic worked as fuel. Although he was walking at a pace that Estela considered intense, he could still manage to talk without showing any signs of tiredness. The doctor kept the same rhythm during the entire walk until they reached the core of Pedra Grande.

The view, however, managed to interrupt him while they enjoyed the fantastic scenery over the Atlantic Forest belt and the thousands of buildings in the concrete jungle that was São Paulo. Far away, they could see the Sea Mountains.

"Awesome!" exclaimed Estela, raising her arms at the top of the massive granite block. "It was worth all the effort to get here. What a fabulous view."

Dr. Jansen got closer to Estela and pointed to the trees below, saying, "Cantareira is responsible for nearly 45 percent of the water that comes out of the taps in São Paulo. We need this forest more than people imagine. I brought you here to talk about important values that we must transmit to our children: respect, honesty, justice, gratitude, generosity, compassion, humbleness, responsibility, and, a very special one, preservation. We must try to change this current conception that everything is disposable. We are facing one of the biggest challenges this planet has ever seen, which is the climatic change that results from pollution and the excessive use of natural resources. We can't delay it any longer; we must act now."

"Can we change that?" asked Estela, raising one eyebrow.

"Yes, considering how quickly technology has been developing during recent decades and if we transform what we usually do, I'm sure we can. I don't see the future as tragic as newspapers and magazines used to describe it a few years ago. They shared a pessimistic vision that didn't help at all. Instead, such a vision paralyzed people."

"If we have no chance, why should we try?" summarized Estela.

"Of course! That conception is freezing. Meanwhile, many scientists today believe that we have alternatives. Negative psychological barriers are being overcome every day by ideas and projects about preservation. However, the academic world can't be the only ones responsible for producing this change, nor can any country alone. We must think about acquiring a planetary conscience to avoid global warming."

Suddenly, Michael stopped talking. Estela looked at him, reading each detail of his facial expressions, and realized that he was looking for the best words to talk about a crucial matter.

"There are state policies that could be very valuable if adopted as a set. I think all the countries should surcharge the excess of carbon and cheapen green energy sources, such as solar energy and wind power. However, they must ally those policies with tax incentives for those who adopt better energy sources. With such policies, we could stop and divert the disaster that is still to come. Naturally, we must not forget that the poorer countries are the ones that need more energy to grow. It's worth mentioning that Pope Francisco insinuated that we humans are responsible for climate change. Thus, we are morally and ethically obliged to prevent it from happening. That conception is marked by the fact that the consequences of global warming are more intense in the countries where the poorest people are already facing hunger and thirst."

"I vividly remember the water crisis that happened in São Paulo from 2014 to 2016[ccix]. It was terrible! The biggest city in the country had no water! Those who had a water tank didn't feel it as much as most people. In the outskirts of the city, the water shortage was a severe problem. Back then, I thought that the levels of the city water reserves would never return to normal."

"And you don't think it will happen again?" asked Dr. Jansen, frowning slightly. "Unfortunately, that event will become increasingly more frequent if we don't take efficient measures regarding preservation. In the United States, hurricanes, which used to happen only 'once in a lifetime,' now return every two years. If we close our eyes to avoid seeing the reality we are facing, and by thinking that the record negative temperatures that hit Chicago in 2019 are proof that global warming doesn't exist, we will be acting like ostriches. It's the same as arguing that São Paulo didn't face a water shortage during the period you were mentioning because at the same time there were floods in southern Brazil. The fact that some areas have a freezing temperature doesn't invalidate the fact that the world average temperature is increasing as a whole."

When people started to appear at Pedra Grande and the place got crowded, Dr. Jansen suggested another walk to a viewpoint that was close to them. While strolling, Estela saw two butterflies flying freely, close to a tree, and exclaimed, "Look, over there! Blue butterflies!"

"And over there, in the top of that tree, a marmoset," added Dr. Jansen.

Once they reached the viewpoint, they stopped to enjoy the majestic view, and Estela said: "I must thank you again for bringing me to Cantareira Park."

"Now you know the way, Estela. You can bring Victor and Sofia here."

"Look, Michael! From here, it is possible to see the pollution of São Paulo!" she said, pointing at a dense fog that was floating above the buildings.

"That is one of the reasons we must start the decarbonization process as soon as possible and reduce gas emissions. Pollution is very harmful to pulmonary health. It can lead to asthma, emphysema, and chronic bronchitis, as well as lung and mouth cancer[ccx]. Not to mention the increased risk of infections, heart attacks, and strokes. All of this is coming from the cars', buses', and trucks' exhausts and the pollutant industries. The worst thing about it is that pollution is not just present in the air. Our water is polluted too. Just to illustrate the problem to you, Estela, during a 1999 North American study, it was demonstrated that the water quality of water streams from thirty different states was compromised. The researchers found traces of chemical and pharmaceutical products in 80 percent of the cases[ccxi]. That was twenty years ago. Imagine how it is nowadays."

"And people drink that water?"

"Yes. Another American study, a more recent one, demonstrated the treated water that supplies about forty-million residents in the US has traces of fifty-six different pharmaceutical products[ccxii]."

"Is that harmful for the population?" inquired Estela.

"They say it isn't, but I have my doubts. Even if I limit myself to only talk about xenoestrogens, which are substances that mimic the action of female hormones, that is still enough to prove the opposite. That's because even very low levels of that substance are enough to create many problems, both in animals and humans, as a result of its endocrine disruptors. We are surrounded by xenoestrogens, which are present in plastics, like bisphenol A and phthalates; BCPs, that are a result of some industrial processes; pesticides; dioxins; and synthetic medicines like contraceptive pills and hormonal replacement therapies. The worst thing about it is that all those substances are present, in different degrees, in the water we drink. High levels of such substances can increase the risk of cervical, breast, and prostate cance[ccxiii]r, reduce fertility, alter thyroid function, cause or worsen endometriosis, and can even influence the development of genitalia in babies[ccxiv]."

"Are you serious?!"

"As I said, that doesn't just affect humans. Fishes like trout, which live in fishing farms that present high xenoestrogen levels, suffered significant modifications[ccxv]. The males became feminized, and they had a high rate of hermaphroditism, having two gonads instead of one. Crocodiles in Florida that were exposed to pesticides presented low levels of testosterone. You can add the fact that male seagulls that were exposed to DDT, a pesticide, during their development stage, are now showing characteristics of hermaphrodites."

"Wow! That is a serious matter!"

Michael Jansen glared at Estela's dark eyes, saying, "Thus, I think it is vital that our children become aware, from a young age, of their responsibilities regarding environmental preservation. We must act! The examples of the past are a clear alert. I can mention some."

"I find it very interesting to bring the past to the present so we can learn and avoid the repetition of harmful actions. So, yes, please mention some!"

"Right. Let's start. Around 1700, the water in the city of New York was so polluted with excrement and trash that a local journalist proclaimed that 'horses from outside of the city could not drink that water.' In London, in 1858, the Thames smelled so badly[ccxvi], due to the pollution produced by industrial waste and domestic sewage, that the UK Parliament had to be closed until the unpleasant smell dissipated. Nowadays, if you walk around London, you can see that the Thames has fish, but it also has many plastic bags and bottles. To become successful regarding the preservation of our planet, we must avoid situations like that. We must be willing to be careful with our environment."

"I think we need to believe that it is possible to make the world a better place."

"It sure is. That transformation starts with ourselves. No matter what we do, we must look forward and think that the future is not so far away from us. It is right here, right now. It is in every child alive, and children are part of the solution. As parents, we must teach them through our actions. For example, when we go to the supermarket, it's important that we bring our green bags, instead of depending on the non-biodegradable bags that are sold there. We can also choose more economical cars to reduce the carbon impact on the atmosphere. Carpooling is also an excellent solution to avoid traffic jams and to reduce gas emissions. Oh! And avoid throwing food away. There are so many reasons to avoid wasting food," said Dr. Jansen while taking a deep breath, as if he was searching for the pure air that was present in that beautiful place, before concluding: "Estela, the small actions add up and, as a whole, can make a huge difference. You, my dear friend, can push that change even further."

"Me?" Estela was scared and took a step backward.

"Yes, you! You have a successful blog and a respectable channel on YouTube. Therefore, you are an influence to thousands of parents. You don't need to be 'eco-boring.' You need to identify the real problems we are facing nowadays and invite people to act in favor of nature."

"I will do it. It is worth it!" she confirmed. "Since you mentioned YouTube, I want to schedule the recording session for the next steps. When can we record them?"

"Estela, do you want my honest opinion?"

"Of course!"

"I think you have enough knowledge and are perfectly capable of talking about the Steps on your own. I enjoy recording with you, but it is not easy to find a good time for both of us. I can't ask you to wait for me because I can't schedule anything soon. It could take months."

"Don't you think it would be strange if I recorded the videos without you?"

"I'm sure it won't. It's your channel. I don't want to become an obstacle to your project. The more videos you record, the more followers you get, and that's very good for everyone! You already have nearly 200,000 followers?"

"To be precise, 185,000."

"Well . . . You should record those next three steps on your own, and you will reach 300,000 followers. You can do it. You always complemented my comments on your blog, and now you can do the same on YouTube."

"I think that's a good idea. I really do," said Estela while considering it. "It will be easier to organize my time that way, and Victor is willing to help me. The ninth step is not very complex since it is about the power of healthy friendships and good influences. I think I will highlight the point you made about the biographies of famous people, which can be role models for children. The tenth step is about deliberate practice, and I want to stress that practice is not enough if it is not properly guided and if we lack a mentor that can identify the things we are doing wrong and how to fix them. I also want to stress that a good mentor is one who helps us visualize our training as if it was not about us and helps us create a mental representation of our actions."

"I think it's a good thing that you value the work of the master, the expert. When we are experts, we look to a situation, and we immediately know if there is a problem there or not. Like doctors, who during emergencies only need to take a look at the electrocardiogram or check the patient to know if they are having a heart attack or not."

"I'm glad you like it. I think I will use the Christmas party as an example to explain the concept of mental representation. I want to explain that if a person has never experienced a Christmas party, that person will have little knowledge regarding the event. However, if the same person experiences the Christmas party every year, he or she will build a mental representation of every element that is a part of it: the tree, the turkey, the family, the presents, the music, the food, the smells."

"Perfect!" exclaimed the doctor.

"And the eleventh step," she continued, "is the one I learned today: encouraging the parents to plant their values in the hearts of their children. I must stress, of course, that this educational process is mainly based on their own actions."

"Don't forget to talk about the value of money," completed Dr. Jansen.

"Oh! Allowance . . . The importance of domestic chores, especially making your bed."

"And above all of that?"

"The value of preservation. We must be a part of the solution, not the problem."

"Exactly! You are more than ready! Just one more thing: remember to mention that our planet is not disposable. You must stress that this is our home and our biggest heritage."

After recording the remaining steps, Estela, Victor, and Sofia traveled to Cancun during the holidays. After several months of hard work, they decided to award themselves with the experience of enjoying paradise. They relaxed in a sophisticated resort in front of the emerald sea and had enough time to visit the Pyramids of Chichen Itza and Coba and the ruins of Tulum, as well as the parks of Xel-ha and Xcaret.

On the way back home, they decided to stay in Mexico City for a few days. When they were landing at the airport, the first thing Estela noticed was the veil of pollution that covered the entire city, like a thick gray mantle. She was used to the pollution in São Paulo but had never seen what she was about to see on the streets of Mexico City: people wearing masks of several colors, some of which had drawings, to cover the nose and the mouth.

She was a little bit worried because of Sofia but managed to calm down, gradually, and find activities for them to do inside, like going to the National Museum of Anthropology, which had many artifacts from the Mayan and Aztec civilizations.

Despite being inspiring, Mexico City's pollution was more than palpable, and the sky was continuously overcast, which seriously bothered them. It didn't take long before Sofia developed a persistent cough.

On the second to last day in the city, when they went to the Pyramids of the Sun and the Moon, in Teotihuacan, a taxi driver explained to them that the pollution was prevalent because people used wood and charcoal to cook. Since it was winter in Mexico, more people were making use of that heat source. Near Zocalo, the historic center, Estela saw electric taxis charging their batteries using solar panels. It was a start, but a small one compared to what was needed.

On their way to the airport, she sighed, unintentionally expressing her desire to get Sofia away from that environment, which was extremely unhealthy in her opinion. Was she exaggerating, as all mothers do? How would her daughter's future be, and all children's, without an effective, sustainable policy? What if . . . ? Questions were assaulting her mind, one by one, and she only had a break when she was leafing through the airplane magazine and saw a sentence, written by Hubert Reeves, a Canadian astrophysicist: "Man is the most insane species. He worships an invisible God and destroys a visible Nature. Unaware that this nature he's destroying is the God he's worshiping."

She analyzed everything that sentence could mean and thought about Dr. Jansen and how right he was, once again. She also kept wondering what the last step would be.

CHAPTER 14 — THE TWELFTH STEP: SELF-KNOWLEDGE

"To thine own self be true."

—William Shakespeare

Estela's Volvo stopped in front of the address that the GPS was indicating: a large lot, completely walled, in the Morumbi neighborhood. Victor and Estela checked the name of the street and the number: 267. They had waited impatiently for that moment: a dinner at Dr. Jansen's place. The unexpected invitation surprised them at first but also made them feel curious and hopeful. They knew that entering that house and the doctor's intimate life was a rare opportunity.

"Is it here?" asked Estela. "It seems like one of those old mansions. I always thought Dr. Jansen would live in a modern house, with a glass façade, like Awake Clinic. I might be wrong."

Victor pressed the intercom button. Immediately, a security guard asked their names.

"Victor, Estela, and Sofia," answered Victor, with his head out the car's window.

The silver gate opened laterally, revealing a small Portuguese pavement road, which passed through the interior of a long garden. The beautiful path gave access to a big Victorian house made of red bricks. The windows were high, framed in white, and the pointy dark rooftop was the final touch of the grand architecture.

"If someone asked me, I would say an Englishman lives here," said Victor, smiling.

When they parked the car, a golden retriever came running in their direction, tail wagging and joyfully barking. Soon after, Dr. Jansen waved from the entrance door, saying, "You have just met Lola, our companion. There's no need to worry; she is quite docile." Dr. Jansen then went closer to the trio and hugged them, saying, "You resemble your mother, Sofia! How many days until you become one-year-old?"

"Ten days, Doctor," answered Estela.

"So she is almost one-year-old, then! It's a pity that Andrea and her husband didn't come with you! I was expecting them."

"They had an obligation today at church and couldn't join us," explained Victor.

"I invited half a dozen employees from the clinic and their respective partners. Two of my children and four of my grandchildren are also here today. Follow me. We will have dinner at our 'Gourmet Space.'"

While walking, Estela looked around and noticed the garden was well-cared for and forested. It also had several kinds of flowers, water fountains and some night-blooming jasmines, which were starting to exhale their sweet scent as the sun set.

"Your house is beautiful! It's an oasis in the middle of São

Paulo," exclaimed Estela, handing Michael a flower arrangement made of orchids.

"Oh! Thank you so much for your gift. I've been living here for the past forty years. The neighborhood used to be much safer; there was no risk at all living here. Nowadays, my children insist that I should move to a private condo. However, for the time being, I will stay here."

Sofia, who was on Victor's arms, pointed her little finger at the dog and said,

"Woof-woof!"

Michael encouraged Sofia to pet her.

After, they walked around the mansion, and Estela noticed that the house had an outbuilding, styled completely differently from the home—much more modern, clean, and wide. They passed by a pool with two streaks of dark-blue tiles, protected by a fence, and met the remaining guests in a structure specifically made for gastronomy.

Dr. Jansen tied the laces of his green apron and said, "Today, I'm cooking paella, to commemorate the fact that the Mediterranean diet was considered the best in the world. I hope you enjoy it!"

Estela observed the doctor washing his hands exemplarily, like a surgeon at a hospital, and returning to his place at the kitchen, where his wife was helping him, stirring the yellowish rice on a big copper paellera. The doctor picked up some olive oil and spread it over the food.

"Michael forgot to mention that," commented Ruth, his wife, "if someone isn't a fan of seafood and fish, I also made *barreado*, which is a common dish from Paraná's seaside. Your wife is from Paraná, isn't she, Bruno?"

"Yes, she is," answered Bruno with a beer in his hand, pulling his partner a little closer to him. "She is from Maringá."

"Everything will be ready in about . . ." the doctor looked at a prominent digital wall clock ". . . half an hour. So, make yourselves comfortable. We have some snacks there, on the table, including chestnuts, fruits, dried fruit, little cakes, salads . . ."

Estela chose ceviche, served on a mini saucer, while Victor took a portion of fried polenta for himself and Sofia.

Ruth walked toward Estela with a large wrapped box in her hands, saying, "We haven't seen each other since that day at the zoo, but I didn't forget about you."

Estela received the gift and unwrapped it carefully. Inside, she found an elegant photo frame, with five pictures of the family. Looking at their pictures from that day at the zoo made Estela emotional.

"It's for posterity," explained Ruth. "I always encouraged my children to take many photos of my grandchildren. After all, time doesn't return, and children only grow."

"You have impeccable taste! The photos are wonderful! Thank you, from the bottom of my heart, for this beautiful surprise."

"We are happy about your success! You are special to us, Estela," said Ruth, touching her face with her hands and kissing her cheeks softly.

"So are you," answered Estela, returning the kisses.

Ruth, as the host, went to spend some time with the remaining guests, and Estela tried to interact with everyone. Gradually, the sky got darker as night came. The garden and the pool illuminated, and dinner was served.

Sérgio, a cheerful little boy, was playing with Pedro, Bruno's son, when Michael said, "Sérgio, can you please go call your mother and father? I told them we would be waiting for them."

"Okay!" said the little boy while running toward the end of the property.

After a few seconds, Tânia and Adriano, two of the domestic workers from Dr. Jansen's house, appeared, holding hands, while the little boy passed through them at high speed. Sérgio entered the house like a jet plane and sat at the table, next to his friend.

"Tânia," said Dr. Jansen, "welcome. Make yourself at home."

The young woman didn't appear to be comfortable until the moment she saw Estela. Then she opened her eyes wide and with a big smile said, nearly shouting, "Are you Estela? The one from the videos?"

"I guess so . . ." answered Estela.

"Oh my God! I love you so much! It's a huge pleasure to meet you, live and in color."

"Did you know Sérgio is following the Steps?" said Michael Jansen. "Tânia does everything perfectly, and Sérgio does his absolute best to be a good boy."

"Estela," said the worker, "I've already watched each one of your videos at least three times. There's only one last Step left. I'm so excited to learn it! When are you recording it?"

"I don't know what the last Step is about," Estela informed with a big smile on her face. "You probably know more about it than me, as you are using it to educate your son."

"I don't," answered Tânia while sitting in a free chair at the table. "The doctor only tells me, 'You must do this and that,' or 'You must act this way.' He never explained the Steps in an orderly way like you do in the videos."

"I act like that precisely because every Step is connected to all the other Steps as if they are a whole," interrupted Dr. Jansen, placing a napkin on his lap. "There is an imaginary division between them, but they are like a guideline for parents, a continuum. The path is revealed, and everyone is free to choose according to their will."

"I have another perspective, Doctor," said Estela. "Each step, singly, adds to the next one, to provide, as a whole, an education proposal that aims at encouraging children to be better and to develop their intellectual and interpersonal skills. Furthermore, the Steps' goal is to develop children's conscience about the importance of values such as honesty, self-esteem, courtesy, optimism, responsibility. Each step might seem small when seen separately, but as a whole, they achieve an unimaginable proportion. We know, for sure, that if applied adequately, the system allows children to achieve above-average cognitive, psychomotor, and affective levels."

"I agree," said Tânia, nodding her head positively.

"They can be seen as small changes that add up to transform

into great results, like a ripple effect," concluded Jansen. "I hope you enjoy dinner!"

At the end of the main dish, Estela looked around the place, carefully observing everyone at the table, and noticed that the meeting was a success. The food was delicious, and they were all having a pleasant conversation in a welcoming environment. What else could she wish for?

Meanwhile, when the dessert was served, Sofia started crying. She was tired because it was almost time to go to bed. Distressed since her daughter was crying, Estela decided to get away from the remaining guests to breastfeed Sofia. She sat in one of the chairs near the pool, which was internally enlightened by blue light beams. Since silence was only interrupted by the wind whispering, Sofia fell asleep in a few minutes.

Estela remained there, observing the leaves of the palm trees dancing above them, hearing the singing of the cicada, and inhaling the scent of freshly-cut grass. Then she noticed an older man who was coming from the balcony toward them. Estela greeted him, nodding, and he sat on a chair next to her, saying: "The doctor swims here, in this pool, every single day at 5:45 in the morning. That's how he stays in such good shape."

Feeling that a stranger was violating her personal space, Estela stood up and said, "His actions match his words."

"Don't get up, ma'am. I'm sorry if I scared you. I'm Vagner, the gardener. I've been working here for the past twenty years."

Estela looked closely to his ruddy face and sat again before asking, "Why didn't the doctor invite you to the party?"

"The doctor knows me," said Vagner, showing his scarce teeth. "I can't be close to alcohol or I will embarrass myself. After two sad episodes, he doesn't invite me anymore."

"He must know you well," she said.

"If there is anyone who can scare me, that's certainly the doctor. He looks at you, and he immediately knows that you did something wrong, that you are hiding something. I've never met someone like him. He has a sixth sense. I remember when the boys were teenagers, he would know just by looking if one of their friends was a bad influence."

"On the other hand, you probably know him well too, am I right?" the journalist wanted to know.

"You could say that. The doctor is a person of habit: he wakes up early in the morning, meditates, swims, and then goes to work. He values family above anything else in this world and only works because he enjoys doing it."

"Interesting. Tell me more about him," said Estela.

"He always helps other people; his heart is huge. Even with me . . . He is constantly supporting me to fight my addiction. He is the most ecologically correct person I know. You know, there used to be a big swimming pool here. When his children left, he made it smaller to use less water, to avoid wasting it. In this garden, everything is sustainable, from the electrical energy that comes from the solar panels to the water system in the garden, which comes from that roof over there, where the rain is captured. The most interesting aspect, in my opinion, is that the water from the taps is reused for the toilet bowls. He is quite responsible!"

"I already imagined that . . ." Estela commented.

"He is a giant, not only because of his height. He notices everything. He is probably already observing us." Vagner slowly stood up from his chair. "I should return to my room. Good night, young lady."

"Good night, Vagner."

Estela returned to the outbuilding when Bruno was asking for a guitar to liven up the party. "Would you play with me, Doctor?" asked Bruno, opening his arms. "Every time I come here, you participate in the show. What about today, Doctor?"

Despite Dr. Jansen trying to decline the invitation, his daughter handed him the violin.

"Let's start with The Beatles, before we visit Coldplay, all right?" announced Bruno. "Which one do you want to hear: 'Yesterday,' 'Let It Be,' or 'Hey Jude'?"

Estela carefully placed Sofia in her stroller, to avoid waking her up, while listening to the two men play a spirited version of "Hey Jude." She asked herself, "Is there anything Dr. Jansen does without giving his very best?

◆ ◆ ◆

Later, while everyone was talking freely, Dr. Jansen asked Victor for permission to take Estela for a walk around the garden.

"After a long path, my dear friend, we are finally on the last step," he said.

"My heart leaped just hearing that," Estela confided. "Are you going to tell me what the last step is about, or should I guess it?"

"Hmm! I'm not sure yet . . ." he said with a mysterious tone. "Do you remember that when we started to talk about the first step, we mentioned the connection between parents and their children?"

"Yes! It's a fascinating and important step," concluded Estela. "I didn't forget it."

"Now, in this last step, I must stress another form of connection: your connection with yourself. 'Know thyself,'" said Dr. Jansen, with a more serious tone than usual. "Such an ancient and meaningful saying, that came from the temple of Apollo, in Delphos, Greece, more than twenty-five hundred years ago."

"And used by Plato, when he wrote about Socrates," completed Estela.

"Yes!" the doctor agreed. "The twelfth step is precisely about that topic: the power of self-knowledge."

"You haven't even started to talk, and I already love it," informed Estela, anticipating the pleasure of acquiring new knowledge to share with her followers.

"According to my experience, and I should tell you that I've already gone through a good portion of the journey, I can firmly state that we all must know ourselves. Know our desires, dreams, fears, and everything that constitutes our identity—acknowledging our virtues and flaws. We must look inside ourselves to understand what brings us joy, sadness, love, and hate.

Analyzing our interior to understand what makes us advance and what frees us. We must understand that we can act according to our thoughts and wishes."

"And when should that search for self-knowledge start?"

"During childhood. Children and teenagers must become familiar with themselves and find their own truths. If they want to be very happy, first, they must learn who they are. They must ask themselves: Who am I? What are my virtues? And my flaws? What do I want? Most of the time, we try to learn about remote galaxies or discover what happens in the deep ocean . . . However, first of all, we must explore our mind, get to know ourselves more, and in better ways."

"How can we know ourselves better?" Estela asked.

"One of the best ways is through meditation."

"Meditation for children?" asked Estela.

"Of course! Teaching meditation and clear focus or, to use other words, mindfulness, helps children become happier and healthier during their teenage years, adulthood, and old age. Since we live in an unhappy world, which brings us down, we must learn more about the value of self-knowledge. It's a feeling that doesn't result from intelligence; it is inside every single one of us already. Thus, we must exteriorize it through wisdom, simplicity, and gratitude."

A call of an owl who was watching her offspring indicated they were entering a forbidden area. Michael lightly touched Estela's arm, whispering, "Come with me. I want to show you the place where I meditate."

They walked to the end of the path and stopped near a simple house, made of wood, which was relatively small. The doctor touched the power switch, lighting the only lamp on the ceiling, which was soft and yellowish, and while taking off his shoes, said, "You can leave your shoes here, at the entrance."

Estela did as he asked, leaving her stiletto-heel sandals at the door. She walked with her naked feet through the room and felt the cold mat floor, made of intertwined straws. The room only had a sideboard, with a glass jug filled with water and covered by a cup, a pink and redolent lily, and a pot with green powder on the inside.

"What is this powder?" asked Estela.

"Matcha; it's made of ground green tea buds," answered Dr. Jansen. "Buddhist monks use matcha to help them focus during long periods while meditating. My first contact with the drink was in Thailand, but this variety is from Japan, which is the one I like the most because it is planted in the shade. It tastes bitter, but it's also soft and flavorful. I don't drink it every day, only when I need more caffeine. I would tell you to try it, but it's late, and it could compromise your sleep."

"That's okay ... Do you spend a lot of time here?"

"I practice meditation quite early, right when I wake up, for forty-five minutes. During that time, I find tranquility, relaxation, and sustainable focus. That time is only for me."

"Don't you think it's a lot of time? I'm sure I can't stand still for that long."

"I'm sure you can, after some training. I tell amateurs to start with shorter amounts of time and increase them gradually until they find their own balance point."

"You know, Michael ... I'm skeptical about meditation," said Estela, passing her hand over her face. "I relate that practice to the image of long-haired hippies and spiritual travelers, with their magic mushrooms and LSD."

"It's a pity you think that way!" exclaimed the doctor sadly. "Meditation is not about esoterism, mysticism, gongs, incense, and far less about drugs. Meditation is a way of returning to our inside, to find ourselves. Most people don't know themselves very well. Since they live according to a denial process, they get away from their true self and lose contact with their bodies and their minds. Especially in a world like ours, which is turbulent and swift, and considering that we never have time for anything. On top of that, we are always attempting to balance work, personal life, and our finances, with little success, and thus we become more frustrated every day. In our lives, we do many things automatically, without thinking. On the other hand, when we meditate, we reach a state of mindfulness; we regain control, and we stop doing everything in a purely mechanical manner. Furthermore, we also acquire self-knowledge, which is a huge help in our search for happiness. Tell me, what is going through your mind right now?"

"I'm thinking about Sofia and imagining how Victor is taking care of her. If he is carefully watching her or distracted by the remaining guests."

"That's it! You also need plain attention. Forget about your preconceptions regarding meditation. Just like you noticed, our mind normally takes us away from the moment we are living and gallops like a wild horse. However, the current moment, now, that's the time in which we should live. Look around you. You are here with me, alone, in the cottage where I practice meditation. This is the space, and this is the moment. You can control that by practicing meditation or through mindfulness, learning how to live in the present, to relax the mind and focus. Besides, this activity can help you calm down in times of high stress and teach you how to understand yourself better, to see yourself completely, naked, with all your nuances. Did anyone ever tell you that meditation changed her or his life?"

"Not that I can remember."

"Then, my dear friend, listen to me. Meditation changed my life! It's not coincidental that it has become a part of my identity, of who I am. Thus, I commit to the practice, and I never fail to meditate, not even a single day. It was through meditation that I better learned how to manage my emotions and how to be clear with my actions instead of reacting irrationally or compelled by feelings. I got rid of my unproductive thoughts, learned how to calm down, focus, breath, and smile more because I understood that I'm lucky to be able to live this wonderful moment, which is now, and to be able to share my journey with the people I've met."

"I didn't know you before," said Estela, "but I believe in you. You are the wisest person I know. If that is a result of meditation, that's the best argument you could use."

"By the way, you shouldn't just trust in my personal experience. To convince you of what I'm saying, I will scientifically explain to you how meditation is efficient."

"Your word is enough, Michael, but all knowledge is welcome. I would like to hear your thoughts."

"Right. In a 2014 magazine, named *JAMA*[ccxvii] [ccxviii], a review and meta-analysis were published, regarding forty-seven solid studies, proving that meditation helps by reducing anxiety, depression, and pain. Another very fruitful study was developed by Gaëlle Desbordes and her peers[ccxix], which demonstrated the changes in the brain activity of individuals who practiced meditation techniques for eight weeks. Their findings suggest that meditation has a prolonged effect and that isn't just restricted to the training session. They managed to show that the amygdalae, which are part of the limbic system and help to detect dangerous events, generating fear and anxiety, are less active in people who practice meditation. With practice, people become less reactive because they relieve those unreasonable worries."

"Like me getting worried about Victor and Sofia?"

"That is an example, among many possible ones. To conclude, I will share the results of other interesting studies, performed by Sara Lazar, a neuroscientist from Massachusetts General Hospital, and her peers[ccxx]. They demonstrated the impact of meditation on several cognitive and behavioral functions. In the brain MRI scan, they found differences in the density of the hippocampus' gray matter, which is related to memory and learning. Furthermore, they noticed a higher functioning of structures associated with compassion, self-knowledge, and introspection. Not to mention the size reduction of the amygdala, which, as I said, plays a vital role in regulating anxiety and stress. Studies also suggest that meditation can reduce brain atrophy in areas that are usually affected by aging . . ."

"That's pretty convincing, Doctor . . ."

"The last time I did some research on the subject, I saw that there are more than nineteen thousand studies about meditation and mindfulness, suggesting that those practices can help improve the quality of relationships in general, which contributes to people's success in their personal lives, besides their professional careers."

"Interesting. I'm curious to know if there is any difference between meditation and mindfulness."

"There is, yes. Meditation is a more structured process that aims at finding inner peace. Like any other skill, it requires time that must be dedicated to practice, as well as the support of a mentor. Deliberate practice will improve our abilities. Normally, we sit according to a correct posture, with our eyes closed, trying to calm down the buzz that lives inside of us. Meditation isn't only about reaching a relaxed state of mind and relieving stress. It is also about cleaning our minds and understanding who we are. Mindfulness is a form of meditation, which stimulates us to focus on our inside, trying to understand our emotions, our thoughts, without interpreting or judging them."

"So," summarized Estela, "being completely focused without judging or criticizing."

"Correct! Mindfulness is about living consciously, in the moment, appreciating life, here and now. The present must be the center of our conscience. We must understand who we are and our vision of the world. Our mind is a boiler filled with countless unique and individual experiences. Thus, we need to go deeper instead of just scratching the surface. It's important that people practice their ability to focus on reality, on the current moment. Buddha taught us a lesson: 'Don't live in the past, don't dream about the future, focus your mind on the present moment.'"

"You said that meditation is more structured. Is mindfulness a more flexible practice?"

"There are two ways to practice mindfulness: formally or informally. In the first, you must reserve some period of the day to sit and meditate, focusing on your body and mind and the things you are experiencing in that exact moment, as well as on your breathing."

"What about the informal manner?"

"The informal technique is for those who think they can't stand still for long periods. They can practice the technique while walking, for example. However, instead of focusing on their thoughts, they must focus on the body: their steps, the way they lift their feet or move their hands, and how they are breathing. Remember: mindfulness is about focusing on the present. Another technique is about focusing hard while eating something, like a raisin."

"A raisin?"

"Yes. Hold it between your fingers, feel its texture, enjoy the way light reflects on it, revealing its shape, asymmetries, each of its grooves as if you have never seen one before. It's important to smell it before eating it, before slowly placing it on your tongue, playing with it without chewing it, trying to notice that moment when your mouth fills with saliva . . . You get my point. After that ritual, bite it, let its flavor invade your palate, and then swallow it."

"I'm amazed! That is enjoying the essence of food. What if we are practicing the formal technique, and for some reason, we want to stop sooner than we previously decided? Say you are aiming at fifteen minutes, but as soon as you reach eight minutes, you feel the desire to stop. What do you do?"

"You must identify where that impulse is coming from. Is it because you are tired after a sleepless night? Is the discomfort of poor posture? Or is it merely impatience? You must interpret your feelings, but you can stop whenever you want, with a clean conscience."

"Well, that encourages me to try it."

"Better than talking about meditation, is practicing it," declared Dr. Jansen. "Should I guide you through a brief session?"

"That would be great!" exclaimed Estela.

"So, let's sit down on the mat."

Estela did as the doctor suggested, while he sat in front of her.

"Now, cross your legs and keep your eyes open. Find a position that makes you feel comfortable, with your back upright, and avoid any tension in your shoulders. Let your hands rest on your knees or legs."

Estela positioned herself accordingly.

"Breathe deeply, calmly, and gently. That's it!"

Once she felt the exaggerated scent of lily in the air of the cottage, Estela escaped that reality. The feeling that invaded her was similar to when she landed at the tropical paradise of her honeymoon.

"While you calm down," said Dr. Jansen, speaking slower than usual, "become aware of your breath and the environment around us. Listen closely to the sounds around and close your visual field. Is it night or day?"

"Night," Estela said impulsively.

"Don't answer, just become aware of it. Are we in a quiet or noisy place?"

Expanding her ears, she managed to identify the sound of cicadas in the background.

"Pay attention to everything, but remember to focus on your breath."

Estela's chest expanded and deflated gently.

"Let's work on breathing as a way to quiet the mind from the usual rambling, set aside the monologues, and relax the body. Close your eyes."

Estela closed her eyes.

"Practicing it daily will help you live in the present. Don't allow your thoughts to wander. The reins of your mind are in your hands. Everyone has a mind that changes between good and bad ideas, either it is walking on the beach, a to-do list, or something similar. That's normal. Compel your focus to your breath. The inhale and exhale movements must bury the avalanche your thoughts produce. Relieve your forehead. You don't need to frown. Relax your neck, shoulders, arms, hands. Feel your body getting comfortable and delighted."

Estela felt increasingly less bothered by inner conflicts and worries, entirely focusing on the moment.

"Keep your focus on your breath. Inhale deeply . . . one . . . two . . . three . . . four . . . five . . . hold your breath . . . and exhale one . . ."

Michael's voice was not disturbing as he gave the simple commands, instilling safety, comfort, and tranquility.

"Very well! Allow your breath to reach its ideal rhythm, not too slow, nor too fast. Notice if you're inhaling and exhaling in a balanced manner. That's it. Excellent! Try to inhale and exhale for similar lengths of time."

Estela's image reflected total tranquility.

"Keep relaxing, feel at peace with yourself, complete happiness. Always remember that you can return to this practice, whenever you want, to restore the tranquility of the mind. Now, gently, open your eyes."

Estela slowly opened her eyes. She saw Dr. Jansen observing her as if he was a father looking at his daughter. He stood up and helped her stand up too.

"What do you think?"

"It's relaxing and, at the same time, invigorating."

"Small actions like these can make a difference in our relationship with the world, always making it better. Living in the current moment helps us to have a better perspective of what is going on inside us. It allows us to ask, "Why am I feeling that?" "Why do I think like this?" Michael carefully considered his next words. Estela looked at him questioningly before he quickly proceeded, "Being in the present moment allows you to face yourself. One of the fundamental elements to living a full life is understanding that everything we feel, even bad feelings, like fear, shame, and envy, are all an invitation for us to see clearer, to access more than the visible, the things that are apparently invisible to our eyes. Many times, we are not able to make our lives match our wishes. If we resist too much, we might hurt ourselves and become resentful. So, it's better to be brave and accept who we are and the moment we are going through. We must keep clarity and our benevolence. The things that disappoint us in the present will pass, without a doubt."

"It's difficult to accomplish that," Estela said.

"Do you know the story of Milarepa[ccxxi], the legendary Tibetan monk?"

"No, I've never heard of him."

"Milarepa lived in a cave. One day, he went to get some food and wood outside of his cave, and when he returned, he noticed it was full of demons. In an attempt to expel them, first, he tried to teach them the Buddhist lessons about compassion. However, they ignored those lessons, and none of them left. Then he sat on the floor and told them he would accept sharing his cave so that they could all live happily together. Confronted with that acceptance, most of the demons disappeared, except for one. Milarepa walked to the demon and jumped on its claws. Instantaneously, the demon disappeared, only leaving a cloud of smoke behind, and Milarepa was once again alone in his cave, where peace reigned again."

Estela thought about the story for a little while and then said, "I understand the message! We must realize that we have internal demons and there's no use in avoiding them. Instead, we should accept them proactively so we can be happy."

"That's exactly the point, Estela! Good interpretation! We must assume the destiny of our happiness, looking at the world with fresh and new eyes. We must not run away from life. Instead, we should feel pain and pleasure. Meditation destroys the barriers we impose internally and likewise, provides a clearer perception of everyone around us. When we focus on the current moment, we can understand things more clearly, acquiring a new sense of self-respect and becoming less influenced by other people. We perceive our weaknesses but also our strengths. Every single person is unique; thus, we are all special. We must acknowledge that there is something precious inside us, and we must work with the things we have to try to improve our current situation. Children and teenagers must be taught to live in reality, in the present, focusing on each moment. We must give them that power. That conquest will bring real benefits for their minds, improving their memory and ability to focus. Furthermore, it will result in better social skills."

"The last step makes perfect sense," said Estela. "In fact, all of the steps make perfect sense."

"An education guided by the Steps will better prepare our children to live in this constantly changing world. They will have their values and will be able to observe and understand themselves. Jointly, the Steps propose a behavioral transformation. The goal is to make children happier, safer, and more capable, making them the leaders we will need in the future. We need trustworthy people with high emotional intelligence, who are generous, compassionate, and disciplined enough to go after their goals and common goals, and to achieve them. Those are the ones who will see the opportunities other people can't. They will have the patience to wait and will know how to manage their own emotions, being proud of who they are. In sum, they will have the skills to achieve their potential."

"And they won't be arrogant…"

"That's right. They will remain humble despite being unbeaten. Since arrogance is a characteristic of the weak, our children won't develop that habit because they will be strong and wise!"

Estela and Michael Jansen returned through the garden after the long talk, without saying a word. Despite the meditation, Estela felt more emotional with each step. She knew it was time to say goodbye. Once they got close to the pool, Estela stopped. She held the doctor's hand and said, "I'm grateful for all these months of knowledge, but at the same time, I'm sad about finishing the Steps. I will no longer have an excuse to see you."

Tears started falling from her eyes, and Estela wiped them with the backs of her hands.

Michael Jansen looked at her without saying a word.

"I'm afraid that since our project is nearly done, we will follow different paths and lose contact. You are always so busy, and so am I. Are we saying goodbye instead of the usual 'see you later'?" she finally said, her voice breaking.

Dr. Jansen held her hands and stared into her eyes.

"We will not say goodbye, my friend. We will have many more projects like this one. Wait and see. We have the Steps for Teenagers, the Steps for Adults, the Steps for Elderly people."

"You are kidding, right?" Estela stopped crying and attempted to smile.

"Who knows how soon we will talk about them..."

CHAPTER 15 — THE CLOSING CYCLE

"At last I have what I wanted. Am I happy? Not really. But what's missing? My soul no longer has that piquant activity conferred by desire . . . Oh, we shouldn't delude ourselves— pleasure isn't in the fulfillment, but in the pursuit."

—Pierre-Augustin Caron de Beaumarchais

Sofia was preparing for her first piano recital. She was six years old, and according to her music teacher's assessment, not only did she work hard, but also she was quite skillful in the music field[ccxxii]. Sofia got immense pleasure from playing her instrument and was able to play by ear. Since Sofia started her piano classes when she was two years old, she developed the ability to play quite naturally because, for her, the musical practice was more about playing than about skills. Therefore, her musical evolution took place gradually until Sofia acquired absolute pitch.

Her life was not limited to music. Regarding her formal studies, she was attending her first year at the bilingual school. She was quite extroverted and kind, so she had many friends. She had developed her English so well that during her last trip to London a taxi driver wouldn't believe she was from Brazil.

Her delicate features, straight hair with bangs, and big eyes framed by full and dark eyelashes gave the impression that Sofia had been drawn—she was stunning!

"You look beautiful, Sofia," her grandmother Sônia would always say.

"Thank you, Grandma!" Sofia would answer, smiling and showing her dimples, just like her mother's. "You are beautiful, too, and I love your scent."

Estela had written Dr. Jansen a short letter, addressed to the clinic, to invite him to the recital. Meanwhile, she was asking herself if he would come since she had not received any confirmation from him. She wanted him to be there. She missed the doctor since they were done with the Steps, and she longed to interact with him. Estela saw him as a second father. She would frequently remember his kindness, courtesy, and above all, his astuteness. His intelligence in noticing and valuing other people's talents was, among other ones, his best quality. Thanks to that, she had discovered new abilities in herself.

When the recital day came, while entering the music school, Estela noticed that Michael had not arrived yet. Since he was quite punctual, her doubts started being replaced by the certainty that he would not be there.

"Do you think Michael will come?" Estela asked Victor.

"He is always so busy . . . I think it's unlikely, if not impossible."

Estela was still hoping to see the doctor. Hence, every time someone entered the music school, she would turn her head to check if it was the doctor. She was restless.

A thousand thoughts assaulted her head. Michael had left her with a remarkable legacy, and the Steps made her famous. Besides the blog and YouTube, where she had more than 1.3 million followers, she was also responsible for writing a daily column in the most prominent Brazilian newspaper. She had also been invited to write a book based on the doctor's teachings. The only reason she had not yet accepted the invitation were her children: William, who was fifteen months old and of course, Sofia. She was already busy with her blog, column, and YouTube page. Working on the book would be too much, at least for now.

The music school was wholly illuminated and decorated for the event. Estela and Victor left Sofia near the stage, after many goodbyes, words of encouragement, and a long good-luck kiss.

Since their seats were in the middle of the theater, Victor had to bring his Nikon, with a telescopic lens, to record this meaningful moment of his daughter's life. All the family was there, but they were dispersed throughout the theater.

While the first group, the beginners, was presented, the eyes of the journalist kept looking for Michael. Nothing!

Finally, it was Sofia's turn. The little girl's teacher appeared on stage, holding hands with Sofia. Estela's heart rate increased, and her eyes focused on her daughter's tiny face . . .

"Wolfgang Amadeus Mozart composed his first minuet, in G major, when he was five years old. It is said that his father helped him because the composition is by no means rudimentary. Instead, there are signs of the musician's geniality in this composition. The musicality is incredible, excellent! Now, right here with me, we have Sofia, who is just six years old and will interpret and execute that same work today. Pay attention to this little girl!"

Sofia flexed her knees, took a bow, and sat straight at the piano. The audience was suddenly silent. Estela crossed her fingers while Victor was recording everything.

Then, Sofia played brilliantly, on the right tempo, calmly, without any mistakes or hesitations.

Estela had tears on her face. She was so proud of her daughter!

A round of applause followed the conclusion of the act. Sofia's teacher returned to the stage and said, "Does anyone disagree with the fact that Sofia is angelical? When I hear her playing, I feel like I'm floating. She is quite skillful and plays with perfect harmony. Do you want to play a second musical piece for the audience, Sofia?"

Sofia nodded her head positively, changed the music score on the piano, and restarted. She played "Für Elise," by Beethoven, at a faster tempo.

This time, the audience gave a standing ovation.

Once again, tears fell from Estela's eyes. She was grateful for being on the right path. Internally, she knew that she and Victor, as parents, were doing their best to educate their children.

After the recital, there was a reception in the school hall. Dr. Jansen finally appeared and walked toward the journalist.

"Congratulations, Estela! Sofia played beautifully," the doctor said quickly before turning to the little girl. "You made my day prettier! Did you know that? I'm quite moved, young lady! You must work really hard to be able to perform that way, am I right?"

"Yes, I do work very hard, don't I, Mommy?" Sofia asked Estela.

"She does!" Estela confirmed. "She is quite dedicated. Not just with the piano; she is always like that. She insists on doing her very best, don't you, my darling?"

The little girl hugged her mother's waist.

"Sônia!" said Dr. Jansen, opening his arms once he saw Estela's mother. "It's been a while!"

Estela looked at the two of them, entirely confused by their familiarity with one another. She couldn't resist her curiosity, so she asked, "Do you know each other? I don't remember . . . When did you meet?"

Her mother suddenly blushed, and when the doctor started to answer the question, Sônia bumped a bowl that was on the table, breaking it once it touched the floor.

"Don't worry about it, I will clean it up," said Michael, who was quick to volunteer, while kneeling. "There are children here that might hurt themselves."

Sônia and Michael picked up the more significant pieces of the glass while Estela looked at them, extremely surprised. The cleaning staff appeared and cleaned the remaining parts.

Then, Michael greeted Victor, while Sônia walked over to Sílvia. Estela was quite curious about their behavior. They looked embarrassed by her question. Several hypotheses formulated in her head—she even thought the two had been lovers, which she soon concluded to be impossible since Michael had married in the United States of America and her mother was quite traditional and defended fidelity. No . . . No . . . Not that . . .

Even so, she felt something in the air, a mystery, an enigma she needed to solve.

She decided to start with her mother because they were family and, thus, closer. She grabbed her arm firmly but without hurting and took her to a corridor which had little to no people and asked, "What was that about? Where do you know Michael from?"

Her mother didn't say a word for a few seconds and kept looking at the floor, avoiding Estela's eyes.

"What? You can tell me! Did you get me my first interview with him, is that it? Am I right?"

Sônia didn't answer. However, when they looked at each other, Estela saw tears in her mother's eyes. She said, in a low tone, nearly a murmur, "I'm sorry."

"Sorry for what? What are you talking about?"

Estela carefully observed the sad expression on Sônia's face. She could perceive anguish emerging from her, overtaking her.

"I'm sorry," her mother repeated. "I must tell you something that I could never say before. An abominable fact with which I've lived until today. A secret that haunts me every single day, especially since you started spending time with Dr. Jansen. I'm going to counseling sessions; I've tried antidepressants and . . ."

"What is it?" asked Estela, feeling scared.

Sônia took a deep breath before starting:

"As you know, I was once an actress. Back then, I felt anxious. I wanted immediate success, and later, I didn't know how to handle it once I achieved it. Thus, I started drinking heavily. Suddenly, I had memory lapses, a hard time trying to memorize my lines, and directors stopped calling me. It was a hard blow that depressed me even more. Drinking became my consolation during that period, and I wouldn't listen to anyone, not even your father, who was my boyfriend back then. I got pregnant, but I didn't know it, I swear to God . . . So I kept drinking."

Estela was looking at the disfigured and wet face in front of her.

"When I finally found out that I was pregnant, I had already drunk too much for too long. Your father married me and provided me all the necessary support so I could get over my addiction, which fortunately I was able to do. However, the damage was already done."

"What damage?" asked Estela.

"I hurt you, my daughter. I did," Sônia sighed, choking with all the tears. "When you were born, the doctors said you had fetal alcohol syndrome. I remember the nurse measuring your head and saying you had microcephaly. She also said your nose and ears were short, your chin was too thin, and you also had congenital clubfoot."

Estela's heart stopped. The scars on her feet, which she always thought to be a consequence of her childhood mischief, were, in fact, a product of the correction surgery.

"Everyone said you would have problems, mental disabilities, that you would never be like the other kids. A friend of mine who was well informed told me about a doctor in São Paulo that could help me. That doctor was Dr. Michael Jansen. Your father and I took a flight to São Paulo, full of hope, to meet him. After the diagnostic, we decided to follow his recommendations, and we stayed here to take care of you. Two and a half years . . . During that period, he taught us what we would have to do for you to have a normal life. When he determined that you were free to go, he asked us several times to follow his guidelines. We followed everything to the last detail. Swimming classes, ballet, English classes, early reading... Everything. Absolutely everything."

While hearing her mother's story, Estela was recapitulating the crucial points of her life: the classes, the reading sessions with her parents after going to bed, their insistence that she practice ballet and track and to go to swimming classes... She had always been healthy, above average; she still stood out in everything. She never imagined, not even for a moment, that she suffered from any consequences of behavior like what her mother just described.

"I never told you before because I was afraid it would affect your self-esteem. When you grew up, you looked so strong, determined, and successful that I thought there was no need to talk about our past. Now, I look at you, so gorgeous, intelligent, and with a brilliant career, and I thank that man over there, every single day. Michael Jansen transformed your life. I made a mistake, and he helped me fix it."

Estela intuitively knew Dr. Jansen was looking at them. She turned her head to the other side of the corridor and even from such a distance, could see his intense gaze. Her mind was like a hurricane at this point. He knew who she was from the beginning? Did he share the Steps with her because of that story? Or would he help her anyway, even if she had never been his patient during childhood? She had all these questions dancing in her head, but only he could answer them.

She looked at her mother. She remembered all the moments they lived together. The fellowship, dedication, love ... What else could she wish for? Before being a mother, she was a woman, a human being, subject to doing wrong and good things. The good things undoubtedly outweighed anything else.

"Mom, if there's a burden that you can remove from your shoulders, this is it. I love my life. I love you, my father, my children, and my husband. I never felt inferior. I always had the chance to grow. I did it! I can say that I feel fulfilled in my life.

And you were—or better, you *are*—the mother I always wanted to be. You always encouraged me. You always wished the best for me. If you did something wrong without being aware of it, forget it. I feel no resentment about it, and you should not feel it either. I'm happy! I'm complete! I can only thank you, Daddy, and Michael for helping me become the woman I am today. I like that woman, as a daughter, a professional, a wife, a mother."

Mother and daughter hugged each other for a long time.

With a glance, Estela saw Michael saying goodbye, waving, and walking away peacefully.

While watching the doctor disappearing, Estela concluded that the Steps would be a part of her forever.

FINAL WORDS

If you believe this book shares an important message to parents and caregivers, please leave your review on Amazon and Goodreads. Reviews are the primary metric people use to judge a book's content. Every single review has a significant impact on others' willingness to read the book. Also, if you enjoyed it, comment with your friends, leave your opinion on the internet and share! A better world starts with us!
Our eternal gratitude,

Andrew Watson & Charles Watson

REFERENCES

[i] https://en.wikipedia.org/wiki/Ibirapuera_Park

[ii] www.sciencedaily.com/releases/2013/04/130407090835.htm

[iii] https://www.ncbi.nlm.nih.gov/pmc/articles/PMC2846100

[iv] https://www.amazon.com/Ice-Storm-Historic-Photographs-January/dp/0771061005/ref=sr_1_fkmr0_1?keywords=A+Historical+Record+in+Photographs+of+January+1998.&qid=1565047844&s=gateway&sr=8-1-fkmr0

[v] https://journals.plos.org/plosone/article?id=10.1371/journal.pone.0107653

[vi] https://www.mcgill.ca/projetverglas/files/projetverglas/1-s2.0-s0013935116301669-main.pdf

[vii] https://www.ncbi.nlm.nih.gov/pmc/articles/PMC3483668/

[viii] http://www.ncbi.nlm.nih.gov/pubmed/12509593?dopt=Abstract&report=abstract

[ix] https://www.ncbi.nlm.nih.gov/pmc/articles/PMC3738999/

[x] https://www.cochrane.org/CD003402/PREG_omega-3-fatty-acid-addition-during-pregnancy

[xi] https://m.acog.org/Patients/FAQs/Exercise-During-Pregnancy

[xii] https://www.ahajournals.org/doi/10.1161/HYPERTENSIONAHA.112.194050

[xiii] https://www.nih.gov/news-events/news-releases/extreme-temperatures-could-increase-preterm-birth-risk

[xiv] https://www.ncbi.nlm.nih.gov/pubmed/25440082

[xv] https://www.ncbi.nlm.nih.gov/pmc/articles/PMC4526182/

[xvi] https://news.harvard.edu/gazette/story/2017/04/over-nearly-80-years-harvard-study-has-been-showing-how-to-live-a-healthy-and-happy-life/

[xvii] https://www.amazon.com/Seusss-Beginner-Collection-Green-Socks/dp/0375851569/ref=sr_1_1?keywords=dr+seuss&qid=1565294879&s=gateway&sr=8-1

[xviii] https://www.ncbi.nlm.nih.gov/pubmed/28673076

[xix] https://www.ncbi.nlm.nih.gov/pubmed/26023793

[xx] Boutwell, B. B., Young, J. T. N., & Meldrum, R. C. (2018). On the positive relationship between breastfeeding & intelligence. *Developmental Psychology, 54*(8), 1426-1433. http://dx.doi.org/10.1037/dev0000537

[xxi] https://www.ncbi.nlm.nih.gov/pmc/articles/PMC2939272/

[xxii] https://www.ncbi.nlm.nih.gov/pmc/articles/PMC2939272/

[xxiii] https://www.ncbi.nlm.nih.gov/pubmed/11988057

[xxiv] https://www.amazon.com/Spectra-Baby-USA-Electric-Hospital/dp/B00BLBLR1I/ref=sr_1_5?keywords=breast+pump&qid=1565306196&s=gateway&sr=8-5

[xxv] https://www.sciencedirect.com/science/article/pii/S0031938408001558?via%3Dihub

[xxvi] https://www.ncbi.nlm.nih.gov/pubmed/28474159

[xxvii] Science 12 Sep 1997: Vol. 277, Issue 5332, pp. 1659-1662 DOI: 10.1126/science.277.5332.1659

[xxviii] https://www.ncbi.nlm.nih.gov/pubmed/16262207

[xxix] https://www.ncbi.nlm.nih.gov/pubmed/9785112

[xxx] https://www.ncbi.nlm.nih.gov/pubmed/31020763

[xxxi] https://www.ncbi.nlm.nih.gov/books/NBK107193/

[xxxii] https://www.nature.com/news/2009/090220/full/news.2009.113.html

[xxxiii] https://www.meaney.lab.mcgill.ca

[xxxiv] https://www.ncbi.nlm.nih.gov/pmc/articles/PMC2682215/

[xxxv] https://www.ncbi.nlm.nih.gov/pmc/articles/PMC2663361/

[xxxvi] https://www.ncbi.nlm.nih.gov/pmc/articles/PMC4286383/

[xxxvii] https://www.tripadvisor.com.br/Attraction_Review-g303631-d3387060-Reviews-Parque_da_Aclimacao-Sao_Paulo_State_of_Sao_Paulo.html

[xxxviii] Hart B, Risley TR. American parenting of language-learning children: persisting differences in family-child interactions observed in natural home environments.Dev Psychol. 1992;28(6):1096–1105
Hart B, Risley TR. Meaningful Differences in the Everyday Experience of Young American Children. Baltimore, MD: Paul H. Brookes Publishing Co; 1995

[xxxix] https://www.aft.org/sites/default/files/periodicals/TheEarlyCatastrophe.pdf

[xl] http://pediatrics.aappublications.org/content/early/2018/09/06/peds.2017-4276

[xli] https://www.ncbi.nlm.nih.gov/pubmed/29457574

[xlii] https://jamanetwork.com/journals/jamapediatrics/fullarticle/570266

[xliii] Brown A; Council on Communications and Media. Media use by children younger than 2 years. Pediatrics. 2011;128(5):1040–1045pmid:22007002
Screening out screen time: parents limit media use for young children. C.S. Mott Children's Hospital National Poll on Children's Health. 2014;21(1):1–2. Available at: www.mottnpch.org/reports-surveys/screening-out-screen-time-parents-limit-media-use-young-children.

[xliv] https://pediatrics.aappublications.org/content/138/5/e20162593#ref-17

[xlv] https://deltacenter.uiowa.edu/sites/deltacenter.uiowa.edu/files/rost_mcmurray.pdf

[xlvi] https://academic.oup.com/bmb/article-pdf/53/1/185/802675/53-1-185.pdf

[xlvii] https://embryo.asu.edu/pages/david-h-hubel-and-torsten-n-wiesels-research-optical-development-kittens

[xlviii] https://www.ncbi.nlm.nih.gov/pmc/articles/PMC4423595/

[xlix] https://www.ncbi.nlm.nih.gov/pmc/articles/PMC3807032/

[l] https://www.pnas.org/content/97/22/11850

[lii] http://dinshi.com/wp-content/uploads/2016/10/Praag-Neural-consequences-of-environmental-enrichment-Nat-Rev-Neuro-2000.pdf

[liii] http://www.scielo.br/scielo.php?script=sci_arttext&pid=S0001-37652001000200006

[liiii] https://www.ncbi.nlm.nih.gov/pmc/articles/PMC1595182/

[liv] https://www.ncbi.nlm.nih.gov/pubmed/9794945

[lv] https://www.ncbi.nlm.nih.gov/pubmed/11144756

[lvi] https://www.iahp.org

[lvii] National Scientific Council on the Developing Child. The timing and quality of early experiences combine to shape brain architecture. 2007. Available at: http://developingchild.harvard.edu/index.php/resources/reports_and_working_papers/working_papers/wp5/.

[lviii] https://www.ncbi.nlm.nih.gov/pubmed/31398551

[lix] https://journals.plos.org/plosbiology/article?id=10.1371/journal.pbio.1000158

[lx] https://www.nature.com/articles/468136d

[lxi] https://journals.sagepub.com/eprint/Wm6JKfkqU9FfTNhgRQ7z/full

[lxii] https://www.ncbi.nlm.nih.gov/pubmed/31396024

[lxiii] https://www.education.vic.gov.au/documents/about/research/readtoyoungchild.pdf

[lxiv] https://www.readingrockets.org/articles/researchbytopic/4862

[lxv] https://www.theguardian.com/us-news/2017/jun/26/jobs-future-automation-robots-skills-creative-health

[lxvi] https://www.forbes.com/sites/vishalmarria/2019/01/11/the-future-of-artificial-intelligence-in-the-workplace/#46ffd7cd73d4

[lxvii] https://www.nytimes.com/2017/03/19/technology/lawyers-artificial-intelligence.html

[lxviii] https://www.amazon.com/Teach-Your-Baby-Gentle-Revolution/dp/0757001858/ref=sr_1_1?keywords=glenn+doman&qid=1565490730&s=gateway&sr=8-1

[lxix] https://www.tinyreaders.com.br

[lxx] Hurwitz SC. To be successful: let them play! Child Educ.2002/2003;79:101–102

[lxxi] https://www.theguardian.com/environment/2016/jul/27/children-spend-only-half-the-time-playing-outside-as-their-parents-did

Dr. Andrew Watson

[lxxii] https://jamanetwork.com/journals/jamapediatrics/fullarticle/1149487

[lxxiii] https://www.barna.com/research/teens-spend-school-hours/

[lxxiv] https://www.nature.com/news/the-myopia-boom-1.17120

[lxxv] https://www.kars4kids.org/blog/health-safety/myopia-epidemic-protecting-your-child/

[lxxvi] https://www.ncbi.nlm.nih.gov/pubmed/28951126

[lxxvii] Frost JL. Neuroscience, play and brain development. Paper presented at: IPA/USA Triennial National Conference; Longmont, CO; June 18–21, 1998.

[lxxviii] Erickson RJ. Play contributes to the full emotional development of the child. Education.1985;105 :261– 263

[lxxix] https://www.amazon.com.br/Flow-Psychology-Experience-Mihaly-Csikszentmihalyi/dp/0061339202

[lxxx] https://www.journalofplay.org/sites/www.journalofplay.org/files/pdf-articles/7-1-article-how-play-makes-for-a-more-adaptable-brain.pdf

[lxxxi] https://www.ncbi.nlm.nih.gov/pmc/articles/PMC3574776/

[lxxxii] https://www.researchgate.net/publication/231827741_Peers_cooperative_play_and_the_development_of_empathy_in_children

[lxxxiii] https://pdfs.semanticscholar.org/7305/71be8ec086c295e07b70fd8bccdfac886368.pdf

[lxxxiv] https://www.ncbi.nlm.nih.gov/pmc/articles/PMC5513638/

[lxxxv] Tamis-LeMonda CS, Shannon JD, Cabrera NJ, Lamb ME. Fathers and mothers at play with their 2- and 3-year-olds: contributions to language and cognitive development. Child Dev.2004;75 :1806– 1820

[lxxxvi] https://pediatrics.aappublications.org/content/119/1/182

[lxxxvii] https://www.frontiersin.org/articles/10.3389/fnsys.2010.00037/full

[lxxxviii] https://www.ncbi.nlm.nih.gov/pmc/articles/PMC140943/

[lxxxix] https://scottbarrykaufman.com/wp-content/uploads/2012/07/Immordino-Yang-et-al.-20120.pdf

[xc] Pellegrini AD, Kato K, Blatchford P, Baines E. A short-term longitudinal study of children's playground games across the first year of school: implications for social competence and adjustment to school. Am Educ Res J.2002;39 :991– 1015

[xci] https://www.journalofplay.org/sites/www.journalofplay.org/files/pdf-

articles/1-4-interview-importance-ofplay-stuart-brown.pdf

[xcii] https://www.ncbi.nlm.nih.gov/pubmed/25010084

[xciii] https://www.tandfonline.com/doi/abs/10.1080/10400419.2015.1087277?
journalCode=hcrj20

[xciv] https://childmind.org/article/pushing-kids-without-pushing-too-hard/

[xcv] https://graphics8.nytimes.com/images/blogs/freakonomics/pdf/
DeliberatePractice(PsychologicalReview).pdf

[xcvi] https://www.nytimes.com/2015/02/28/business/dealbook/
the-rhythm-of-great-performance.html

[xcvii] https://www.spring.org.uk/2009/10/how-rewards-can-back-
fire-and-reduce-motivation.php

[xcviii] https://www.psychologytoday.com/intl/blog/the-baby-
scientist/201806/motivating-children-without-rewards

[xcix] https://www.ncbi.nlm.nih.gov/pubmed/19678872

[c] https://www.ncbi.nlm.nih.gov/pubmed/20339972

[ci] https://www.cnn.com/2018/02/16/health/longevity-intergenerational-
care-elderly-children-intl/index.html

[cii] https://www.tripadvisor.com.br/Attraction_Review-g303631-d317785-Reviews-
Zoologico_de_Sao_Paulo-Sao_Paulo_State_of_Sao_Paulo.html

[ciii] https://www.amazon.com/Sigma-150-600mm-5-6-3-Sports-Canon/dp/B00NJ9SCOK

[civ] https://www.amazon.com/Canon-50mm-Lens-Digital-Cameras/dp/B000I1YIDQ

[cv] https://www.ncbi.nlm.nih.gov/pmc/articles/PMC2917081/

[cvi] https://www.ncbi.nlm.nih.gov/pubmed/28616997

[cvii] https://www.theguardian.com/science/2014/sep/05/teenage-
brain-behaviour-prefrontal-cortex

[cviii] https://www.sciencedaily.com/releases/2016/05/160511080728.htm

[cix] https://digitalcommons.unl.edu/cgi/viewcontent.cgi?
article=1173&context=sociologyfacpub

[cx] https://psycnet.apa.org/doiLanding?doi=10.1037%2F0012-1649.26.6.978

[cxi] https://effectiviology.com/stanford-marshmallow-experiment-self-control-willpower/

[cxii] https://www.sciencedaily.com/releases/2011/08/110831160220.htm

[cxiii] https://www.psychologytoday.com/intl/blog/peaceful-parents-happy-kids/201506/8-steps-help-your-child-develop-self-control

[cxiv] http://www.mdpi.com/2075-4698/4/3/506

[cxv] https://www.ncbi.nlm.nih.gov/pmc/articles/PMC4736542/

[cxvi] https://news.stanford.edu/news/2007/february7/dweck-020707.html

[cxvii] The Perils and Promises of Praise" by Carol Dweck in Educational Leadership, October 2007 (Vol. 65, #2, p. 34-39)

[cxviii] Hallmann E. The influence of organic and conventional cultivation systems on the nutritional value and content of bioactive compounds in selected tomato types. Journal of the Science of Food and Agriculture. 2012;92:2840-2848. DOI: 10.1002/jsfa.5617

[cxix] https://www.researchgate.net/publication/265263313_Does_Organic_Production_Enhance_Phytochemical_Content_of_Fruit_and_Vegetables_Current_Knowledge_and_Prospects_for_Research

[cxx] https://www.parentingforbrain.com/4-baumrind-parenting-styles/

[cxxi] https://www.ncbi.nlm.nih.gov/pubmed/24766881

[cxxii] https://www.ncbi.nlm.nih.gov/pubmed/31373292

[cxxiii] https://www.fda.gov/food/consumers/questions-answers-fdaepa-advice-about-eating-fish-women-who-are-or-might-become-pregnant'

[cxxiv] https://www.sciencedaily.com/releases/2018/04/180412141014.htm

[cxxv] https://www.health.harvard.edu/blog/regular-exercise-changes-brain-improve-memory-thinking-skills-201404097110

[cxxvi] https://www.ncbi.nlm.nih.gov/pmc/articles/PMC6222249/

[cxxvii] https://www.bbc.com/news/technology-32067158

[cxxviii] https://pediatrics.aappublications.org/content/138/4/e20161372

[cxxix] https://www.huffpost.com/entry/adhd-exercise-b_4835640

[cxxx] https://www.cdc.gov/ncbddd/adhd/data.html

[cxxxi] https://www.additudemag.com/statistics-of-adhd/

[cxxxii] https://www.sciencedaily.com/releases/2016/05/160504121641.htm

[cxxxiii] https://www.ncbi.nlm.nih.gov/pmc/articles/PMC3441937/

[cxxxiv] https://www.medicalnewstoday.com/articles/325352.php

[cxxxv] https://www.hindawi.com/journals/np/2016/6391686/

[cxxxvi] https://www.ncbi.nlm.nih.gov/pmc/articles/PMC3894304/

[cxxxvii] https://www.ncbi.nlm.nih.gov/pmc/articles/PMC4915811/

[cxxxviii] https://www.ncbi.nlm.nih.gov/pmc/articles/PMC3622473/

[cxxxix] https://www.ncbi.nlm.nih.gov/pubmed/9795193

[cxl] https://www.ou.org/life/health/one-small-change-turned-these-19000-students-into-fittest-smartest-us-alan-freishtat/

[cxli] https://www.ncbi.nlm.nih.gov/pubmed/31130853

[cxlii] https://journals.plos.org/plosone/article?id=10.1371/journal.pone.0124859

[cxliii] https://www.johnshopkinshealthreview.com/issues/fall-winter-2017/articles/the-rise-of-teen-depression

[cxliv] https://www.ncbi.nlm.nih.gov/pmc/articles/PMC2746750/

[cxlv] https://www.ncbi.nlm.nih.gov/pmc/articles/PMC3674785/

[cxlvi] https://www.ncbi.nlm.nih.gov/pubmed/29882074

[cxlvii] https://health.gov/news/blog-bayw/2018/04/promoting-family-fitness/

[cxlviii] https://www.sciencedirect.com/science/article/pii/S1359178917300976

[cxlix] Morand, Matthew K., et al. "The Effects of Mixed Martial Arts on Behavior of Male Children with Attention Deficit Hyperactivity Disorder." Hofstra University, Hampstead, NY (2004).

[cl] https://www.amazon.com/Teach-Physically-Superb-Gentle-Revolution/dp/0757001920

[cli] https://www.amazon.com/Grit-Passion-Perseverance-Angela-Duckworth-ebook/dp/B010MH9V3W/ref=sr_1_1?keywords=grit+angela+duckworth&qid=1565716220&s=books&sr=1-1

[clii] https://www.ncbi.nlm.nih.gov/pubmed/17547490

[cliii] https://www.ncbi.nlm.nih.gov/pubmed/30224491

[cliv] https://www.ncbi.nlm.nih.gov/pubmed/29331059

[clv] https://www.ncbi.nlm.nih.gov/pubmed/26867111

[clvi] https://www.ncbi.nlm.nih.gov/pubmed/26855479

[clvii] https://www.ncbi.nlm.nih.gov/pubmed/30531053

[clviii] https://www.ncbi.nlm.nih.gov/pubmed/29180140

[clix] https://www.nytimes.com/1985/02/12/science/about-education-how-talent-can-be-nurtured.html

[clx] https://www.kumon.com

[clxi] https://www.researchgate.net/publication/280568975_Persevering_with_Positivity_and_Purpose_An_Examination_of_Purpose_Commitment_and_Positive_Affect_as_Predictors_of_Grit

[clxii] https://www.ncbi.nlm.nih.gov/pubmed/30550597

[clxiii] https://www.ncbi.nlm.nih.gov/pubmed/26796576

[clxiv] https://www.ncbi.nlm.nih.gov/pubmed/30819462

[clxv] http://www.acasinhafeliz.com.br/indexFrameset.htm

[clxvi] https://www.ncbi.nlm.nih.gov/pmc/articles/PMC3583091/

[clxvii] https://www.ncbi.nlm.nih.gov/pmc/articles/PMC4295724/

[clxviii] https://academic.oup.com/cercor/article/26/7/3196/1745819

[clxix] https://www.newamericaneconomy.org/press-release/demand-for-bilingual-workers-more-than-doubled-in-5-years-new-report-shows/

[clxx] https://www.amazon.com/Enlightenment-Now-Science-Humanism-Progress-ebook/dp/B073TJBYTB/ref=tmm_kin_swatch_0?_encoding=UTF8&qid=&sr=

[clxxi] https://www.researchgate.net/publication/319059631_Theory_of_mind_empathy_and_bilingualism_The_effect_of_metalinguis-tics_and_early_bilingualism

[clxxii] https://www.ncbi.nlm.nih.gov/pmc/articles/PMC4000604/

[clxxiii] https://www.researchgate.net/publication/264466802_The_Role_of_Bilingualism_in_Creative_Performance_on_Divergent_Thinking_and_Invented_Alien_Creatures_Tests

[clxxiv] https://www.ncbi.nlm.nih.gov/pmc/articles/PMC3033609/

[clxxv] https://www.ncbi.nlm.nih.gov/pmc/articles/PMC4709424/

[clxxvi] https://nouvelles.umontreal.ca/en/article/2017/01/09/bilingualism-may-save-brain-resources-as-you-age/

[clxxvii] https://www.amazon.com/Bilingual-Revolution-Future-Education-Languages/dp/1947626000

[clxxviii] https://www.psychologytoday.com/intl/blog/smores-and-more/201112/the-gift-failure

[clxxix] https://www.ncbi.nlm.nih.gov/pubmed/25566389

[clxxx] https://www.amazon.com/dp/B005JSSAH8/ref=dp-kindle-redirect?_encoding=UTF8&btkr=1

[clxxxi] https://www.ncbi.nlm.nih.gov/pmc/articles/PMC1775687/

[clxxxii] https://www.nejm.org/doi/full/10.1056/NEJMsa066082

[clxxxiii] Boutwell, Brian & Meldrum, Ryan & Petkovsek, Melissa. (2017). The role of general intelligence in friendship selection: A study of preadolescent best friend dyads. Intelligence. 64. 10.1016/j.intell.2017.07.002.

[clxxxiv] https://www.psychologytoday.com/intl/blog/the-peak-experience/201109/what-was-maslows-view-peak-experiences

[clxxxv] https://www.amazon.com.br/Search-Meaning-English-Viktor-Frankl-ebook/dp/B009U9S6FI

[clxxxvi] https://www.amazon.com/Who-Abraham-Lincoln-Janet-Pascal/dp/0448448866/ref=sr_1_2?crid=295DHOZ7HO55W&keywords=who+was+books&qid=1565643010&s=gateway&sprefix=Who+Was%2Caps%2C328&sr=8-2

[clxxxvii] https://www.amazon.com/You-Have-Brain-T-H-I-N-K-B-I-G/dp/0310745993/ref=sr_1_1?keywords=You+Have+a+Brain&qid=1565643178&s=books&sr=1-1

[clxxxviii] https://www.amazon.com/Think-Big-Unleashing-Potential-Excellence-ebook/dp/B002SVQCY2/ref=sr_1_1?crid=2R1NXV7XE3BD9&keywords=think+big+ben+carson&qid=1565643207&s=books&sprefix=Think+Big+Ben%2Cstripbooks%2C274&sr=1-1

[clxxxix] https://www.amazon.com/Gifted-Hands-Cuba-Gooding-Jr/dp/B019F95VW8

[cxc] https://www.amazon.com/Story-My-Life-AmazonClassics-ebook/dp/B077P9GLN9/ref=sr_1_3?keywords=Story+of+My+Life+kindle&qid=1565643276&s=books&sr=1-3

[cxci] https://www.amazon.com/gp/product/B01MT1Z2YG/ref=series_rw_dp_sw

[cxcii] Naja Ferjan Ramirez et al, Bilingual Baby: Foreign Language Intervention in Madrid's Infant Education Centers, Mind, Brain, and Education (2017). DOI: 10.1111/mbe.12144

[cxciii] https://www.sciencedirect.com/science/article/pii/S0010027718300994

[cxciv] https://pt.wikipedia.org/wiki/Oca_(Parque_do_Ibirapuera)

[cxcv] http://www.niemeyer.org.br

[cxcvi] https://en.wikipedia.org/wiki/Bras%C3%ADlia

[cxcvii] https://www.amazon.com/gp/product/B071Y385Q1/ref=dbs_a_def_rwt_hsch_vapi_tkin_p1_i0

[cxcviii] https://www.audible.com/pd/Leonardo-da-Vinci-Audiobook/B071VTQZYT

[cxcix] https://journals.sagepub.com/doi/abs/10.1177/0305735612463948

[cc] https://en.wikipedia.org/wiki/Printing_press

[cci] https://graphics8.nytimes.com/images/blogs/freakonomics/pdf/DeliberatePractice(PsychologicalReview).pdf

[ccii] https://www.amazon.com/Outliers-Story-Success-Malcolm-Gladwell-ebook/dp/B001ANYDAO

[cciii] https://www.ncbi.nlm.nih.gov/pmc/articles/PMC18253/

[cciv] https://www.amazon.com/Peak-Secrets-New-Science-Expertise-ebook/dp/B011H56MKS

[ccv] https://en.wikipedia.org/wiki/Cantareira_State_Park

[ccvi] https://www.tripadvisor.com.br/Attraction_Review-g303631-d3860053-Reviews-Parque_Estadual_da_Cantareira_Nucleo_Pedra_Grande-Sao_Paulo_State_of_Sao_Paulo.html

[ccvii] https://journals.sagepub.com/doi/pdf/10.1177/039463200902200410

[ccviii] https://www.amazon.com/Make-Your-Bed-Little-Things-ebook/dp/B01KFJGT50/ref=tmm_kin_swatch_0?_encoding=UTF8&qid=1566257277&sr=8-2

[ccix] http://www.scielo.br/scielo.php?script=sci_arttext&pid=S1414-753X2016000100003

[ccx] https://www.ncbi.nlm.nih.gov/pmc/articles/PMC5615585/

[ccxi] https://toxics.usgs.gov/pubs/FS-027-02/

[ccxii] https://www.medicalnewstoday.com/articles/100038.php

[ccxiii] https://ehjournal.biomedcentral.com/articles/10.1186/1476-069X-11-S1-S8

[ccxiv] https://www.ncbi.nlm.nih.gov/pmc/articles/PMC1469672/

[ccxv] https://www.sciencedirect.com/science/article/pii/S0160412016304494

[ccxvi] https://en.wikipedia.org/wiki/Great_Stink

[ccxvii] https://jamanetwork.com/journals/jamainternalmedicine/fullarticle/1809754

[ccxviii] https://jamanetwork.com/journals/jamainternalmedicine/fullarticle/2110998

[ccxix] Desbordes, Gaelle & Negi, Lobsang & W W Pace, Thaddeus & Alan Wallace, B & Raison, Charles & Schwartz, Eric. (2012). Effects of mindful-attention and compassion meditation training on amygdala response to emotional stimuli in an ordinary, Nonmeditative State. Frontiers in human neuroscience. 6. 292. https://www.researchgate.net/publication/232814367_Effects_of_mindful-attention_and_compassion_meditation_training_on_amygdala_response_to_emotional_stimuli_in_an_ordinary_Nonmeditative_State/citation/download

[ccxx] https://www.frontiersin.org/articles/10.3389/fnagi.2014.00076/full

[ccxxi] https://www.amazon.com/Life-Milarepa-Biography-Eleventh-Century-Spiritual/dp/B019G5EY6A/ref=sr_1_4?keywords=milarepa&qid=1566260171&s=gateway&sr=8-4

[ccxxii] https://www.ncbi.nlm.nih.gov/pmc/articles/PMC3957486/

Printed in Great Britain
by Amazon

15060149R00164